ONE
NATION
AFTER
TRUMP

ONE
NATION
AFTER
TRUMP

A Guide for the Perplexed,
the Disillusioned, the Desperate,
and the Not-Yet Deported

E. J. DIONNE, JR.,
NORMAN J. ORNSTEIN,
& THOMAS E. MANN

St. Martin's Press
New York

www.stmartins.com

The Library of Congress Cataloging-in-Publication Data
is available upon request.

ISBN 978-1-250-16405-6 (hardcover)
ISBN 978-1-250-16406-3 (ebook)

Our books may be purchased in bulk for promotional, educational,
or business use. Please contact your local bookseller or the Macmillan
Corporate and Premium Sales Department at 1-800-221-7945, extension
5442, or by e-mail at MacmillanSpecialMarkets@macmillan.com.

First Edition: September 2017

10 9 8 7 6 5 4 3 2 1

In loving memory of Matthew Harris Ornstein

Are we to be one people bound together by common spirit, sharing in a common endeavor; or will we become a divided nation? For all of its uncertainty, we cannot flee the future.

—Barbara Jordan

CONTENTS

PART TWO
The Way Forward

When a Crisis Is an Opportunity

The Perils of Trumpism and the Call to Engagement

Amerian democracy was never supposed to give the nation a president like Donald Trump.

We have had more or less ideological presidents and more or less competent presidents. We have had presidents who divided the country and presidents whose opponents saw them as a danger to everything they believed in. But we have never had a president who aroused such grave and widespread doubts about his commitment to the institutions of self-government, to the norms democracy requires, to the legitimacy of opposition in a free republic, and to the need for basic knowledge about major policy questions and about how government works. We have never had a president who daily raises profound questions about his basic competence and his psychological capacity to take on the most powerful and challenging political office in the world. We have never had a president who spoke more warmly of dictators than of democratic allies, and whose victory came with the assistance of a foreign power that meddled in our election.

We have, in short, never had a president who, from his first day in office, plainly showed that he had *no business being president.*

Trump arouses anger, yes, but also fear—fear about whether our institutions can survive a leader who praises strongmen abroad and sees them as a model for bold leadership; fear about the instincts and commitments of a narcissistic politician who assails and insults revered national heroes, from John Lewis to John McCain, simply because they refuse to fall in behind him; fear about the future of a tolerant, multiracial, and multiethnic nation under a leader who freely demeans whole groups of Americans; fear about an incompetent executive branch staffed by loyalists with contempt for government and little understanding of its critical functions; fear about the country's standing in the world, given his cavalier and often hostile attitude toward long-standing alliances and toward many of our closest friends; fear about the future of gender equality under a president who shamelessly demeaned women and bragged about assaulting them; fear of the likelihood of corruption on the part of a chief executive who refuses to separate himself from his business empire in any meaningful way; and, finally, fear for the future of the United States' great experiment in freedom and democracy.

In his duplicitous reaction to Russia's efforts to undermine our democracy, he has shown us how the dysfunction of our politics puts our nation *directly* at risk. It makes us vulnerable to outside efforts to use our internal divisions to sow chaos and weaken our nation. Trump uses terrorist attacks to personal advantage, as when he responded in June 2017 to the death of seven people and the injury of dozens of others in London by criticizing the city's mayor and trying to score points in our domestic debate on gun control.

And far from bringing us together, Trump demeans his office by regularly turning its power to petty and often cartoonish assaults on his enemies, particularly in the media. Thus, his sexist Twitter outburst against MSNBC's Mika Brzezinski and his posting of a video two days before the nation's July 4th holiday of his violently wrestling a figure labeled "CNN." These and other episodes we describe in these pages reveal a presidency devoted to the interests, proclivities, and will to power of one man, not to the needs of the nation.[1]

Yet precisely because the crisis created by Trump's rise is so profound, we believe that the popular mobilization and national soul-searching he has aroused could be the occasion for an era of democratic renewal. If Trump is a threat to our democracy and the product of its weaknesses, the citizen activism he has inspired is the antidote, the way to vindicate our long experiment in self-rule. Opposition to Trump is calling millions of Americans to a new sense of citizenship.

We offer *One Nation After Trump* to encourage this new engagement and to insist that the movement against Trumpism needs not only tactics and strategies but also a vision—a hopeful and unifying alternative to his dark and divisive assessment of our country's prospects. His opponents need to offer clear, compelling, and practical ideas that respond to a distemper that led many of our fellow citizens to feel such disgust with the status quo and such anger about their place in it that they were prepared to risk empowering a deeply and obviously flawed demagogue.

We also propose answers to what we see as questions our country must face. In some cases, we suggest that the conventional responses to them are wrong or incomplete. In others, we highlight what we feel are the underappreciated insights of historians and political scientists who draw our attention to the long-term nature of the problems we confront. At the same time, we also acknowledge the very good work that journalists and scholars have done in a short time to help our country understand how we came to this moment and what we face now.

We thus ask: Where did Trumpism come from? Why were nearly 63 million Americans persuaded to vote for him? What is the nature of Trump's threat to our free, democratic republic, and how can those who would protect it take him on? How can we defend those whose rights he undermines? How can we create a politics that is not a zero-sum game pitting Americans against each other along the lines of race, class, gender, region, and background? And how can we begin solving the problems and responding to the legitimate grievances that gave rise to Trump in the first place?

If Trump represents a unique hazard, he did not single-handedly create the circumstances that made him president. He did not become the dominant figure in the Republican Party simply because of his mastery of reality television, cable news, tweets, and the power of the oft-repeated lie, as helpful as these were to his unlikely ascent.

Rolling back the Trump threat requires seeing that *he represents an extreme acceleration of a process that was long under way*. It involves the decline of basic norms in politics, governing, and the media as well as the decay of institutions that are central to republican government. The radicalization of the Republican Party and its primary electorate began three decades ago. Absent these forces, Trump would still be a loudmouthed developer and brand-peddler far removed from the levers of power.

Trumpism can be understood as a protest movement among a minority of Americans to long-term changes in the country's social, economic, religious, and political life. It is, in the literal sense of the term, reactionary. This separates it not only from progressivism but also from a traditional conservatism that, in principle at least, always accepted what Edmund Burke, the first conservative, taught: that preserving what is best in a regime and a society means accepting that change and reform are inevitable.

Burke recommended "a disposition to preserve, and an ability to improve." Trumpism looks backward, not forward.[2]

Trump took advantage of a trend in American politics toward minority rule, or what might be called "non-majoritarianism." Our system is now biased against the American majority because of partisan redistricting (which distorts the outcome of legislative elections), the nature of representation in the United States Senate (which vastly underrepresents residents of larger states), the growing role of money in politics (which empowers a very small economic elite), the workings of the Electoral College (which is increasingly out of sync with the distribution of our population), and the ability of legislatures to use a variety of measures, from voter ID laws to the disenfranchisement of former felons, to obstruct the path of millions of Americans to the ballot box. Trump profited from this bias against the majority, becoming president despite losing the popular vote by the largest margin ever for an Electoral College winner.

But he also exploited the seething rage created by economic changes that left significant parts of our country devastated and the citizens of these regions angry enough to turn to a charlatan whom they saw as at least articulating their sense of discontent. Trump's opponents will not prevail if they ignore the roots of this unhappiness. The conversion process requires listening as well as preaching. It mandates self-criticism and self-examination if the call on others to think differently is to have any chance of being heard. It's true that some of his enthusiasts have expressed views about African Americans, women, immigrants, and Muslims that demand condemnation. But while denouncing Trump's supporters for "voting against their interests" or for being "backward" or "reactionary" may be emotionally satisfying to his opponents, it will not persuade any of them to reconsider the choice they made. Worse still, some of the hostility that Trump's critics express toward those who voted for him merely mirrors the attitudes encouraged by his own strategists, who would intentionally divide our nation for their own political purposes.

Republican leaders confront an even more profound moral reckoning in acknowledging their role in enabling Trump's ascendancy. For decades, they had taught their supporters to mistrust Washington and hate government. They exploited the Tea Party and other mass movements on the right for electoral gain. Their rhetoric opened the way for Trump's nihilism and his promise to take a wrecking ball to the very system in which these Republican officials were complicit. For the Republican establishment, Trump's triumph ratified John F. Kennedy's warning in his inaugural address: "Those who foolishly sought power by riding the back of the tiger ended up inside."

The times were well suited to a candidate prepared to combine elements of populism, nationalism, nativism, and protectionism, and to marry these to the promise of strongman leadership ("I alone can fix it"). Paradoxically in light of who Trump is, a man deeply immersed in the world of high-level influence peddling, he cast himself as an implacable opponent of powerful moneyed interests and as the guardian of working people. That his own party had championed the role of large donations and that a conservative Supreme Court had struck down long-standing limits on their influence did not deter him.[3]

His nationalism and his forays into old-style "America First" isolationism played to a country exhausted by long and unsuccessful wars in Iraq and Afghanistan. His protectionism was welcomed by many voters—especially in the pivotal states of Michigan, Pennsylvania, Wisconsin, and Ohio—after the disappearance of millions of well-paying manufacturing jobs, many of them to China. His nativism responded to the unease among many native-born

Americans about the rise in the proportion of immigrants in our population over the last four decades. And the Republican Party's success in obstructing Barack Obama's agenda contributed—again paradoxically—to a popular desire for strong leadership that showed little regard for rules or norms.

Trumpism represents something far more important than the scheming of one man. To see clearly where Trumpism comes from is to understand that this worldview did *not* just suddenly sweep the country, does *not* command vast support among the American people, and does *not* represent an irresistible wave of the future. But for Trump and Trumpism to be defeated, Americans must understand the nature of the threat that he poses, the shortcomings in our society that he exploited, and the dangers of his overt and covert appeals to racism and xenophobia. They must also embrace public engagement—from demonstrating and attending town meetings to organizing a precinct, registering voters, working on campaigns, running for office, and, of course, voting itself. Saving our democracy requires citizens to devote themselves to the messy, sometimes frustrating, but ultimately gratifying work of self-government.

Trump poses a challenge for Republicans and Democrats alike. With some courageous early exceptions, Republicans in large numbers were willing to work with Trump and overlook or apologize for even the shabbiest aspects of his presidency in the hope of winning policy victories that have eluded them for more than a decade. Republicans who know better have also been intimidated by the very forces they helped unleash within their own party. They fear primaries, and they fear assaults from the conservative media. They worry that the GOP really has become Trump's party and are thus willing to accommodate him in order to hold on to the power they have.

The Democrats' path has, in one sense, been easier. Opposition to Trump runs so deep among so many Americans that standing up to him has turned out to be the best way to mobilize new forces into politics that could herald a revival of the center-left and the Democratic Party. But Democrats face a complex set of choices, partly because many of their senators, especially those up for reelection in 2018, come from states where pro-Trump feeling ran strong; partly because they are seeking to win over and work with at least some conservatives who may agree with certain Trump policy initiatives but share the center-left and left's deep concern about his authoritarianism and unfitness; and partly because defeating Trump will require both a vigorous defense of the rights of racial, ethnic, and religious minorities—including American families endangered by Trump's hostility to immigrants—and an understanding of the legitimate grievances of white working-class voters who expressed their frustrations by supporting him. Empathy can be hard in a period of profound political polarization, but it is indispensable. At the same time, warm feelings are not the same as coherent policies, and we hope here to show where they can be found.

The first part of *One Nation After Trump* analyzes the meaning of Trump's ascendancy and the dangers it poses. We open by insisting that Trump's opponents should take heart from the fact that he has never represented an American majority. A large share of the Trump vote was a negative verdict on the status quo (and, in the general election, on Hillary Clinton). His election was not a mandate for Trumpism. Understanding what did *not* happen in 2016 is as essential as understanding what did for moving forward.

So is an understanding of the complicated role of the media. The paradox is that the media, particularly television, facilitated Trump's election and yet is now one of the most powerful forces holding him accountable. We vigorously defend the role of a free and independent media while also pointing to the problems in our media system, the failures of journalism during the 2016 campaign, and the historical roots of Trump's attacks on the press's legitimate and essential role. Truth is the ally of both a free press and our democracy, and it is not well served by the temptation of false balance, the insistence that both sides are equally at fault even when this is plainly not the case.

We then offer three closely related chapters on the decay of the norms essential to democratic government, how this decay can lead to lawbreaking and the rise of autocracy, and how Trump has used populist appeals to gain power, even as his economic policies strongly favor society's most privileged sectors. We use these chapters to detail many of Trump's abuses during his first six months in office. Our purpose is to make clear that Trump's is not a normal presidency, that he lacks the self-restraint a functioning democracy requires of its leaders, and that his ethical misconduct raises systematic doubts about his capacity to govern in the public interest.

Norms, we argue, are often more important than formal rules in ensuring the functioning of a constitutional republic. Trump has violated these basic understandings of how our democracy works in an unprecedented way, yet his behavior is rooted in the evolving politics of the American right. In briefly revisiting arguments we made in our recent books (*Why the Right Went Wrong* and *It's Even Worse Than It Looks*), we trace how democratic norms have been under a sustained attack for decades by an increasingly radicalized Republican Party and conservative movement. Trump is less of an outsider than he seems, and he was building on rather than resisting recent trends within the GOP. This history helps explain why so many Republican leaders are reluctant to call out Trump's excesses and to acknowledge the risks he poses to our political system. Defeating Trumpism will require reversing longer-term political trends.

This norm-breaking is not simply a matter of political nicety. It is part of Trump's larger assault on our institutions, his tendency to think in autocratic terms, his abusive attitude toward the judicial system, and his disrespect for civil servants and the day-to-day work of government. We show how Trump's words and behavior parallel those of authoritarian leaders, past and present. We also deal with the curious contradictions of the Trump presidency. In many ways, it embodies weakness, the result of his refusal both to engage himself in the details of government and to appoint qualified men and women to the second and third tiers of his administration. Yet it also makes vast claims to power.

Because Trump sometimes resembles the authoritarian populists of other nations and other periods of history, we next discuss the difficulties with populism as a concept, describe the many forms it can take, and examine how the term can be overused and misapplied. We conclude that to the extent that Trump is a populist (in many ways an absurd label for a well-born billionaire developer), he fits into the category of those who define "the people" in an exclusionary way. His purpose is to cast political opponents and members of minority groups as the people's enemy. And whether or not Trump can fairly be called a populist, his policies make clear that he is a phony friend of the working class.

We close the first part of the book by taking on a debate that is of central importance both to understanding our country and to developing strategies for effective opposition to Trump: whether his support depended more on economic discontent or on a backlash rooted in race, culture, religion, and nativism. It is a debate that often divides Trump's opponents. After examining a raft of postelection studies, we conclude that while the cultural-backlash thesis explains a very large share of Trump's support, the economic backdrop of 2016 was critical to his victories in the key Rust Belt states. We thus point to the dangers of two forms of denial: the temptation to underplay the large role of race, immigration, and cultural conservatism in his campaign and his appeal, *and* the danger of overlooking the desire of many of his supporters to strike back against their sense of economic dispossession. Dealing with both is essential to moving beyond Trumpism.

This leads directly to the second part of our narrative. If we hope to encourage successful opposition and resistance to Trump and Trumpism, our purpose here is also forward-looking. We offer a substantive agenda because we agree with those who say that Trump's opponents have an obligation to offer a coherent alternative vision. At the same time, we insist that those who oppose Trump do so precisely to *affirm* a series of values he has put in jeopardy—about what political leadership demands, how politics should be carried out in a free republic, and how Americans should treat each other across our many differences. Trump's ascent to power is a warning sign pointing to the need for national renewal. The answer to Trump—the way both to defeat him and to solve the problems that led to his presidency—will be found, we believe, in efforts to forge a new economy, a new patriotism, a new civil society, and a new democracy.

It should not have taken Donald Trump to remind us of the profound imbalances in our national economy or to demonstrate that many Americans have been left behind over the last 30 years. Trump-style protectionism galvanized many voters because advocates of trade agreements regularly broke their promises of new paths to prosperity for communities and individuals distressed by globalization.

Trumpian discontent is typically defined as the product of an angry *white* working class that has suffered as manufacturing jobs have been moved overseas or supplanted by new technologies. True, Trump's supporters were and remain overwhelmingly white, and his appeal was inflected with a white ethno-nationalism. But the process of deindustrialization affects Americans across all races—and, it should always be remembered, a very large share of the American working class is not white but African American and Latino. As the sociologist William Julius Wilson noted in his book *When Work Disappears,* the vanishing of blue-collar jobs in a globalized and technologically sophisticated economy began wreaking havoc in our nation's inner cities long ago.[4]

A new economy will rise from an honest reckoning with the growing inequality and despair in many kinds of communities across our country, and also from an effort to build on the many economic advantages the United States enjoys. It will deal with the legitimate sources of discontent felt both among Trump's supporters and in the neighborhoods and precincts most strongly opposed to him. We do not pretend to offer a full-fledged economic program in these pages, but we do lay out a framework for dealing with the structural barriers to a more just economy. We propose a *Charter for American Working Families,* a *GI Bill for American Workers,* and a *Contract for American Social Responsibility* to offer ways of improving incomes, increasing social mobility, and strengthening communities caught on the wrong end of the economy. Responding to the grievances of the working class—white and nonwhite alike—must be part of the response to the economic struggles of all Americans. Trump's opponents cannot engage in a false-choice argument about whether to maintain their commitment to the rights of our country's ethnic minorities or to focus entirely on the white working class. Their task is to find policies that serve the interests of both groups, and of all Americans.

A new patriotism is the alternative to Trump's nationalism. It is ironic that despite Trump's calls for "America First," he has imported into American politics a blood-and-soil nationalism far removed from the United States' pluralistic and constitutional traditions. Despite many bouts of nativism, American patriotism has always returned to a definition of national identity rooted in constitutional republicanism and democratic institutions. A new patriotism would defend our commitment to pluralism while also stressing ideals shared across all of our differences. *E pluribus unum*—out of many, one—is our brilliant national motto that stresses both the "many" and the "one." Our pluralism must speak to all Americans, upholding both our right to express particular identities and our shared commitment to an equality that Martin Luther King Jr. insisted was "a dream deeply rooted in the American dream." A new patriotism would also reaffirm the United States' commitment to democratic values and renew our alliances with other democratic nations. A foreign policy that walks away from international structures that are themselves products of creative American statecraft is not a form of "realism." It is short-sighted and self-defeating.

And a new patriotism requires that our country rediscover empathy as the antidote to Trumpian division. Left, right, and center have contributions to make in the task of reweaving our nation's social bonds and in insisting that empathy cannot be selective. The injustices confronting African Americans in inner cities and rural areas must bring alive our social consciences, and so too should the anguish in declining and predominantly white communities in Appalachia and the old factory towns across the Northeast and Midwest.

Recognizing that the economic and social anxieties Trump exploited are fueled by a sense of dislocation and alienation, we also call for a new civil society. Trumpism thrives on division and seeks to deepen rather than heal the polarization in our politics. Trump's approach to politics always requires an enemy. This is true in a personal sense, as was obvious in his, by turns, vitriolic and mocking attacks on President Barack Obama, Hillary Clinton, and his Republican primary opponents. He also needs a collective enemy, whether at home ("the dishonest media" and Mexican Americans as "rapists") or abroad (ISIS, which truly is an enemy, but also our European allies, whom he regularly denigrates).[5]

It is an irony of Trump's appeal that while his combative rhetoric made him anything but a unifier, many rallied to him out of a yearning for forms of community and solidarity that they sense have been lost. Economic change has ravaged not only individual living standards but also cities and towns that once created thriving forms of civil society through churches and labor unions, veterans' organizations and service clubs, sports leagues and ethnic associations. It is not mere nostalgia to miss the forms of sociability and mutuality that are far more difficult to maintain when communities lose the vitality of a strong economic base. Writers as varied in their views as Robert Putnam, Charles Murray, and J. D. Vance have shown that economic decline is often implicated with family breakdown and the decay of social institutions. Family and community disruption, in turn, push many toward alcoholism, opioid abuse, and suicide, setting off a vicious generational cycle that is hard to break. The rise of what economists Anne Case and Angus Deaton have called "deaths of despair" among middle-aged whites is a national tragedy and a national emergency. This should be recognized, but so too should the deep hurts in African American and Latino communities. Here again, casting one group's pain against another's is a recipe for division and inaction.[6]

Finally, a new democracy requires answering political dysfunction and a pervasive sense of political cynicism with reforms that would make our system more inclusive and more democratic. As long as so many citizens see the system as rigged (a word Trump used to great effect), they will be reluctant to embrace the work of self-governance. This is why we call for institutional reforms to reduce the power of big money in politics and to protect the voting rights of all Americans.

But all this will only be possible if citizens once again join the democratic fray in large numbers. Trump's election called forth an extraordinary mobilization and drew millions of Americans to political engagement. This new era of civic commitment is essential to stopping Trump and reversing the effects of Trumpism. It is also a prerequisite to healing the wounds in our body politic that allowed him to reach the White House.

We are aware that events during the Trump presidency have moved with an unprecedented speed that far outpaces book-publishing schedules. However, absent a miraculous change in Trump's character we believe the story we tell here will be consistent with further developments. The damage that Trump has inflicted on our system will need repair no matter when he actually leaves office. That is why much of this book is forward-looking. Our nation must begin devising a new politics to move us beyond the chaos he has sown.

Our title consciously echoes the final words in the Pledge of Allegiance, "one nation under God, indivisible, with liberty and justice for all." We certainly make no claims to speak for the

Almighty, but the last seven words of the pledge define our hopes. The battle against Trump is a fight against national division—for the idea that we still are "one nation"—and a defense of liberty and justice. Restoring our capacity to work together to protect these values is the best way to put Trump and Trumpism behind us.

PART ONE

Trump and Trumpism

Trumpian Misconceptions

*What Trump's Election Meant, What It Didn't,
and Why Trumpism Doesn't Own the Future*

Two moments define Donald Trump's rise to power.

March 2011: Trump initiated his long entanglement with birtherism, the false claim that President Obama had not been born in the United States and was therefore ineligible to be president. In a March 17 interview on ABC's *Good Morning America,* he told Ashleigh Banfield: "If I ever got the nomination, if I ever decide to run, you may go back and interview people from my kindergarten, they'll remember me. Nobody ever comes forward. Nobody knows who he is until later in his life. It's very strange. The whole thing is very strange." Six days later, on *The View,* Trump asked Whoopi Goldberg and Barbara Walters, "Why doesn't he show his birth certificate?" He added: "I wish he would because I think it's a terrible pall that's hanging over him. . . . There's something on that birth certificate that he doesn't like."

The outbursts crystallized all that was wrong with Trump—and also how he would get to the White House. He was a shameless liar, and unapologetically demagogic. He would rally the angriest wing of the Republican Party by exploiting its racial and religious fears and prejudices.

June 10, 2014: In a Republican primary result almost no one expected, Eric Cantor, the House Republican majority leader, was ousted by a little-known college professor named Dave Brat. The routing of a thoroughly conservative Republican leader by the Tea Party, a movement Cantor himself had extolled, was a sign of how vulnerable traditional Republican politicians were to challenges from inside their party. No matter how much they tried to appease the GOP far right, more would be demanded of them. Brat's campaign was a prototype of what was to come.

He fiercely attacked Cantor as beholden to the party's moneyed interests and soft on immigration. "Eric is running on the Chamber of Commerce and Business Roundtable principles," Brat told an audience of Tea Party supporters. "They want amnesty for illegal immigrants. They want them granted citizenship. And it's in the millions—40 millions—coming in."

Brat, the prototype of a new nationalist, populist-sounding far right, explicitly denounced Cantor as a tool of Wall Street. "All the investment banks in the New York [*sic*] and D.C.—those guys should have gone to jail. Instead of going to jail, they went on Eric's Rolodex, and they are sending him big checks," Brat said. "They get cheap labor," he added of big business, "but everyone in the 7th district gets cheap wages."

John Judis, a journalist who closely followed the Tea Party and other populist movements, accurately noted at the time that Brat, a libertarian, would likely end up being far more business-friendly than he advertised himself in the campaign. But Judis added presciently that "in defeating Cantor, Brat echoed the age-old, darker, and more complicated themes of right-wing populism. These themes will continue to resonate, even if Brat abandons them."[1]

They did, for Donald Trump. At the time, the front-running Republican presidential candidates did not make the connection.

In 2016, this would prove to be politically fatal for Jeb Bush, Marco Rubio, John Kasich, and even Ted Cruz. In more moderate tones in the cases of Bush, Rubio, and, especially, Kasich, and with a harder edge in Cruz's, all would count on a mainstream conservative message to deliver them the party's nomination. Cantor might have warned them that a large contingent of the GOP rank and file was looking for something more incendiary.

Because Trump's rise to the presidency surprised nearly everyone (including the authors of this book and, it would appear from the evidence, Trump himself), he and his supporters have taken to scoffing at any and all analysts who, since his victory, have pointed to the underlying weakness of his position: his loss of the popular vote, his low favorability ratings throughout the campaign, and his record-low approval numbers on Inauguration Day. The idea seems to be that those who saw Trump as an unlikely president before Election Day are doomed to be wrong about everything they say now about the trouble he faces.

Humility is certainly a virtue, and it's fair to preach its benefits in the wake of the difficulties prognosticators confronted in 2016. But in fact, the predictions that Trump would never appeal to a majority of Americans were correct.

It is important to remember the basic facts of 2016. Trump's victory was a very close-run thing—a matter of 77,744 votes in three crucial states, almost certainly enabled by the intervention at the end of the campaign by then–FBI Director James Comey, who made Hillary Clinton's controversial use of email central to the dialogue in the final ten days before voting. Trump was also helped immensely by the interference of the Russian government and the heavy play throughout the fall of disclosures from hacked

Democratic emails. There was also evidence that the two events overlapped—that Russian disinformation about the Obama Justice Department's handling of the email investigation may have prompted Comey's aggressively critical public comments about Clinton.[2]

And it was no trivial matter that Trump lost the popular vote to Clinton by some 2.9 million ballots and ran nearly 11 million votes behind the combined Democratic, Libertarian, and Green totals. Trump received 62,984,824 votes, a gain of 2,051,167 over Mitt Romney's 2012 total. Nationwide, Clinton received 65,853,516 votes, just 62,419 fewer than Obama. A monumental shift in the nature of the nation's political leadership was enabled by relatively modest shifts in the electorate.

Trump's victory was less an endorsement of his program than a rejection of Clinton. Exit polling found that in the electorate that made Trump president, 60 percent had an unfavorable view of him; only 38 percent had a favorable view, which suggests how small his core support was on Election Day. But Clinton's numbers were nearly as bad, as 55 percent had an unfavorable view of her. Here is what should be seen as the decisive piece of data about the 2016 election: Among voters who had an unfavorable view of both Trump and Clinton (nearly a fifth of the electorate), Trump won decisively, 47 percent to 30 percent. Among the quarter of voters who explicitly said that the main motivation of their choice was dislike of the other candidate, the numbers were similar: 50 percent for Trump, 39 percent for Clinton. The 2016 election was a negative verdict, not a mandate for Trumpism.[3]

These numbers are critical for understanding how fragile Trump's hold on the public is and why he began his term with the lowest approval ratings of any new president in the history of modern polling. They explain why his disapproval numbers increased so quickly after he took office and why a large-scale grassroots movement rose up against him so rapidly. Trump did not speak for the country, and Trumpist ideology—to the extent that he even has a consistent ideology—does not command majority support.

Through all of the controversies in Trump's early months in office, political analysts regularly argued that despite his problems, Trump was still hanging on to support from his "base." But his base was a minority, and Trump showed little capacity for expanding beyond this core. This will have consequences in the long run, and it should give heart to Trump's foes.

Moreover, as the political analyst Nate Silver has shown, Trump's supporters are not blind to his failures or indifferent to his most questionable actions. Silver wrote: "The current conventional wisdom is that while President Trump might not be popular overall, he has a high floor on his support," and his "sizable and enthusiastic base—perhaps 35 to 40 percent of the country—won't abandon him any time soon." The problem with this conventional wisdom? It "isn't supported by the evidence." Silver found that the proportion of Americans who strongly approve of Trump fell from around 30 percent in February 2017 to just 21 or 22 percent of the electorate in May. Trump's real base may amount to a mere one-fifth of the American electorate.

Trumpism is thus no juggernaut. Trump's opponents should have the confidence of knowing that he does not speak for anything like the majority of the American people and that his own supporters are not inured to his shortcomings. The experience of Trumpism in practice has bolstered the positions of his opponents. This certainly seemed to be the Trump effect in Europe, where far-right movements in Austria, Holland, and, most significantly, France fell back as more moderate political forces were victorious. There has been, as *Boston Globe* columnist Michael A. Cohen observed, "a backlash to the backlash," a rallying to the defense of liberal democracy and openness. As we will see, this "backlash to the backlash" in the United States has taken the form of unprecedented political mobilization and engagement.[4]

But what of the argument that Trump has become the authentic tribune of the white working class? We will have much more to say on working-class discontent later in the book, but it is clear from both the exit polls and the raw vote count that these voters did make Trump's narrow victories in Wisconsin, Michigan, and Pennsylvania—and thus his presidency—possible.

Erie County, Pennsylvania, a once-booming manufacturing center that has been hit hard by deindustrialization, is a representative example. Barack Obama defeated Mitt Romney by a large margin in the county: 68,036 for Obama to 49,025 for Romney. But in 2016, Trump carried Erie County with 60,069 votes to 58,112 for Clinton. Comparable swings were delivered by demographically similar counties in all three crucial states, as well as in Ohio.

The exit polling told a related story. Obama, for example, carried Wisconsin in 2012 and won 45 percent of the vote among whites without college degrees. Clinton managed only 34 percent among such voters, and lost the state.

Notice something here: Even in victory, Obama lost the white working-class vote in Wisconsin. He lost it by even larger margins nationwide. The movement of such voters to the Republican Party had begun long before the rise of Donald Trump. Overall, Trump overwhelmed Clinton among whites without a college degree, 66 percent to 29 percent. But Obama performed only slightly better. He lost these voters to Romney in 2012, 61 percent to 36 percent. Clinton's gains among white college graduates were not large enough to offset these losses.

These figures demonstrate that there was not some immense wave of white working-class voters moving toward Trump. He built on existing trends rather than engineering something entirely new. In many working-class counties outside the Northeast and Midwest, Trump did no better and no worse than Romney did.

Further—this is often lost in the focus on the white working class's role in 2016—a large share of the Trump constituency was affluent or at least comfortable, made up of traditional conservatives and Republicans. As the political scientists Nicholas Carnes of Duke University and Noam Lupu of Vanderbilt University showed, about a third of Trump's supporters in the primaries made $100,000 or more annually. In the general election, they found, about two-thirds of Trump voters "came from the better-off half of the economy."[5]

Within the white working-class, hostility to Clinton was as much or more of a driving force in Trump voting as it was in other groups. Many of the counties in Michigan and Wisconsin that Clinton lost to Trump were also counties she lost to Bernie Sanders in the Democratic primaries. It was a warning the Clinton campaign did not take seriously enough. It should be said that some of the anti-Clinton vote was certainly rooted in sexism, and we will later point to some early postelection studies suggesting its role in her defeat. Trump himself certainly played on gender prejudice throughout the campaign—for example, by regularly attacking her alleged lack of "stamina." While separating sexism from other factors is difficult, it would be a mistake to ignore misogyny's role in 2016.

The essential point is that Trump's seemingly singular appeal to the white working class should be neither exaggerated nor underestimated. He may only have built on the appeal Republicans and conservatives already had to working-class white voters, but the legitimate discontents bred by deindustrialization, trade, and technological change no doubt helped him increase his margins. And what has often been cast as a populist rebellion in the economically stressed former factory centers in the United States has parallels across the West. It was reflected, for example, in support for Brexit in Britain and for Marine Le Pen's National Front in France. It *should* worry Democrats and the center-left elsewhere that so many working-class voters feel unrepresented by parties and politicians once seen as their champions. Writing about both the United States and Britain in his timely book *The New Minority,* Justin Gest observed that "social and economic forces have isolated the white working class as a political constituency, to the extent that many in this demographic feel like a peripheral afterthought in a country they once defined."

Still, as the Democratic pollster Guy Molyneux noted in a postelection analysis, it's just as important to remember that the white working class is not monolithic. By Molyneux's estimates, about half of the white working-class vote is reliably Republican, perhaps a sixth is reliably Democratic, and a little more than a third might be seen as a swing electorate, cross-pressured on many issues. Trump's gains among white working-class voters were achieved through a combination of sweeping policy promises and appeals to cultural and social anxiety. Even assuming his demagogic style allows him to retain some of these voters, Trump's support could be vulnerable if he fails to restore manufacturing jobs and if his agenda on health care, taxes, and government spending turns out to be—as it has been so far—traditionally conservative in its orientation toward the wealthy. Martin Wolf, the legendary economic columnist for the *Financial Times,* called Trump's ideology "pluto-populism," which he defined as "policies that benefit plutocrats, justified by populist rhetoric." If even a significant minority of Trump's working-class supporters reach the same conclusion, his pluralities in key states will evaporate.[6]

The 2016 outcome must also force a reckoning with a crisis in our democracy that conventional accounts of our elections too often ignore: our political system increasingly allows a minority to prevail over the majority. This is obviously true of the Electoral College, but it is also true of a Senate that vastly underrepresents the larger states and of a gerrymandered House of Representatives. The system empowers the old over the young, whites over nonwhites, and declining rural regions over growing metropolitan areas. Supreme Court decisions weakening the protections afforded by the Voting Rights Act and strengthening the hand of concentrated money in politics have aggravated all of these problems.

Begin with the Electoral College. In the 172 years from the widespread adoption of popular voting for president in 1824 through 1996, there were 44 elections. In only three of them did the winner of the popular vote differ from the winner of the Electoral College. Two of those cases were idiosyncratic. The election of 1824 was a four-way race held after one system of party competition had broken up and the new one had yet to take hold. Even in 1824, Andrew Jackson, the popular vote winner, won a plurality in the Electoral College. But because he lacked a majority, the election was thrown into the House of Representatives, which chose second-place finisher John Quincy Adams. Partly because of outrage over the outcome, Jackson handily defeated Adams four years later. In 1876, the election returns from three southern states were hotly disputed, and it is hard to know with any precision what the popular vote was. Only 1888, when President Grover Cleveland lost reelection even though he won the popular vote by 0.8 percent of the total, provided a clean case of an Electoral College/popular vote split in this long period.

But two of the five elections between 2000 and 2016 have involved a disparity between the popular and the electoral vote.

> Our political system increasingly allows a minority to prevail over the majority.

Why has an occasional problem in our past become a semichronic issue now? It has to do with a major demographic change over the last 50 years in which an ever-larger proportion of the population has moved from rural areas to more populous metropolitan regions.[7]

In 1960, 45 percent of Americans lived in large U.S. metropolitan areas, and another 18 percent lived in smaller metropolitan areas, a total of 63 percent. By 2010, the proportion living in large metros had risen to 55 percent, while smaller metros accounted for 29 percent. In other words, over a 50-year period, the metropolitan share of the American population rose by 21 percentage points, to 84 percent.

In the Electoral College, every state, small or large, gets two electors automatically (for their two members of the U.S. Senate). Again, regardless of size, every state gets at least one elector for its representative in Congress. Small states, which tend also to be rural, thus gain an enormous advantage over larger states. Candidates preferred by metropolitan voters can run up huge margins in cities and suburbs but not see these advantages reflected in their electoral vote count.

To pick the extreme but most revealing example: California has 67 times more people than Wyoming does. (In the first Census, the ratio between the largest state and the smallest was only

13-to-1.) California gets one elector for every 713,637 people, Wyoming one for every 195,167. Thus, in real terms, a Wyoming voter has more than *three-and-a-half times* the electoral power of a California voter.

In the case of the 2016 election, the Electoral College's distance from the popular vote was aggravated because so many Clinton voters cast ballots in large, reliably Democratic states like California and New York. Her big margins in these states had no payoff in the electoral vote.

We will have more to say about the problems of the Electoral College. And it is only one aspect of our system that increasingly promotes minority rule. Consider as well the makeup of the Senate, where the small-state bias is even more pronounced than it is in the Electoral College. The election of 2016 produced a Senate with 52 Republicans and 48 Democrats, a number that includes two Independents who caucus with the Democratic senators. Because more-populated states tend to vote Democratic, the 48 Democrats actually represent 55 percent of the nation's population. And this speaks only to the partisan bias introduced by the Senate's system of representation, which also privileges rural interests over urban and metropolitan concerns. On gun control votes, for example, the minority of senators who back more stringent firearm regulations consistently represent a majority of the people—a fact reflected in polling showing broad support for reforms such as background checks. Budgets also demonstrate this tilt: farm subsidies are far harder to cut than urban revitalization efforts.[8]

In April 2017, *The Washington Post*'s Philip Bump published an article underscoring just how unrepresentative the Senate has become. He noted that theoretically, "a bill or nomination could pass out of the Senate with the support of senators representing only 16.2 percent of the population. If the two senators from the

25 smallest states agreed to support a bill—and Vice President Pence concurred—the senators from the other 25 states and 270 million people they represent are out of luck."

When Justice Neil Gorsuch was confirmed for a lifetime appointment to the Supreme Court after a bitter battle, Bump wrote, the senators voting for him represented only 44.4 percent of the population. In putting the then-49-year-old, very conservative Gorsuch on the Court, senators representing a minority of Americans made a decision that could influence the direction of American jurisprudence for decades.

This representation problem will only get worse. David Birdsell, a political science professor and dean at Baruch College, predicts that, by 2040, 70 percent of Americans will live in the 15 largest states. "That means that the 70 percent of Americans get all of 30 Senators and 30 percent of Americans get 70 Senators," Birdsell told Adam Wisnieski of *City Limits*.

And the House of Representatives—theoretically, as its name suggests, the most representative branch of government—has become much less so because of partisan gerrymandering. Gerrymandering is an old American story. In its basic form, the majority party in a state legislature, seeking to maximize its representation, packs supporters of the minority party into a relatively small number of districts that the opposition consistently wins by enormous margins. The minority party's supporters "waste" their votes in these landslide elections. The mapmakers then draw themselves into an even more secure majority by creating districts that their own candidates win by solid but smaller margins.

Both parties have played at gerrymandering, but because of the Republicans' 2010 sweep, they controlled the most recent redistricting process in nearly all the key swing states. Republicans already enjoy an advantage over Democrats in the House because of the concentration of Democratic votes in urban areas. Aggressive Republican gerrymandering has intensified this bias. David Wasserman of *The Cook Political Report* calculated that Democrats won 50.5 percent of all major-party votes cast in House elections in 2012 but just 46.2 percent of the seats. In 2014, Democrats won 47.1 percent of the vote but 43.2 percent of the seats. Wasserman estimates that "Democrats might expect to consistently receive about four percent fewer seats than votes."

Ending gerrymandering would be no cure-all for our political system. But eliminating it would certainly produce fairer and more robust competition. In May 2017, the Brennan Center for Justice offered a powerful response to those who downplay the impact of partisan redistricting. The center's report, titled *Extreme Maps,* found that in 26 states that account for 85 percent of congressional districts, Republicans derive a net benefit of at least 16 seats from partisan bias in mapping. At the time the report was published, Democrats needed a swing of only 24 seats to regain a majority in the House—meaning that two-thirds of the GOP's margin could be ascribed to gerrymandering.[9]

Democrats have learned from their 2010 catastrophe that they need to focus as shrewdly as Republicans have on winning state legislative seats. Less-partisan districting can be forced if parties divide control of state legislatures, or if one party can counter the other's legislative majorities by winning governorships.

The gerrymandering problem is important not only for Congress but also for the state legislatures themselves. The skewed district lines that help Republicans overall also often disempower cities, particularly in GOP-controlled states. This is true in spite of the "one person, one vote" court rulings that require roughly equally populated legislative districts. And when authorities in urban areas enact policies at odds with conservative preferences at the state level, legislatures dominated by nonurban forces often veto these decisions, or pass broad preemption laws reducing the power of cities or counties. The controversy in North Carolina over a state law requiring transgender people to use the bathroom corresponding to their assigned sex at birth arose because the state legislature was overriding the preferences of the city of Charlotte. Paradoxically, in such cases, it is conservatives—committed in principle to the idea that government closest to the people works best—who are moving power away from local jurisdictions.

Conservative legislatures have further tilted the electoral playing field with measures that make it harder for African Americans, Latinos, and young people to vote. Trump's claims of massive voter fraud are cruelly ironic given that there is no evidence to support them, even as the evidence mounts that voter ID laws and other efforts to make voting more difficult plainly discriminate against Democratic-leaning groups.[10]

Absent reform, an increasingly diverse and metropolitan nation will find itself with steadily less-representative governments.

Of all the claims made on behalf of Trump, one of the least persuasive is the idea that his election was a realigning political earthquake. On the contrary, he did not revolutionize politics as Franklin Roosevelt did in 1932 or Ronald Reagan did in 1980. Trump won in the Electoral College largely because he was the Republican Party's nominee. His primary constituency was the Republican base: the exit poll showed he won 88 percent of the ballots cast by Republican voters, and 81 percent from self-described conservatives.

His victory was the logical outcome of a transformation in the nature of Republicanism and conservatism over the last several decades. Cantor's defeat was a leading indicator of how the party leadership's pact with extremism would turn on its authors.

Trump is more than a product of his own gifts for self-promotion, more than an accident of the electoral system, and more than the beneficiary of unprecedented interventions by a hostile foreign power and an FBI director. Trump's success also reflected a gradual radicalization of the Republican primary electorate and the decisions of a party leadership willing to tolerate and stoke resentment, conspiracy theorizing, and the demonizing of opponents and the media. Republican leaders built their own Jurassic Park: they created the conditions for a candidate like Trump, and then lost control over what they had created.

> Republican leaders built their own Jurassic Park: they created the conditions for a candidate like Trump, and then lost control.

As the Trump presidency moved forward, this reality created a stark split between the party's congressional wing and many of its leading thinkers. The latter understood that Trump was creating a crisis for both the conservative movement and the country. Michael Gerson, the *Washington Post* columnist who previously served as chief speechwriter for President George W. Bush, used blunt language to describe the disaster that had befallen the right:

> The conservative mind, in some very visible cases, has become diseased. The movement has been seized by a kind of discrediting madness, in which conspiracy delusions figure prominently. Institutions and individuals that once served an important ideological role, providing a balance to media bias, are discrediting themselves in crucial ways. With the blessings of a president, they have abandoned the normal constraints of reason and

compassion. They have allowed political polarization to reach their hearts, and harden them. They have allowed polarization to dominate their minds, and empty them.

Writing at the end of a week during which Trump embraced Saudi monarchs and scolded longtime European democratic allies while a Republican congressional candidate in Montana body-slammed a reporter who had asked a simple question about health care, conservative blogger Jennifer Rubin argued that Republicans could no longer pretend Trump and Trumpism were foreign bodies that had invaded their party:

> Conventional wisdom says that Trump executed a hostile takeover of the GOP. What we have seen this week suggests a friendly merger has taken place. Talk radio hosts have been spouting misogyny and anti-immigrant hysteria for years; Trump is their ideal leader, not merely a flawed vehicle for their views. Fox News has been dabbling in conspiracy theories (e.g., birtherism, climate-change denial) for decades; now Republicans practice intellectual nihilism. Nearly every point of criticism raised against the left—softness on foreign aggressors, irresponsible budgeting, identity politics, executive overreach, contempt for the rule of law, infantilizing voters—has become a defining feature of the right.

Rubin concluded that the Republican Party "now advances ideas and celebrates behaviors antithetical to democracy and simple human decency. Center-right Americans, we have become convinced, must look elsewhere for a political home."[11]

Yet inside Congress, Republican politicians continued to be fearful of Trump's support among their party's primary voters and kept hoping that appeasing Trump might bring them the tax cuts that remained their single unifying cause.

There was no better example of how Trumpism had been normalized early on than birtherism itself. Most Republican leaders were not birthers and did not claim that Barack Obama was a Muslim. And a few (including John McCain during his 2008 campaign) actively pushed back against the false claims. But more typical of the leadership's behavior was a performance by then–House Speaker John Boehner during a 2011 appearance on *Meet the Press*. Boehner was shown video of a focus group in which one participant declared of Obama, "I believe that he is a Muslim." Given an opportunity by the host, David Gregory, to push back, Boehner declined. "David," Boehner said, "it's not my job to tell the American people what to think." The Speaker allowed, somewhat grudgingly, "The president says he's a Christian. I accept him at his word." But pressed again, he was thoroughly open-minded about the untruth. "The American people have the right to think what they want to think," he said. Trump took the right Boehner conferred upon him to the political bank.[12]

The spectacle around birtherism—and the Republican leadership's refusal to disavow it from the start—catapulted Trump into conservative star status. Trump's skill at mobilizing and exploiting the media was essential to his success. Paradoxically, so too was his campaign to cast the media as his enemy.

TWO

When the Truth Doesn't Matter

*The Crisis of the Media and
the Rise of "Alternative Facts"*

It did not take long for the country to understand that Donald
Trump would have a very different relationship with the free
press and the facts than any previous president. All presidents tan-
gled with journalists, but only Trump echoed autocrats through
the generations in labeling the media (or at least the many parts he
didn't like) "the enemy of the American people." His chief strategist delivered the same message in a *New York Times* interview
early on. "I want you to quote this," Steve Bannon said. "The media here is the opposition party."[1]

Trump's attacks on society's information-gatherers and ac-
countability-seekers began long before he was elected. But becoming president did nothing to mellow him. His first attack came
within hours of his inauguration. Trump's crowd was about average—not minuscule, but not, to use one of his favored words,
huge. And the photographic evidence made clear that compared
with the throngs that gathered to celebrate both of Barack Obama's
inaugurations, Trump's turnout was much smaller. But plain and
convincing evidence did not stop Trump from insisting otherwise.

"We had the biggest audience in the history of inaugural speeches," he declared, furious over confronting any contradiction.

Trump was inaugurated on a Friday, and it fell to Sean Spicer, his new press secretary, to call in the press the next day for a dressing-down. Spicer carried out his first assignment loyally. But defending the new president's factually indefensible claim was an impossible task and a very unfortunate opening act for a new White House spokesman. It was also a sign of things to come. Spicer's job would be defined by his willingness to back up Trump's fictions and, when this failed, to deflect, distract, and confuse. (Eventually, Trump would end televised White House briefings, and Spicer would largely cede his public role.)

The statement that would define Trump World's attitude toward truth came the day after, on Sunday morning, when Kellyanne Conway, Trump's senior counselor, appeared on NBC's *Meet the Press*. Challenged by host Chuck Todd as to why Spicer was asked to go to the podium to offer patent untruths, Conway answered with a formulation that might have embarrassed George Orwell had he included it in *1984* (which became Amazon's number-one bestseller during Trump's early weeks in office).

"Sean Spicer, our press secretary," she declared, "gave alternative facts."

"Alternative facts?" an astonished Todd exclaimed. "Alternative facts are not facts. They're falsehoods."[2]

In his powerful book *On Tyranny,* the historian Timothy Snyder offered 20 lessons that twentieth-century history had to teach us in the Trump era. Lesson 10 was at once basic and essential: "Believe in truth."

"To abandon facts is to abandon freedom," Snyder insisted. "If nothing is true, then no one can criticize power. . . . You submit to tyranny when you renounce the difference between what you want to hear and what is actually the case."[3]

In the battle against Trumpism, the fight for truth may be the most important struggle of all.

The journey to "alternative facts" and to what would be called "the post-truth world" began long ago. It involved severe financial challenges to traditional media institutions and the rise of alternative conservative outlets whose power was never matched by liberal alternatives. Beginning in the Nixon-Agnew era, the right made the "liberal media" its enemy, and over the next four decades, mistrust hardened into a deep hostility that Trump aggravated and exploited. Social media made it ever easier for citizens to inhabit their own information worlds, free not only from challenges to their views but also from correction of error and misunderstanding. Technology made everything more efficient, including the spreading of lies.

In this new environment, the dedication of the older news outlets—the established newspapers and television networks—to "balance" became more and more problematic. What "balance" was owed falsehood? What was to be done if one political candidate was outlandishly and shamelessly willing to make up facts and level a steady stream of unsubstantiated charges while the other candidate was merely flawed in the ways all candidates are flawed? And how could television executives, particularly those running the cable outlets, resist a man who was a ratings machine? It turned out that they couldn't.

It is one of the ironies of our moment: Trump has made the media his enemy even though the media—above all television—helped make him president. The largely uncritical and mostly unmediated coverage he received in his campaign's early stages helped turn an implausible candidacy into a juggernaut.

The tracking firm mediaQuant calculated that as of mid-March 2016, Trump had received $1.898 billion worth of free media—six times the coverage of Ted Cruz, who ranked number two in free media among Republican presidential candidates. In that same period, the value of the airtime of Democratic front-runner Hillary Clinton was calculated at $746 million, less than half the attention given to Trump.

Some media executives were entirely candid about why they turned the news into Trump State Television: the showman was pure magic in building audience share. Leslie Moonves, the board chairman, president, and CEO of CBS, came to regret how candid he was about the Trump bonanza. "It may not be good for America," Moonves told a conference of investment bankers in February 2016, "but it's damn good for CBS." Later Moonves tried to pull back. "It was a joke! It was a joke!" he insisted in October. But it was no joke to Trump's opponents, or the country.[4]

Trump also owed a great deal to the media for its treatment of Clinton. She was badly hurt by the continuous coverage given to the same three stories involving her use of a private email server as secretary of state, her large speaking fees from Wall Street firms, and the content of emails stolen from Democrats by Russian hackers.

It cannot be said that the media ignored Trump scandals. On the contrary, critical coverage picked up once he secured the Republican nomination. But the genuinely tough investigative reporting on Trump did not begin in earnest until later in the election season, even as Clinton got a going-over not only throughout her campaign but also long before. The anti-Clinton narrative was fed for several years by selective and often-misleading leaks from Republicans on Capitol Hill. Trump frequently criticized the media for underestimating his chances of winning, but these low expectations almost certainly helped him by delaying inquiries into his background even as the negative cycle of stories continued unabated and dented Clinton's standing.

A study of election reporting released in December 2016 by Harvard University's Shorenstein Center on Media, Politics and Public Policy was revealing. It showed that in the general election, coverage of Trump was 77 percent negative, 23 percent positive. For Clinton, the coverage was 64 percent negative, 36 percent positive. The tough stories on Trump eventually did kick in. But Trump got a head start on Clinton because he was treated far more generously than Clinton in the early part of the campaign. Thus, for the campaign as a whole, according to the Shorenstein analysis, 62 percent of Clinton's coverage was negative, compared with just 56 percent for Trump.

The study found that on topics related to fitness for office, coverage of the two candidates was virtually identical: 87 percent of the stories about both of them were negative. Thomas Patterson, a professor at Harvard's Kennedy School of Government and the author of the report, wondered: "Were the allegations surrounding Clinton of the same order of magnitude as those surrounding Trump? It's a question that political reporters made no serious effort to answer during the 2016 campaign."

Democrats were certainly upset about the flow of the news. A Pew survey in September 2016 found that 43 percent of them thought the media was "too easy" on Trump, compared with only 27 percent in their party who thought this about coverage of Mitt Romney in 2012, and 22 percent who said John McCain's treatment in 2008 was too easy.[5]

Complaints about how Clinton came in for tougher scrutiny than Trump went beyond partisan circles. A September forum in which NBC's Matt Lauer interviewed Clinton and Trump back-to-back was emblematic. In a critical analysis, *New York Times* media writer Michael Grynbaum noted "what has become a common complaint about media coverage during this election: that news organizations and interviewers treat Mrs. Clinton as a serious candidate worthy of tough questions, while Mr. Trump is sometimes handled more benignly."

During the event, as Grynbaum noted, Lauer "devoted about a third of his time with Mrs. Clinton to questions about her use of a private email server, then seemed to rush through subsequent queries about weighty topics like domestic terror attacks." Lauer was also taken to task for not challenging Trump's statement that "I was totally against the war in Iraq" when, as Grynbaum pointed out, Trump "initially said he supported the war."

And it was only after the election—when Russia's engagement in the campaign on Trump's behalf framed the defining scandal of his young presidency—that the media seriously pondered a question that the Clinton campaign had tried and failed to put front and center before November 8: Was it a mistake to focus far more on the contents of the various emails stolen from the Democratic National Committee and Clinton campaign leader John Podesta than on the fact of Russia's involvement in obtaining them?

Journalists will inevitably publish new information as it becomes available. This is what those who stole the emails counted on. Nonetheless, the media could have covered the email leaks differently. David Leonhardt of *The New York Times* noted the sharp contrast between the U.S. media's near-constant reporting on Clinton campaign emails and the relatively subdued response from the French media when emails were released from front-runner Emmanuel Macron's campaign just days before France's presidential election. In the United States, Leonhardt wrote, the "overhyped coverage of the hacked emails was the media's worst mistake in 2016."

Once Trump did come under real scrutiny during the campaign, the results were devastating—or so it seemed. Investigative reporters spent long hours over several months digging up the details on Trump's falsehoods and the complicated workings of various parts of his empire. *The Washington Post*'s David Fahrenthold won a well-deserved Pulitzer Prize for his coverage of the Trump Foundation's faux charitable donations. He found that "many of Trump's philanthropic claims over the years had been exaggerated and often were not truly charitable activities at all." The *Post* continued its investigations of Trump across a wide field, particularly his campaign's relationship with Russia, and, once he became president, engaged in a healthy, old-fashioned war-for-scoops with an increasingly aggressive *New York Times*.[6]

The list of scandals unearthed *before* the election was so extensive that David Graham of *The Atlantic* later produced what he called "A Cheat Sheet" summarizing them. Heading the list was "Sexual-Assault Allegations," with the nature and timing of the allegations described as "Various, 1970s-2005." The best known of these was Trump's infamous interview with Billy Bush on *Access Hollywood*. Graham's list went on to describe Justice Department charges of racial discrimination against Trump and his father at 39 sites around New York for refusing to rent or negotiate rentals "because of race and color" (the Trumps eventually settled the case). There were beauty pageant scandals; accusations of Mafia ties; tenant intimidation; his four bankruptcies; and numerous complaints from contractors, waiters, dishwashers, and plumbers who said he stiffed them out of pay they were rightly owed.

Especially revealing is the saga of Trump University, seemingly little more than a vehicle for separating the credulous from their money. Trump's claims about Trump U bore more than a passing resemblance in language and tone to those he would make in his campaign. "At Trump University, we teach success. That's what it's all about, success. It's going to happen to you," Trump said in a promotional video. He went on:

> We're going to have professors and adjunct professors that are absolutely terrific—terrific people, terrific brains, successful, we are going to have the best of the best. And honestly, if you don't learn from them, if you don't learn from me, if you don't learn from the people that we're going to be putting forward—and these are all people that are handpicked by me—then you're just not going to make it in terms of the world of success.[7]

The media also carefully documented Trump's many outrages on the campaign trail. During the summer, the headlines and airwaves were, for a while, dominated by Trump's public feuding with Khizr and Ghazala Khan, an American Muslim family whose son, Humayun, was killed in Iraq. On July 28, 2016, the final night of the Democratic National Convention, Khizr Kahn offered a powerful tribute to his son's service as a U.S. Army captain and declared: "If it was up to Donald Trump, he never would have been in America." Khan held up a pocket Constitution, offering to share it with Trump. "Let me ask you," he thundered, "have you even read the United States Constitution?"

In this instance, Trump's standard tactic of smearing anyone who dared criticize him became a major liability. In a July 30 ABC News interview with George Stephanopoulos, Trump asked of Khan's speech: "Who wrote that? Did Hillary's scriptwriters write it?" And astonishingly, Trump compared his own "sacrifices" to those of a soldier who had given his life for the country. "I think I've made a lot of sacrifices," said the man who moves from one of his luxury properties to another on a private jet. "I work very, very hard."

The Trump campaign recognized how much damage Trump was causing himself in the Khan controversy and sent out a memo to surrogates in early August entitled "URGENT PIVOT" about the need to control it. Scott Mason of the Trump campaign knew where to place the blame. "As usual, the media is working against our efforts and our messaging," he wrote.[8]

Yet the cascade of investigative stories bunched together in the late summer and fall may have had a perverse effect: Trump became the first candidate in history to succeed in fending off one scandalous story with another. Where Trump offered a kind of scandal potpourri, coverage of Clinton constantly kept coming back to and driving home the same compact list of sins and shortcomings. All the reports on Trump certainly left him a very unpopular man—witness his record-low approval rating for an election winner. But the coverage overall may have hurt Clinton more because of its long-term nature and its persistent focus on the same issues.

In the Harvard study, Patterson detailed how the negative tone of the coverage was not confined to the candidates. On the treatment of immigration, Muslims, health policy, and the economy, coverage was overwhelmingly negative as well: from a "low" of 70 percent on the economy to a "high" of 87 percent in its treatment of Muslims. Since many of the stories on health policy were negative tales about the Affordable Care Act (aka Obamacare), and since, as Patterson pointed out, the negative reporting on the economy came in the face of the economic recovery, the broader tone of the news fit closely with Trump's nightmare rhetoric, which culminated in his inaugural address's most resonant word: "carnage."

Patterson's conclusion is depressing for the media. "The car wreck that was the 2016 election had many drivers. Journalists were not alone in the car, but their fingerprints were all over the wheel."[9]

With both Clinton and Trump seen negatively by the voters and with the media reinforcing this view, the candidate who was most at the center of the news at any given time tended to lose ground. And it was Clinton's misfortune that, in the volley of scandals, she was the last to be on the media griddle because of then–FBI Director James Comey's decision, against all Justice Department protocols and traditions, to insert himself into the campaign in its final days. On October 28, he wrote a letter to Congress announcing that new emails had been discovered on the server belonging to one of Clinton's aides. The Clinton story dominated the end of the campaign, even though Comey, on the weekend before the election, announced that there was nothing new in the emails after all. Trump's campaign was floundering when Comey wrote to Capitol Hill. The FBI director gave Trump his closing argument, and Trump's advertising in the waning days focused heavily on exaggerated distortions of what Comey had actually announced. It was enough.

How did a man who had no business being president of the United States reach the Oval Office? As we argued in chapter 1, an antiquated and increasingly unrepresentative electoral system was a major part of the story. Tactical and strategic errors by the Clinton campaign undoubtedly played a role. But the media would do well to engage in self-reflection. Brian Beutler, a senior editor at the *New Republic*, offered a sharp assessment, published on Election Day, before the results were known. It was titled "Shame on Us, the American Media." Beutler's critique is worth citing at some length:

The inability of political media to process and communicate asymmetry between the parties is a genuine crisis for the industry and our political culture. I believe both that if Trump were to become president, it would be a consequence of that crisis, and also that the media would do a much better job covering a Trump administration, outside the context of a horserace, than it did when he was running against a Democrat. But the way this campaign has been covered gives me incredible pause about the latter assumption. And even if it's correct, the double standard makes no sense. There's no way to justify systemically misinforming people about the stakes of an election, and then clarifying the consequences after it's over.[10]

Even journalists who might take issue with Beutler's conclusions would be hard-pressed to argue that the 2016 campaign marked the media's finest hour. It was a year when fake news stories gained wide attention and readership, and in which websites on the far right forced their distorted version of events (as well as nonevents) into the mainstream coverage. Like so much else in the Trump Moment, the attitude of his administration and his allies toward facts and the media's role in providing them was rooted in developments on the right over the previous half century. And conservative agitation against the media influenced the media itself, leading journalists toward defensiveness against charges of "liberal bias" at the very moment when they most needed to be fearless.

The long conservative campaign against "the liberal media" began in the 1960s and hit its stride during the Nixon administration, when Vice President Spiro Agnew attacked those who labored in the news business as "nattering nabobs of negativism." Nixon, pushed by his shrewd and sharp-edged aide Pat Buchanan, decided he would never win over the mainstream media—then the Big Three television networks (ABC, CBS, and NBC) and the major newspapers. So he would demonize them and cast them not as fact-gatherers but as political enemies.

The strategy certainly had its cost for Nixon. Traditional journalism continued to do its work, and in the end, the media (and particularly *The Washington Post* in the era of Woodward, Bernstein, and Bradlee) played a large role in bringing Nixon down in the Watergate scandal. But what Nixon started in the conservative world long outlived Watergate, and the legacy of his antimedia campaign would dramatically alter the way Americans discuss politics.

One of the first fruits of the Nixon-Agnew-Buchanan push was the proliferation of op-ed pages in which newspapers offered views quite different from those advanced in their editorials. (The term "op-ed," which goes back to early in the twentieth century, refers to "opposite editorial.") There had long been conservative columnists, of course, but the search for more conservative voices in what had been moderate or liberal papers helped launch distinguished careers, including those of George F. Will in *The Washington Post* and the late William Safire, a former Nixon speechwriter, in *The New York Times*. In 2016, Will became one of Trump's most biting conservative critics, and he changed his voter registration from Republican to "unaffiliated" the day after House Speaker Paul Ryan endorsed Trump. Safire died in 2009, leaving a rich legacy of writing on, among other things, writing and words themselves. He also fired one of the first salvos in the campaign to discredit Hillary Clinton in a 1996 column that described her as "a congenital liar."

If the only impact of the antimedia campaign had been an expansion of the viewpoints available to readers, it could be considered salutary (although the diversity of views it encouraged opened more space on the right than it did on the left of conventional liberalism). More important is the fact that conservatives targeted the parts of the news system tasked with providing neutral information and analysis, not just opinion. Journalists were not only assumed to be liberal; they were also assumed to inject their bias into their reporting. It was the beginning of an era of conservative denial.

There were other immediate effects in the 1970s. As the liberal writer Eric Alterman noted in his book *What Liberal Media?*, one of the most visible was the transformation of reporter roundtables on the Sunday morning interview shows as the traditional networks began adding conservative commentators. This was an unwitting step toward a false balance that reflected a kind of internalization of the right's critique by many producers and editors. Journalists who might or might not be liberal were assumed to hold left-of-center views simply because they were journalists. But precisely because they were nonpartisan journalists, they were constrained in expressing their opinions. Their right-leaning colleagues on the panels felt no such constraints.

Over the years, the panels diversified to include openly liberal voices, but the constant fear of being labeled "liberal" led network executives (as well as newspaper editors) to be especially assiduous in looking over their right shoulders. With time, this would have larger corrosive effects, which were especially visible in the 2016 campaign, and panel discussions frequently included former Trump staffers who had never sundered their ties to his campaign. Particularly when conservatives, but not liberals, were violating long-standing norms, or when Republicans were taking demonstrably more radical positions than Democrats, a retreat into the language of "everybody does it" or "they're both extreme" disguised rather than clarified the developing realities of American politics.[11]

Still, none of the concessions to conservatives quelled their rage at the media. In the late 1980s, the repeal of the Fairness Doctrine (it had required broadcasters to present contrasting views on controversial matters), combined with AM radio's search for programming as music migrated to the better sound of FM, opened the way for new conservative media empires. Pioneer Rush Limbaugh first went on the air in 1984; his show took off in 1988 when he began syndication from WABC in New York City. (He now broadcasts his show from Palm Beach, Florida.) After two years of syndication, Limbaugh was drawing 5 million listeners.

William F. Buckley Jr., not Limbaugh, was the first conservative media star. His *Firing Line* launched in 1966, the beginning of a 33-year run. Buckley's approach differed vastly from Limbaugh's. It was consciously highbrow (the musical introduction was Bach's Brandenburg Concerto No. 2), and Buckley, who liked argument, not simply assertion, often jousted with a prominent voice of the left. Limbaugh, who understood radio from his time as a nonideological broadcaster, went for popular rock music and unapologetically lowbrow humor, and he did not seek out sparring partners. He quickly spawned many imitators. One of the earliest signs of the power of Limbaugh and the radio talkers was their campaign to kill a pay raise for Congress, judges, and top government executives in late 1988 and early 1989, which attracted immense attention—and booming ratings.

Conservatives quickly colonized large parts of the AM dial. In many communities, the stations that carried Limbaugh offered 24 hours of conservative talk (broken up in some cases by a lone moderate or liberal who represented "balance"). A 2007 study by the liberal Center for American Progress found that 91 percent of political talk radio broadcast each day on the 257 news/talk stations owned by the five largest commercial station owners was conservative. And of those 257 stations, 236 broadcast no progressive programming.

Liberal efforts to challenge conservative radio dominance largely failed, even if at least two important careers, those of Senator Al Franken and MSNBC's Rachel Maddow, were furthered by talk radio stints. Part of the liberal problem, as we will see, is that liberals were drawn to more traditional news. But liberals also argued that media companies owned by conservatives consciously pushed the right's agenda. (This may become an even more serious issue over time with the concentration of ownership of local network affiliates. When *Guardian* reporter Ben Jacobs was body-slammed by Republican congressional candidate Greg Gianforte on the eve of the Montana special congressional election in May 2017, Missoula's NBC affiliate, recently acquired by the conservative media giant Sinclair Broadcasting, refused to cover the story. The station's news director, Julie Weindel, explained the decision by saying that Jacobs was "a reporter for a politically biased publication.")

One person who took careful note of the conservative talk radio boom was Roger Ailes, the man who taught Richard Nixon how to master television during his 1968 campaign and who later helped elect Ronald Reagan and George H. W. Bush. He left political consulting in 1991 and first entered the cable news world as president of CNBC. In 1992, Ailes brought Limbaugh to late-night TV with a syndicated half-hour show. While the show only lasted four years, Ailes knew he was on to something, and, with Rupert Murdoch's encouragement, he put Fox News on the air in October 1996. At its launch, it reached 10 million households. A mere four years later, boosted by conservative viewers who flocked to the network during the Clinton impeachment saga, it had spread to 56 million homes. And in 2002, aided in part by George W. Bush's post-9/11 popularity, it would become the nation's number-one cable news network, with an audience that for many years regularly beat the combined viewership of CNN and MSNBC. If Fox's promise of "fair and balanced" news struck those outside the conservative orbit as entirely false, it spoke to how conservatives wanted their news. "Fair and balanced" meant "conservative."[12]

There is a profound irony in this story. Trump, the candidate Fox eventually came to champion, triumphed despite charges of sexual harassment—and his own admissions. Fox, on the other hand, was shaken, quite literally to its foundations, when Ailes was forced to leave the network in 2016 amid sexual harassment allegations. Then, in April 2017, Bill O'Reilly, the network's ratings star, was pushed off the air by similar, well-documented charges.

Fox's troubles coincided with a surge by MSNBC. The network turned in a liberal direction during George W. Bush's presidency and vastly increased its market share as progressives sought an alternative to Fox and the ideologically indistinct CNN. MSNBC pulled back from its clear ideological branding toward the end of Obama's presidency. But as its prime-time anchors became voices of opposition, resistance, and reporting in response to the new Trump presidency, MSNBC soared, temporarily reaching the number-one spot in the cable news primetime rating wars in late May. MSNBC's resurgence was yet another sign of where energy in American politics was moving: Trump was demobilizing many conservatives even as progressives (joined by the anti-Trump right) girded for battle. In the four-decade-long struggle over the media, it was a rare moment of liberal ascendancy—and a potential turning point. This was true even though MSNBC included in its ranks conservative hosts and many conservative commentators.

There are two important lessons from the history of the conservatives' war on the media. The first is that the profound difference in how conservatives and liberals approach the mainstream media is the result of long-standing habits, not an innovation of the Trump years. Conservatives felt a need to create their own new media forms. Liberals, on the whole, did not do so until much later. Even then, at least until Trump's presidency, they did not embrace their partisan outlets as fiercely as conservatives did Fox and the talk radio shows. Liberals retained loyalty to a diverse array of traditional media offerings. When pollsters inquire, self-identified conservatives overwhelmingly list Fox News as their most trusted media source. Liberal preferences, by contrast, are widely scattered and include the older news outlets. Many reasons have been offered for why conservatives so dominate talk radio, but one of them is that liberals seem to prefer news to ideological talk.

But the other effect of the conservative mistrust of traditional media was more profound, and it reached a crisis point in the Obama and Trump years. Conservative talk radio host Charlie Sykes, who became a leading anti-Trump voice on the right, described the problem with precision in a December 2016 essay in *The New York Times:*

> One staple of every radio talk show was, of course, the bias of the mainstream media. This was, indeed, a target-rich environment. But as we learned this year, we had succeeded in persuading our audiences to ignore and discount *any* information from the mainstream media. Over time, we'd succeeded in delegitimizing the media altogether—all the normal guideposts were down, the referees discredited.

That left a void that we conservatives failed to fill. For years, we ignored the birthers, the racists, the truthers and other conspiracy theorists who indulged fantasies of Mr. Obama's secret Muslim plot to subvert Christendom, or who peddled baseless tales of Mrs. Clinton's murder victims. Rather than confront the purveyors of such disinformation, we changed the channel because, after all, they were our allies, whose quirks could be allowed or at least ignored.

We destroyed our own immunity to fake news, while empowering the worst and most reckless voices on the right.

This was not mere naïveté. It was also a moral failure, one that now lies at the heart of the conservative movement even in its moment of apparent electoral triumph.[13]

The road to "fake news" was paved by the disdain in a large part of the conservative movement for real news. The trail to "alternative facts" was blazed by a mistrust of those whose jobs and professional ethics required them to report and rely on real facts.

The conservative war on the media did not take place in a vacuum. Its early offensives, from the 1970s to the late 1990s, were launched when traditional media outlets were economically strong. But the era since the turn of the century has been a time of struggle for network news and of financial near-catastrophe for the newspaper business. The weaknesses of the old media system opened the way for the flourishing of false "news" stories and the further balkanization of information sources. It was, in short, the ideal climate for what Trump (and Russia's disinformation specialists) needed to do.

Cutbacks in the news divisions of the Big Three television networks were common as their competition with each other was expanded to include a struggle for audience with hundreds of cable and online offerings. In November 1980, the year CNN launched, 75 percent of television sets in use were tuned to one of the three nightly network newscasts during the dinner hour. By 2003, the figure had dropped to 40 percent. In 1980, 52.1 million Americans watched one of the three evening news programs. In the first quarter of 2017, that figure was 25.0 million. Network television news remains important. The Big Three still have excellent reporters, and, even with much smaller audiences, their evening news programs still draw far larger viewership than any of the cable news shows. But they have lost the dominance they once enjoyed.[14]

The financial problems facing the television networks, however, are dwarfed by those confronting newspapers, which had dominated the nation's political discourse for much of our history. Paul Starr, one of the wisest students of the American media, noted in 2009 that for three centuries "newspapers have been able to develop and flourish partly because their readers have almost never paid the full cost of production." From the eighteenth century through the mid-nineteenth century, newspapers were subsidized by the state or by political parties. "Then, as consumer markets expanded, newspapers increasingly sold not just news to readers, but also readers to advertisers. . . . The key to the rise of independent and powerful newspapers in the United States in the nineteenth and early twentieth centuries was their role as market intermediaries—that is, in connecting large numbers of sellers (advertisers) and buyers in a local area."

> The road to "fake news" was paved by the conservative movement's disdain for real news.

Those under the age of 30 or 35 have little experience holding a print newspaper in their hands, and those under 40 or 45 might never know that afternoon newspapers were once a central part of the daily lives of many Americans. The afternoon papers died off because they no longer fit the work-life schedules of most Americans and could not sustain themselves in competition with television. Many cities thus came to be served by a single newspaper. The results were monopoly profits. Starr paraphrases Warren Buffett's comments in his 2006 annual letter to Berkshire Hathaway stockholders to the effect that "until the Internet, newspapers had been as easy a way to make huge returns as existed in America."

And in the case of newspapers, private monopoly profits helped to finance a public good: large staffs of reporters whose job it was to inform democratic citizens and to report on various levels of government as well as private institutions and hold them accountable. One need not romanticize this past. Some newspapers and some reporters were better than others. Some newspapers spoke truth to power, and others reinforced it. But the result was many eyes on governments and politicians, and at least some attention to how businesses were behaving.

Metropolitan newspapers began losing economic ground before the rise of the Internet. Early blows were the death of the downtown department store (whose consumer base was almost perfectly matched to local newspaper readership) and the rise of malls whose businesses relied increasingly on direct mail and other forms of advertising and promotion. And then came the Internet, the ultimate market intermediary. Classified advertising fled to the web, undercutting one of the most profitable sectors in the newspaper business. Craigslist did more damage to newspapers than any government censor ever did.

The result has been a massive decline in the number of newspaper reporters on the job. In the American Society of News Editors report for 2015, the number of newsroom jobs was down to

32,900 from a peak of 56,900 in 1990. Total newspaper employment dropped even more dramatically. According to the Bureau of Labor Statistics, it fell from 457,800 jobs in June 1990 to 183,200 in March 2016. This loss was only partly offset by the rise in employment in Internet publishing and broadcasting—from 29,700 in June 1990 to 197,800 in March 2016.

To mourn the troubles faced by old newspapers without celebrating the extraordinary achievements of online media would be both nostalgic and shortsighted. The lives of the authors of this book have been enriched no less than those of others by the ready availability of news, analysis, scholarship, and information of all kinds—about politics, science, sports, movies, comedy, the arts, food, and countless other subjects. Paradoxically, traditional newspapers, particularly those with large national and international audiences, are now more widely read than ever thanks to the Internet, even if a business model has yet to be found to make this readership as lucrative as their old localized print circulations.[15]

The new online world places a heavy premium on opinion, which is far cheaper to produce than detailed, reported pieces. Here again, nostalgia is dangerous. Today's more opinionated forms of journalism are not new to the media or our public life. They take us back in our history to a time when most journalism was partisan and raucously engaged on one side or another in our political battles—sometimes corruptly so. The purpose of the newspapers was to mobilize support for parties all year round. From the beginning of our republic in the 1790s and through much of the nineteenth century, American newspapers were, for the most part, the organs of political parties. There was no ideal of objectivity.

Moreover, it's important to stress that opinion journalism never went away. Even in the heyday of objective journalism, opinionated columnists were an important part of what traditional

newspapers had to offer. The country has been blessed throughout
its history with thoughtful magazines of opinion. Among the most
durable: *The Nation,* founded in 1865; the *New Republic,* founded
in 1914, during the Progressive Era; and *National Review,* founded
by Buckley in 1955 in what proved to be one of the most important
steps in creating the modern conservative movement.

It also needs to be said that the concern over the fate of truth
and fact is not a sudden preoccupation of the Trump era. In 1994,
Michiko Kakutani, the *New York Times* literary critic, wrote a
powerful essay that could be republished in 2017 with no altera-
tion. "Throughout our culture," she wrote, "the old notions of
'truth' and 'knowledge' are in danger of being replaced by the new
ones of 'opinion,' 'perception,' and 'credibility.'" Kakutani warned
of "a universe in which truths are replaced by opinions" as citizens become "increasingly convinced of the authenticity of their
own emotions and increasingly inclined to trust their ideological
reflexes." The problems we face today were a long time in coming.

And if nostalgia can lead us to assume, falsely, that today's
difficulties are unique to our moment, it can also make us miss
the resurgence of major newspapers and the ways in which new
websites have picked up at least some of the reporting slack. Moreover, journalism is now far more adept than it used to be at using,
reporting, presenting, and explaining data. In the Internet era,
many outlets have managed, often brilliantly, to maintain a strong
allegiance to fact and truth while presenting both in the context of
a clearly articulated political viewpoint. The list of such efforts is
long; we will cite just a few. On the progressive side, for example,
Vox offers careful policy and data analysis that has pushed mainstream outlets to do more of this work themselves, while *Talking
Points Memo* has built credibility for its reporting and investigations. On the other side of politics, the conservatives at *National*

Affairs magazine and its website are similarly disposed to holding fast to the traditional rules of policy inquiry while being unapologetic—but also often nuanced—in their allegiance to the politics of the center-right. (One of the authors of this book is closely associated with the journal *Democracy,* which does similar work from the progressive side.)

One of the most widely cited observations in an era when even facts (and "facts") seem to have a political allegiance is the late Daniel Patrick Moynihan's coinage: "Everyone is entitled to his own opinion, but not to his own facts." There is a need for a corollary to Moynihan's rule: *Opinion journalism cannot be called journalism if it is not based on fact.* In our time, a defense of *factually based* opinionated commentary is as important as a defense of traditional reporting itself.

In an ideal world, a journalism of verification and fact would live side by side with an enriched (and factual) opinionated sector. There are genuine grounds for hope that this might yet be our future. But technology does not stand still. There will continue to be more opinion available than ever, combined with a greater capacity on the part of individuals to select only the point of view they share—and, in the name of enhancing the online experience, a tendency of social media platforms to push people toward others who are like them and agree with them.

It is problematic enough, Cass Sunstein argues in his book *#republic: Divided Democracy in the Age of Social Media,* that because people have "a growing power to filter what they see," technology can foil what John Stuart Mill believed was a central aspiration for debate in a democratic republic: "placing human beings in contact with persons dissimilar to themselves, and with modes of thought and action unlike those with which they are familiar." Combine this with fake news, and you create circumstances in which basic facts are denied, phony "facts" are manufactured, and fictional accounts are offered as truth.[16]

The media environment, in other words, was perfectly set up for Trump. Many conservatives had already cut themselves off from the mainstream media. New forms of right-wing media (notably Steve Bannon's *Breitbart News*) could take advantage of this by being more aggressive than ever in promoting not only alternative story lines, common enough in any campaign, but also nonfactual, phony narratives.

This was the conclusion of a study published in March 2017 by Yochai Benkler, Robert Faris, Hal Roberts, and Ethan Zuckerman from the Berkman Klein Center for Internet and Society at Harvard University and MIT's Center for Civic Media. Their research into 1.25 million stories published online between April 1, 2015, and Election Day concluded that "a right-wing media network anchored around Breitbart developed as a distinct and insulated media system, using social media as a backbone to transmit a hyper-partisan perspective to the world. This pro-Trump media sphere appears to have not only successfully set the agenda for the conservative media sphere, but also strongly influenced the broader media agenda, in particular coverage of Hillary Clinton."

And selective consumption of information (and "information") was especially common on the right. "While concerns about political and media polarization online are longstanding, our study suggests that polarization was asymmetric," the authors wrote. "Pro-Clinton audiences were highly attentive to traditional media outlets, which continued to be the most prominent outlets across the public sphere, alongside more left-oriented online sites. But pro-Trump audiences paid the majority of their attention to polarized outlets that have developed recently, many of them only since the 2008 election season."

The study points to a central truth many would prefer to evade: the problem presented by Trumpism is not the creation of broad, general trends that have nothing to do with party or ideology. It is not the product of technology itself. *The loss of a common conversation is largely the result of habits on the political right, deeply engrained since the late 1960s.* Trumpism was not created by liberals or moderates, even if liberals and moderates can certainly be faulted for not seeing the threat clearly or responding to it adequately. It was enabled, as Sykes insisted, by conservatives' habit of rejecting information that was not congenial to their side and denying the legitimacy of the sources of inconvenient facts.

The Harvard/MIT study was clear in noting that technology alone cannot be held responsible for fragmenting public discourse. If this were true, the authors wrote, "we would expect to see symmetric patterns on the left and the right." But this was not the case. In fact, "different internal political dynamics in the right and the left led to different patterns in the reception and use of the technology by each wing." Social media, such as Facebook and Twitter, were especially important in enabling "right-wing media to circumvent the gatekeeping power of traditional media."

Perhaps even more disturbing was the study's finding that the mainstream media itself was deeply influenced by the accounts developed on the right. Here again, chasing the right did not help the mainstream media win credibility among those who had no interest in engaging with it. But doing so did distort the picture mainstream journalism presented of the campaign. The campaign's story was told far more in terms set by Trump than in terms set by Clinton.

"The right-wing media was . . . able to bring the focus on immigration, Clinton emails, and scandals more generally to the broader media environment," the study found. "Donald Trump's substantive agenda—heavily focused on immigration and direct attacks on Hillary Clinton—came to dominate public discussions. Coverage of Clinton overwhelmingly focused on emails, followed by the Clinton Foundation and Benghazi."

An April 2017 ABC News/*Washington Post* poll further confirmed that conservative attacks on the mainstream media had dramatically shaped the perceptions of Trump voters. According to the poll, 78 percent of Trump supporters thought that news organizations regularly produced false stories. But only 17 percent thought the same of the Trump administration. On his liberal *Plum Line* blog at *The Washington Post,* Greg Sargent argued that it was "hard to avoid the conclusion that Trump is accomplishing one of his key goals. In the minds of his voters, at least, his project to obliterate shared agreement on the legitimate institutional role of the media in informing the citizenry proceeds apace."[17]

Those who would preserve the mainstream media's traditional role—as providers of facts, fair mediators of policy and political debates, and investigators who hold power accountable—do not need to accept the right wing's insistence that they are biased political actors and enemies of conservatism. On the contrary, preserving ground for the neutral arbitration of what's true is essential, and so is restoring some consensus on what facts actually are and how they are to be determined. For the mainstream media to give up on these aspirations—the legendary columnist Walter Lippmann said journalists should seek to emulate "the patient and fearless men of science who have labored to see what the world really is"—would be a great loss to democratic deliberation. The increasing resistance in the media to the administration's trafficking in untruth was a sign of health. And the rallying of many citizens who put their money on the line through tens of thousands of new subscriptions to traditional news outlets demonstrated that journalism's role in preserving democracy and liberty is more widely recognized than ever.

Defending those engaged in the work of establishing verifiable truths—whether they are specialists in government agencies who collect and disseminate accurate information, scientists and others in the academy who subject their work to critical scrutiny, or the practitioners of old-fashioned journalism—is essential to carrying out all the other tasks of democracy. Disorienting the public by blurring the line between fact and falsehood, Alexander Hamilton warned, is the trick of the despot whose "object is to throw things into confusion that he may 'ride the storm and direct the whirlwind.'" It should now be clear that false balance does not serve the truth, defensiveness does not preserve journalism's values, and trying to appease critics who have no interest in the truth only compromises journalism's purposes.

> False balance does not serve the truth, defensiveness does not preserve journalism's values.

Trump's hundredth day in office brought clarity to the battle the free media face. He chose to be the first president in 36 years to skip the White House Correspondents' Association Dinner— and Ronald Reagan failed to attend in 1981 because he was recuperating from an assassination attempt. Instead, Trump traveled to Harrisburg, Pennsylvania, where he denounced "fake news" and called journalists "incompetent, dishonest people."

But the assembled scribes back in Washington did not turn the other cheek. Bob Woodward and Carl Bernstein, heroes for their Watergate reporting, spoke of journalism's responsibilities, and that sent a message. And Jeff Mason, the president of the association, addressed directly the threat the media confront. "We cannot ignore the rhetoric that has been employed by the president about who we are and what we do," Mason said. "We are not fake news. We are not failing news organizations. And we are not the enemy of the American people." The standing ovation that greeted his words signaled an understanding that a crisis point had been reached.

Václav Havel, the brilliant Czech dissident who became his country's president, was alive to the challenge to facts and truth from his time resisting a Stalinist dictatorship. "When a truth is not given complete freedom," Havel said, "freedom is not complete."

It is to the dangers to freedom and democratic norms that we turn next.[18]

THREE

Bad Behavior

The Disappearing Norms of American Politics

When President George H. W. Bush departed the White House in January 1993 after a bitter election loss to Bill Clinton, he left behind a handwritten note for his successor:

Dear Bill,

When I walked into this office just now I felt the same sense of wonder and respect that I felt four years ago. I know that you will feel that, too.

I wish you great happiness here. I never felt the loneliness some Presidents have described.

There will be very tough times, made even more difficult by criticism you may not think is fair. I'm not a very good one to give advice; but just don't let the critics discourage you or push you off course.

You will be our *President when you read this note. I wish you well. I wish your family well.*

Your success is now our country's success. I am rooting for you.

Good luck,

George

Bush did not have a legal requirement to leave that kind of message. But in writing it, he reflected America's long tradition of orderly succession after an election and the deeper need for the country to come together after a fierce campaign. George W. Bush adopted a similar practice after leaving office: he went out of his way to avoid questioning or disparaging Barack Obama. "I think that not criticizing my successor is a statement unto itself, in terms of trying to create an environment where people are able to have a meaningful discussion or debate without trash talk," Bush explained.[1]

Fast-forward to March 4, 2017.

"Terrible! Just found out that Obama had my 'wires tapped' in Trump Tower just before the victory. Nothing found. This is McCarthyism!"

Even for Donald Trump, this particular tweet, sent at 6:35 a.m. that Saturday morning, marked a new low. And the largely uncritical response to this baseless claim from Trump's Republican colleagues represented the triumph of partisanship over the fundamental democratic norms that had guided generations of politicians on both sides of the aisle.

The occupant of the Oval Office had accused the previous president of the United States of violating the law in spectacular fashion. And matters didn't stop there. His first message was one of four he would issue against Obama. (Self-obsessively mixing show business and government business, he also offered an attack on Arnold Schwarzenegger for his stewardship of Trump's old TV show, *Celebrity Apprentice*). Here is what Trump tweeted at 7:02 a.m.: "How low has President Obama gone to tapp [*sic*] my phones during the very sacred election process. This is Nixon/Watergate. Bad (or sick) guy." The double *p* on the word normally spelled "tap" was, perhaps, an indication of how little thought and care

Trump put into this outburst. Watching this undisciplined and insecure man call his calm, confident, and popular predecessor "bad" and "sick" made it hard not to ponder the word "projection."

Did Trump know something about Barack Obama that the rest of us didn't? Trump's most loyal advisers could offer no proof for Trump's claim because there was none. After the fact, Trump would send the White House counsel and other staffers rummaging through security information to find support for charges he couldn't back up himself. He left it to Congress to investigate his accusation.

And Congress itself would be corrupted by Trump's trafficking in falsehood. In late March, Representative Devin Nunes, the chair of the House Intelligence Committee that was investigating Russia's interference in the 2016 election and the possible complicity between Russia and Trump's campaign, rushed to the White House and held a news conference to say that Trump officials had been caught up in incidental surveillance by intelligence agencies during the transition—and that their names had been "unmasked," or shared within the intelligence community and the Obama White House. Nunes cited classified reports that, violating standard practice, he did not initially share with his committee members. Later, it emerged that Trump White House officials had been instrumental in getting the information to Nunes. The bizarre episode blew up on the Intelligence chair. In April, when the House Committee on Ethics said it was investigating whether Nunes "may have made unauthorized disclosures of classified information," he temporarily removed himself from the Russia inquiry. It later emerged (to the rage of Democrats on the committee) that he had continued to issue subpoenas in a related inquiry into the "unmasking" of Trump campaign officials by intelligence agencies. The "unmasking" charge—about activities that were neither unusual nor particularly suspicious—was itself an effort to distract attention from Trump's troubles.

Many in Trump's party were dumbfounded by his charges against Obama, though most were reluctant to take him on. They knew from prior episodes that conservative media and most of their own voters would not break ranks, and would not take kindly to any condemnations of the president's remarks.

One Republican who did speak out was Senator John McCain, showing that sometimes courage simply requires stating obvious truths. "This is unprecedented," McCain said. "I have never heard of a president of the United States accusing his predecessor or any other president of the United States of violating the law." McCain said that Americans "have a right to know on what basis" Trump made his charge and "should demand it."

"I haven't seen anything like this," he added.[2]

There was good reason why McCain (who was also critical of Nunes) had not ever "seen anything like this." All of Trump's predecessors had observed certain norms of behavior. One of the singularly dangerous aspects of Trump's rise is how destructive he has been to the standards of politics, governing, and even basic human conduct. Bret Stephens, then a *Wall Street Journal* columnist who later migrated to *The New York Times,* wrote after Trump's Obama outburst that the president was engaged in the "methodical corruption of the presidency—or, more accurately, the *concept* of the presidency."

There had been ample warnings that a President Trump would be exactly as Stephens described him: "an intemperate and verbally incontinent 70-year old man, prone to believing dubious conspiracy theories." His indifference to truth went far beyond spin or the usual political exaggeration. Never had a public figure, let alone a president, caused a vigorous debate in the press over when his pronouncements should be called "lies," and when they should merely be labeled as "untruths" or "unproven" charges. Trump's mendaciousness was disorienting to the journalists covering him because they had expected that, like all the presidents before him, he would act in accordance with the established norms and traditions of the office.

In politics, there is far more talk about "breaking the rules" than "violating the norms." The rules that govern political comportment are vital. But norms may be more precious. Many of the virtues we ask of our fellow human beings cannot in practice be legislated or, at best, can be codified only imperfectly and incompletely.

Norms are defined as "a standard or pattern, especially of social behavior, that is typical or expected of a group." They are how a person is *supposed* to behave in a given social setting. We don't fully appreciate the power of norms until they are violated on a regular basis. And the breaching of norms often produces a cascading effect: as one person breaks with tradition and expectation, behavior previously considered inappropriate is normalized and taken up by others.

> Trump is the Normless President, and his ascendancy threatens to inspire a new wave of norm-breaking.

Trump is the Normless President, and his ascendancy threatens to inspire a new wave of norm-breaking.

This would be bad enough if he were entirely a one-off, an amoral figure who suddenly burst onto the scene and took advantage of widespread discontent and an electoral system that tilts outcomes in the direction of his politics. But Trumpism has long been in gestation. His own party, sometimes consciously, sometimes not, has been undercutting the norms of American politics for decades. As the traditionalist conservative Rod Dreher has written, "Trump didn't come from nowhere. George W. Bush, the Republican Party, and movement conservatism bulldozed the field for Trump without even knowing what they were doing."

Our nation has to hope that in the long run, more Republicans will join the ranks of the conservatives who already understand the damage Trump's indifference to informal ethical benchmarks is inflicting on our political system. But to do so effectively, they will, as Dreher suggests, have to reexamine their own past and the deterioration in the standards of political behavior that took root in their party. And this will only happen if Republican officials come to see altering the course of the modern conservative movement as a political imperative.[3]

In his 1960 book *U.S. Senators and Their World,* the political scientist Donald R. Matthews described the informal dos and don'ts that shaped senators' behavior to make the institution function and fit into its place in the constitutional orbit. Matthews's work was pathbreaking in political science. He understood that these unwritten guides to behavior are essential to the vibrancy and health of a political system. They fill in the many gaps left by formal rules and ensure that people with vastly different political interests can work together to advance the common good.

In a chapter entitled "The Folkways of the Senate," Matthews listed habits and customs crucial to the functioning of the body (and antithetical to Trumpism): legislative work (putting substance over show); specialization (learning in depth some areas of expertise); courtesy (ensuring that policy and politics not become personal); apprenticeship (deference early on to more senior senators); and most important, institutional patriotism (protecting your institution's responsibilities, prerogatives, resources, and integrity).[4]

A core part of institutional patriotism is respect for "regular order," the sometimes esoteric practices and rules observed by members of the Senate to reach decisions in a body that relies heavily on unanimous consent and that respects the rights of the minority. These include deference to individual members who seek to delay the timing of a vote, or who have strong reservations about judicial or executive nominations, and giving all senators an opportunity to ask questions during a hearing. In return, individual senators are expected not to delay the body's work unreasonably by indefinitely denying unanimous consent to move forward, or by offering killer amendments.

The most important formal rule in the Senate is the filibuster. It involves the ability of the minority to keep the Senate from voting on an issue or nomination until a supermajority of 60 senators agrees to support a motion to stop debate and move to a vote, a process called cloture. The formal rule was previously backed by the widely shared norm that the filibuster would be used only rarely, ensuring that the rights of the minority party would be respected but that the majority would be able to act in most cases without fear of unreasonable obstruction and gridlock.

Norms themselves are not static. They evolve in response to changes in society. One need only look at our willingness to share things about ourselves online (a practice that politicians themselves frequently follow), or to use language in public that a generation ago would have been considered unacceptable, to see how expectations of behavior shift over time. The same is true of political norms. The norm of apprenticeship, for example, disappeared as senators increasingly rejected the idea of automatic deference to their older colleagues. Power dispersed throughout the body. More senators became what their traditionalist critics derided as "show horses" as media opportunities expanded and provided individuals with leverage over policy agendas. Fundraising became a more important and time-consuming activity for individual senators (as well as House members), crowding out time for substantive legislative work. Policy specialization was subverted by the growing value of soundbites and slogans prized by television news.

But norms such as courtesy toward fellow officials and, especially, institutional patriotism remained strong in the Senate, House, and Supreme Court. In the 1970s, for example, senators such as Democrat Adlai Stevenson of Illinois and Republican Pete Domenici of New Mexico devoted enormous time to reexamining and reworking the Senate committee system. This project brought little direct benefit to their constituents or their careers. They participated chiefly because they wanted to improve the institution of which they were a part.

The presidency and the executive branch had their own norms, sometimes bolstered by formal rules. They included respect for the majesty of the Oval Office and its history; acceptance of law and precedent; avoidance of conflicts of interest to maintain the credibility of the president and presidency; an understanding of the division of labor among the branches; acknowledgment of the essential role of the free press, even when it is harshly critical; and a commitment to insulating the FBI, the IRS, and law enforcement from political pressure or intervention. It's true that those norms were at times violated, sometimes shockingly so, as in the case of the Watergate scandal. But other actors inside the institutions eventually acted to restore a sense of balance.

Yet today, many of the broader norms that once surrounded deliberation, discourse, and the basic functioning of the American political system, whether in the legislative or executive branch, have collapsed. These changes did not occur overnight with the election of Donald Trump; they were set in motion much earlier. Still, Trump's brazen disregard for the truth, his highly unconventional and often offensive campaign, his behavior as president, and the "See No Evil, Hear No Evil" response so far from his fellow partisans in Congress present the most serious challenges to the norms of our democracy since the period leading up to the Civil War, which traced many of the same lines of division in politics we now face.

Parties, from the beginning of the Republic, have been a central force in American politics, clarifying the policy choices available to American voters. They provide the basis for organizing elections and political power in the institutions of government even as they compete constantly for loyalty and fealty with the institutions themselves. Members of Congress loyal to the president's party sometimes reflexively follow his lead, denying or papering over his failings and failures. At other moments—driven by personal beliefs or constituency interests, by electoral imperatives, and sometimes, at least, by faithfulness to the public interest and the fundamentals of the Constitution—they keep their distance from him. And members of the party opposed to the president often challenge his positions.

But during some periods of divided government, when one party controls the White House and the other has a majority in the House, the Senate, or both chambers, cross-party coalitions where parties share responsibility for governance have thrived. As the political scientist David Mayhew showed, divided government during the decades following World War II produced significant legislative achievements—and arguably did so as or more often than when a single party held all the reins of power.[5]

Strong Democratic majorities in Congress in the 1930s voted for sweeping New Deal legislation—but many Democrats joined with Republicans to block Franklin Roosevelt's attempt to enlarge the Supreme Court. Republicans in the majority in 1947–48 vigorously opposed most of Harry Truman's agenda—leading to his famous campaign in 1948 against the "Do-Nothing Republican Congress." But the same Congress joined with Truman to enact the Marshall Plan, as well as a historic and (to this point, at least) enduring reorganization of the national security apparatus that created the National Security Council and made it easier to coordinate defense and foreign policies. Most Democrats in the Reagan era opposed his initial plans to slash government and cut taxes, but conservative Democrats provided enough votes for Reagan to enact an early package. Then, in subsequent years, Democrats bargained with him to increase taxes to combat the burgeoning deficit his program produced and to stave off further spending cuts.

So what happened? Parties have certainly become more polarized, shaped by the great ideological and geographical sorting that began in the 1960s. The South, realigned by Lyndon Johnson's commitment to civil rights, lost its status as nearly uniformly Democratic and gradually became the GOP's most important power center. New England and the West Coast had once been strongholds of an often moderate brand of Republicanism. They became bastions of Democratic strength. A repolarized partisanship solidified by the 1990s and became even more pronounced after 2008.

Polarized parties encouraged polarized policymaking, but room still existed for occasional cross-party cooperation. The State Children's Health Insurance Program (S-CHIP), which covered almost 9 million children in 2016, would never have been enacted without the odd-couple partnership between the loyally liberal

Senator Ted Kennedy of Massachusetts and the faithfully conservative Senator Orrin Hatch from Utah. Over four decades in Congress, from 1975 to 2015, Representative Henry Waxman, a staunch liberal, found common ground for compromise with conservative Republicans—including Reagan. The results: groundbreaking policies in health care and the environment. Waxman also conducted bipartisan investigations during the Bush administration in cooperation with Republican Representative Tom Davis of Virginia.

The norms inculcated over many decades led to an elaborate language of respect ("my distinguished colleague") toward fellow legislators that often seemed out of place during particularly emotional and intense debates. They could also lead to amusing understatement. In the 1960s, House Speaker John McCormack of Massachusetts would express his distress over the behavior of a Republican on the floor by saying: "I hold the distinguished gentleman in minimum high regard."[6]

Tribalism, which cast members of the opposing party not as worthy adversaries but as dangerous enemies, swept that respect away. The change began with Newt Gingrich, who came to Congress in 1979 determined to nationalize congressional elections and convince voters that Washington was so dreadful and corrupt that anything would be an improvement over the status quo. When he recruited candidates, he offered them a language of partisan militancy. "You're fighting a war," Gingrich characteristically told a group of college Republicans in 1978. "It is a war for power. . . . Don't try to educate. That is not your job. What is the primary purpose of a political leader? To build a majority." And he did, winning an extraordinary victory in 1994 that gave Republicans control of the House for the first time in 40 years. That heralded a period of intense competition for control of the House and Senate, which itself fueled the hyperpartisanship that came to characterize national politics more generally.

Gingrich transformed the Republican Party in Congress. His recruits came in believing what Gingrich had taught them. Although he had a deep interest in science, Gingrich launched an attack on the use of science and facts in public policy that would be picked up by other Republican politicians in the years to come. One of the more enduring norms of Congress was that evidence vetted by acknowledged experts would frame debate and deliberation. Lawmakers could differ sharply on policy solutions, but all would share facts curated by the experts. As Speaker, Gingrich abolished the Office of Technology Assessment, a blue-ribbon congressional agency that had been established for scientists to offer objective analysis on issues ranging from defense and space to climate and energy. The new majority defended shuttering the office's doors as a cost-saving measure, and it was part of Gingrich's broader (and largely successful) effort to centralize power in the Speaker's office. But the move also sent a message that ideological commitments would trump evidence.[7]

Although Gingrich's tenure as Speaker ended in 1998, the atmosphere he helped to create persisted and was amplified by his less colorful successor, Dennis Hastert. Goaded by his lieutenant Tom DeLay (who was, in many ways, the real leader of the House), Hastert and House Republicans culminated their sustained assault on the Clinton presidency by pushing for impeachment of Bill Clinton, a move that most Americans saw as aggressively partisan.

And when George W. Bush succeeded Clinton, the Hastert-led House transformed itself into an arm of the executive, creating a custom that became known as the "Hastert Rule." Closing off the option of broad bipartisan coalitions in support of legislation, the "Rule" declared that the House would now rely only on

Republican votes to pass bills, and they would reach the floor only if they secured a "majority of the majority." To promote the Bush agenda, Hastert also bent both the existing rules and customs of the House. There would be few amendments permitted; bills would be written not in committee but by party leaders; and open processes (such as conference committees to reconcile differences between bills passed in the House and the Senate) would be discouraged. In a particularly flagrant episode, Hastert and DeLay held open a roll call vote to pass George W. Bush's prescription drug benefit under Medicare for three hours, rather than the customary 15 minutes, in order to avoid defeat. They secured the final vote for the bill, but DeLay was later admonished by the House Ethics Committee for offering to a retiring GOP House member an endorsement for his son, who was seeking to succeed the father, in an effort to secure his vote and get the bill passed.

The Republican Party's disregard for political norms intensified further with President Obama's election. Immediately after Obama's inauguration in 2009, Senate Republican leader Mitch McConnell and his colleagues embarked on a deliberate strategy of obstruction across a broad range of policies. McConnell made his objective clear in a comment that came to epitomize his approach: "The single most important thing we want to achieve is for President Obama to be a one-term president." Republicans tried to cast their response as a reaction to purported aloofness and high-handedness on the part of Obama and his congressional allies. In fact, as Republican Senator George Voinovich explained, McConnell from the start had advised his colleagues of Obama, "If he was for it, we had to be against it."

McConnell bent the norms of the Senate to a degree the body had never seen before in his use—and misuse—of the filibuster. As congressional scholar Sarah Binder has pointed out, motions for cloture to end a filibuster (an imperfect but helpful measure of how often the filibuster was used to block Senate business) were filed rarely in the 1970s—in some years, they averaged less than one per month. During the Obama era, Democratic Majority Leader Harry Reid took to filing for cloture more than once a week. And in 2013, when a frustrated Reid decided to eliminate the filibuster for all presidential nominations except for the Supreme Court, a Congressional Research Service study showed how dramatic the abuse had become. In all of American history, it found 168 cloture motions had been filed on presidential nominations—and nearly half of them, 82, happened during Obama's presidency.

Reid did not take this action lightly. It came only after another threat, when McConnell made clear that no matter whom President Obama nominated to fill the three vacancies on the D.C. Circuit Court of Appeals, Republicans would filibuster the nominees through the entire Obama term to preserve the Court's conservative majority.[8]

But there was no better example of extreme partisanship than McConnell's refusal to consider any nominee Obama put forward to replace Supreme Court Justice Antonin Scalia after Scalia's sudden death in February 2016. McConnell argued that the "American people should have a voice in the selection of their next Supreme Court Justice" and that "this vacancy should not be filled until we have a new president."

McConnell fractured the norms of the Senate with his use—and misuse—of the filibuster.

This was a radical departure. Supreme Court nominees had been rejected before, but except for those who withdrew, none in recent memory had been denied both a hearing and a vote. That it was justified with a risible claim to being democratic, as if the

American people hadn't reelected Obama for a full four-year second term, showed just how far McConnell was willing to go. And
nearly all of McConnell's colleagues overwhelmingly supported
this strategy, one by one announcing that they, too, would seek to
delay hearings and a vote on a nominee until Obama had left the
White House. This even included Senator Orrin Hatch of Utah,
who had once praised Garland as a "consensus nominee."[9]

Upon taking office, Trump quickly nominated Tenth Circuit
Court of Appeals judge Neil Gorsuch to fill Scalia's seat. Democrats moved to filibuster Gorsuch's nomination, citing their opposition to Republican treatment of Garland and Gorsuch's staunch
conservative record. Immediately, McConnell invoked the "nuclear
option," as Reid had earlier, this time allowing Supreme Court
nominations and not simply lower-court, cabinet, and subcabinet
confirmations to be pushed through on a simple majority vote. The
Republicans succeeded, and Gorsuch was confirmed. But a line
had been crossed. It became increasingly difficult to avoid seeing
the Court itself as merely another partisan institution.

McConnell's disregard for Senate norms was not limited to his
use and abuse of filibusters. When the effort to repeal Obamacare
came to the Senate in May 2017, McConnell created a process that
had virtually no precedent when it came to considering a major
policy change. He named a group of 13 Republican senators as a
health policy task force, bypassing the committees that have ju-
risdiction over the issues at stake. They met in complete secrecy.
McConnell made clear that he would not bring Democrats into the
process at all. He would not hold a single hearing. His plan was to
rush the bill to passage with as little debate as possible, on the accurate assumption that the more the public knew about the details
of the plan, the less likely it would be to pass. The gambit failed in
its initial objective. A Congressional Budget Office estimate that

the bill would throw 22 million Americans off the insurance rolls led to resistance among key Republican senators from states that had benefited from Obamacare. McConnell had to put off a quick vote and rewrite the proposal during the summer.

The contrast with the process by which Obamacare was considered and enacted—a process Republicans had assailed, in McConnell's words, as "a disservice to the American people"—could not have been more stark. *The New York Times*'s Robert Pear noted that "in June and July 2009, with Democrats in charge, the Senate health committee spent nearly 60 hours over 13 days marking up the bill that became the Affordable Care Act." The Senate Finance Committee, he wrote, had worked on the legislation for eight days, "its longest markup in two decades." Before passing the Affordable Care Act on December 24, 2009, the Senate debated it for 25 days, "considered more than 130 amendments and held 79 roll-call votes." That the Senate in the Trump years would set out to upend the American health care system largely in secret was a dramatic and genuinely shocking example of how the decay of norms is not an abstract problem. It threatens the most basic commitments of our democracy.[10]

House Republicans started the Obama years in the minority and without the weapons available to their counterparts in the Senate. But they took an equally deliberate approach to blocking, stalling, and discrediting the new president's program. Led by Eric Cantor, Kevin McCarthy, and Paul Ryan—they called themselves the "Young Guns"—they sought and usually achieved perfect party discipline against every major Democratic initiative. This was of immense help to their campaign to delegitimize the president and his policies. They could refuse to vote for any Democratic bills—and then accuse Obama and the Democrats of governing in a partisan way.

The GOP base was already inflamed by Obama's election, angry over the economic downturn that began under Bush, and convinced that Bush had failed because he had governed as a "big-government Republican." The result was the Tea Party's mobilization: a marriage of grassroots right-wing activism and the politics of money as Charles and David Koch and other large conservative contributors fueled and directed the anger on the ground. With the economy recovering sluggishly, Republicans won a landslide in the House in November 2010, picking up 63 seats and a new House majority.

Buoyed by their victory, Republicans pressed their strategy of delegitimizing Obama further. They used their newfound power to conduct repetitive hearings charging the administration with dark and scandalous behavior. Examples included allegations of corruption in the Troubled Asset Relief Program and in Afghanistan, and claims that the IRS had targeted conservatives. The latter led to an effort to impeach IRS Commissioner John Koskinen, something even many Senate Republicans saw as a dangerous overreach. The hearings typically produced no results beyond news stories critical of Democrats, but that was the point. One of their prime targets was Hillary Clinton. The party conducted eight different congressional inquiries into the Benghazi attack in Libya, without producing any truly damaging information (though the investigations did indirectly unearth the fact that Clinton had used a private email server). In his campaign, Trump only picked up on the demolition work begun long before in Congress.

Yet for Republicans, the strategy might be seen as having worked too well. The sense that government was broken deepened. So did the mistrust of elites. In 2016, Gallup found that trust in political leaders had a hit a new low. Only 42 percent of American expressed a "great deal" or a "fair amount" of trust in them, down 21 points since 2004. Donald Trump, the outsider's outsider, would benefit immensely from his party's spadework. When he declared, "What the hell do you have to lose?" he was talking about African Americans, who had little interest in his candidacy. But many other voters—frustrated with rising inequality, stagnant wages, shifting social dynamics, and gridlocked, divisive government—were ready to respond.[11]

The election of Trump in 2016 represented both the culmination of the GOP's war against norms and its dramatic escalation. During the campaign, Trump defied all the previously accepted assumptions and conventions about how presidential candidates should act. He demeaned many different groups of Americans: from Mexican immigrants to women, from a disabled reporter to a Gold Star family. He embraced religious discrimination with a call for a total ban on Muslims entering the country. And he converted the dog-whistle appeals of the late twentieth century into bullhorn-style racial politics that harkened back to the time of George Wallace. When Trump spoke of the "hell" of America's inner cities and promised to restore "law and order," he claimed to be appealing for African American votes. In fact, he was describing the world as seen by his political base.

No one was safe from Trump's assaults. He went out of his way to ridicule and attack the Speaker of the House, Paul Ryan, with the same vigor he directed against his primary opponents. Once Trump was elected, Ryan fell into line and served, at times, as one of the new president's most enthusiastic champions. He made clear that the Republican Congress had no interest in serving as a counterweight to Trump's excesses. Even as evidence mounted of Russia's unprecedented interference in the 2016 election to aid

Trump, the GOP exercised a shocking indifference. "There's no need to ask what Republicans would be doing if the shoe were on the other foot—if the Russians had intervened to help elect the Democratic nominee," wrote Robert Kagan, an anti-Trump neoconservative scholar. "They would be demanding a bipartisan select committee of Congress, or a congressionally mandated blue-ribbon panel of experts and senior statesmen with full subpoena powers to look into the matter." Instead, Kagan said, they joined Trump in "covering up."

John Thune of South Dakota, an influential Senate Republican, made the dynamic inside the GOP clear. "There's a widely held view among our members that, yes, he's going to say things on a daily basis that we're not going to like," said Thune, "but that the broad legislative agenda and goals that we have—if we can stay focused on those and try and get that stuff enacted—those would be big wins." In other words, if Republicans in Congress could get tax cuts, demolish regulations, and install pro-business Supreme Court justices, anything else would go.[12]

Indeed, the 115th Congress started with a deeply troubling sign that Republicans would treat their own ethical transgressions with the same indifference as they would Trump's. On the evening of January 2, 2017, just hours before a new rules package was to be adopted in the House, there was a surprise effort led by Ryan ally Bob Goodlatte, the House Judiciary Committee chair, to gut the independent Office of Congressional Ethics (OCE), created in 2008 to oversee allegations of ethics violations by members and staff.

After Republicans voted to defang the OCE, the public backlash was immense, and Ryan and his colleagues were forced to back down. "House Republicans," *The New York Times* wrote in an editorial, "made it clear that they had no real intention of draining the Washington swamp." Even Trump saw the damage the House was doing, speaking out against not the action (he called the office "unfair") but its timing. In a sign of the chaos to come in his White House, shortly before Trump tweeted his views, his counselor Kellyanne Conway went on TV to defend House Republicans and criticize the OCE for its "overzealousness."[13]

Republicans also signaled that they would tolerate previously unacceptable and unethical behavior in the new administration. Trump entered the White House with more significant conflicts than any president in recent American history. While he correctly asserted that many anti-corruption laws do not apply to the president, his unwillingness to present even the appearance of propriety was without recent precedent.

Ignoring the steps that had become routine for presidential candidates, Trump flatly refused to release his tax returns during the campaign. He said (falsely) that he could not do so because he was under audit. After the election, he continued to rebuff calls for disclosure of his tax information with the justification that "the only one that cares about my tax returns are the reporters." The polling showed otherwise: a *Washington Post*/ABC News survey on the eve of his inauguration found that 74 percent of Americans wanted him to release them. And on April 15, 2017, major rallies were held around the country to call on Trump to release his taxes. In typical Trump fashion, he questioned the legitimacy of the protests, tweeting on Easter Sunday: "Someone should look into who paid for the small organized rallies yesterday. The election is over!"[14]

Trump also eschewed presidential norms in failing to divest fully from his business interests around the globe. Instead, he placed the Trump Organization into a trust operated by his sons Donald Jr. and Eric. Ethics advisers to previous administrations of both parties sharply criticized his approach, pointing out that anything short of full separation between Trump and his corporate empire would open his administration up to all manner of ethical quandaries. Trump only reinforced the notion that he cared little about keeping distance between his presidential responsibilities and his family's personal business dealings when he took to Twitter early in his presidency to blast Nordstrom after the company announced it would be phasing out his daughter Ivanka's line of clothing and accessories.[15]

Transparency took another blow when the administration announced it would no longer release the White House visitor logs. True, this specific practice had only become routine during the Obama years, but it operationalized a much more enduring norm. Its purpose was to allow the public to know who was meeting with the president and his staff. Evidently keeping the American people informed about the president's appointments with outside influencers was not a component of Trump's promise to "drain the swamp."

And the one area touted regularly by Trump and his team as demonstrating their commitment to transparency and ethical behavior—his executive action requiring all White House staff to sign a five-year postemployment ban on lobbying—proved to be a sham. As ethics watchdog Craig Holman noted, the order defined the ban narrowly to encompass only efforts to influence the legislative branch, not work with executive branch agencies. And as Sarah Posner reported in *The Washington Post,* the administration also allowed waivers to be granted, brought in wealthy individuals like financier Carl Icahn as "special advisers" to whom the rules were not applicable, and, as a consequence of delays in nominating senior political appointees at agencies, temporarily filled hundreds of key positions with so-called beachhead teams whose members may not be subject to the order at all. In late May, OGE reported that the administration had issued dozens of ethics waivers. And the Trump team initially sought to keep the waivers secret; its hand was finally forced only by pressure from the Ethics Office.[16]

In April, new questions arose about the Trump family's financial entanglements when the Chinese government gave preliminary approval to three trademarks that enabled Ivanka Trump to sell her branded jewelry, bags, and spa services there. The approval happened to come on the same day she met with President Xi Jinping. Even if the timing was simply accidental, the episode highlighted the significant interests the Trumps have in the Chinese economy. And in May, it was reported that Jared Kushner's family had name-dropped him to potential Chinese investors for a real estate development project in New Jersey. Kushner's sister told the investors that the project "means a lot to me and my entire family" and promised that if they were to invest at least $500,000, they would qualify for the special EB-5 visa program. As ethics experts Norm Eisen and Noah Bookbinder wrote in a *Washington Post* op-ed, "There can be little doubt now that both Kushner and [Ivanka] Trump face at least the appearance of a conflict—indeed, of multiple conflicts—when it comes to China policy."[17]

Republicans in the Senate, in the meantime, chose to ignore a wide array of legal and financial concerns involving Trump's cabinet appointments. They disregarded questionable stock trades and purchases by Republican Representative Tom Price of Georgia, nominated to be secretary of health and human services. Legitimate worries about the divestiture of assets by nominees such as Betsy DeVos at the Department of Education and Wilbur Ross at the Commerce Department were swept aside in the rush to confirmation. So too were EPA nominee Scott Pruitt's conflicts of interest related to the fossil fuel industry. Pruitt would later be the lead defender of Trump's decision to leave the Paris climate accord.

As Oklahoma's attorney general, Pruitt had refused for years to follow freedom-of-information requirements to release all his emails and correspondence related to multiple lawsuits he had filed against the agency he was nominated to head. But a judge set a deadline for the release while his confirmation was pending. Senate Republicans forced a vote days before the documents were made available, and he was confirmed by a narrow margin. When the documents came out soon thereafter, it became clear that Pruitt had lied to Congress: he said he had conducted no official business at all using a nongovernmental email account, which was false. That revelation—along with the fact that many of his legal filings were drawn directly from documents sent to him by energy lobbyists—came too late for the Senate to consider.

Democrats responded to a small group of Trump nominees, including Price and Treasury's Steve Mnuchin, with a kind of guerrilla tactic, boycotting the key hearings in the Senate Finance Committee, which under the committee rules meant there was no quorum to allow votes. Republicans responded by suspending the rules to jam the nominations through committee and then on to the Senate floor. Finance Chair Orrin Hatch called the Democrats "idiots." Senate Majority Leader Mitch McConnell chose more elegant language. "The first thing we have to do is move beyond this us-and-them mentality that has so often characterized the last eight years," he said on the Senate floor. "We're all in this together. We rise and fall as one." But authentic institutional patriotism means real vetting of nominees. McConnell, who embraced precisely such an "us-and-them" mentality under Obama, was paradoxically advancing exactly that approach by turning back legitimate Democratic demands for more care in the vetting process.[18]

The congressional leadership reacted in a similarly partisan way when Trump issued his initial refugee ban, which was itself a reworking of the "Muslim ban" he had promised in his campaign. The result: chaos at American and foreign airports, hundreds of stories of family separations and heartache, blocked green-card holders, and the revocation of the valid visas of over 100,000 people. (Administration officials later claimed the number was 60,000.) In drafting the executive order, the Trump administration violated long-standing practices followed by previous presidents. Such orders are supposed to be crafted deliberately, with drafts vetted for legality and constitutionality by not only the Office of Legal Counsel and the Justice Department but also the relevant executive departments to make sure they are workable. This order was simply pushed through. Key agencies were taken by surprise.

Ryan had said flatly in June 2016: "I do not think a Muslim ban is in our country's interest." But in late January, after Trump issued the order, Ryan endorsed it. "President Trump is right to make sure we are doing everything possible to know who is entering our country," he stated. McConnell also supported the action.

Even after it became known that House Judiciary Committee staffers had worked secretly with the White House on the order while Republican congressional leaders were kept in the dark, there was no pushback against this remarkable breach of norms and the disrespect it showed for congressional leaders and for the institution itself. (Adding to the insult, the staffers signed confidentiality agreements about their work with the administration.) There was also little protest among Republicans when Trump denounced the judge who issued a broad injunction against the ban as a "so-called judge," and then publicly assigned him blame for any deaths that might result from terrorist attacks that occurred while his travel ban was blocked.[19]

Trump's refusal to abide by normal standards of presidential conduct had devastating unintended consequences and undermined his own efforts. His tweets attacking judicial injunctions against both the first and second iterations of the travel ban— including one in which he contradicted his own legal arguments and specifically said it was a ban, not a readjustment in screening entrants to the country—were subsequently used by the courts in their deliberations and decisions.

The shooting of House Republican Whip Steve Scalise and three others at a practice for the congressional baseball game initially drew thoughtful calls for bipartisan concord from both Paul Ryan and Nancy Pelosi. President Trump's first response was similar. "We may have our differences," he said, "but we do well, in times like these, to remember that everyone who serves in our nation's capital is here because, above all, they love our country." But the spirit of concord quickly gave way, suggesting how much old norms of behavior have frayed. The president's supporters— including many prominent members of Congress—blamed the shooting on Trump critics and on the left. (The shooter, a clearly disturbed individual who was killed in the attack, had posted anti-Trump messages.) Trump said nothing in response to these charges. By the next morning, he had left conciliation behind, tweeting angrily about the Russia investigation.

Just as troublesome was the willing complicity of members of Congress charged with investigating Moscow's influence. Responding to a *New York Times* report of communications between Trump campaign officials and the Russians, White House Chief of Staff Reince Priebus communicated directly with top FBI and other intelligence officials to try to get them to talk to reporters to knock down the stories. The White House also asked the chairs of both the House and Senate Intelligence Committees, who are supposed to provide independent oversight of the executive, to do the same. Both chairs complied.[20]

Then, in May, Trump suddenly fired FBI Director James Comey. Appointed to lead the nation's top law enforcement agency by President Obama in 2013, Comey had served less than four years of his ten-year term. Trump's decision violated the long-standing tradition that the FBI should remain autonomous of the White House. Since ten-year terms had been instituted for the FBI directorship in 1976, only one director had been sacked early (William Sessions, who was fired in 1993 as a result of ethics violations). Hours after the announcement, *The New York Times* reported that Comey had met just a week earlier with Deputy Attorney General Rod Rosenstein to ask for additional resources for the FBI's probe into Russian interference. At first, Trump (ironically) used a memo from Rosenstein criticizing Comey's handling of the Clinton case as a pretext for the firing. But later in the week, Trump further strengthened claims that he was engaging in obstruction when he dropped the cover story and told NBC's Lester Holt that "this Russia thing" was on his mind when he dismissed the FBI director.[21] And *The New York Times* reported that Trump had told Russian officials in a White House meeting that month that by firing Comey, whom he called a "nut job," he would no longer face "great pressure because of Russia."

It is difficult to avoid comparisons between Trump and former president Richard Nixon. The Watergate scandal was in its time, and remains today, the most egregious example of a president violating both rules and democratic norms. Nixon's willingness to distort the truth systematically and to push aside anyone who dissented with his version of events led to what came to be known as the "Saturday Night Massacre." Nixon's order to have the independent special prosecutor Archibald Cox sacked forced the resignations of his attorney general and deputy attorney general, who refused to do Nixon's bidding. Many saw echoes of the Massacre when Trump fired Acting Attorney General Sally Yates after she ordered the Justice Department to refuse on constitutional grounds to defend the travel ban. The circumstances were quite different, but the appearance of retribution was even clearer when it emerged that Yates had earlier warned administration officials that National Security Adviser Michael Flynn had lied about the nature of contacts he had had with Russian officials. It was not until further disclosures by *The Washington Post* that Flynn was fired.

Comey's dismissal had even more direct parallels to Nixon's efforts to deflect and ultimately obstruct Watergate inquiries. His firing prompted the deputy attorney general, Rod Rosenstein, to name Robert S. Mueller III, a former FBI director, as special counsel to oversee the investigation into ties between Russia and Trump's campaign.[22]

The ousted FBI director did not sit by in silence. His testimony to the Senate Intelligence Committee on June 7 gave new ammunition to Trump's critics and enraged the White House. While Comey would not say directly that he saw Trump's actions as obstruction of justice—he left any conclusions to the special counsel—he made it clear that Trump had asked him to drop the investigation of Flynn. He was also very direct in explaining why he kept careful notes of his discussions with Trump in a way he had not done when he had conferred with Presidents Bush or Obama.

"I was honestly concerned he might lie about the nature of our meeting," Comey said of Trump.

The FBI director raised further suspicions about the president and those around him by saying several times that he could only answer some questions in a closed session. And Comey signaled how worried he was about the future of the investigation by acknowledging that after he was fired and out of office, he had arranged the leaking of his (unclassified) memos about his conversations with Trump "because I thought that might prompt the appointment of a special counsel."

Characteristically, Trump responded to Comey's testimony via Twitter, alleging that the former FBI director had simultaneously lied to Congress and cleared the president of all wrongdoing: "Despite so many false statements and lies, total and complete vindication . . . and WOW, Comey is a leaker!"[23]

The story continued to take bizarre and potentially ominous turns into the summer. When Trump's friend and ally Chris Ruddy, CEO of Newsmax Media, said Trump was considering firing Mueller, the White House shot the story down even as Kellyanne Conway tweeted an attack on the integrity of Mueller and his team. And when *The Washington Post* subsequently reported that Mueller was investigating Trump himself for obstruction of justice and many of those around him for financial crimes, Trump turned on Rosenstein. Playing off Rosenstein's original memo about the Clinton investigation, Trump tweeted: "I am being investigated for firing the FBI Director by the man who told me to fire the FBI Director! Witch hunt."

Trump's obsession with the Russia inquiry only fed suspicions that he feared where the investigation might lead. The revelations in July that Donald Trump, Jr., had eagerly agreed during the campaign to a meeting with a Russian emissary—knowing explicitly that the encounter grew out of Russian government efforts to tilt the election toward Trump—suggested that the president had reason to worry. But Trump's efforts at damage control (through attacks on investigators and his political enemies) had the opposite effect: they became exercises in damage enhancement. Toward the end of the 2016 campaign, Trump had predicted that Clinton's election would bring "an unprecedented and protracted constitutional crisis" because of the investigations she would confront. "She'll be in court for her entire tenure, and she'll be convicted," he said. It was a statement with eerie echoes for his own presidency.[24]

Analogies between Trump and Richard Nixon are necessarily imperfect (and, on the matter of being serious about policy, they could be seen as unfair to Nixon). Still, Watergate serves as an instructive counterpoint to how Trump's behavior has been addressed so far. Most congressional Republicans defended Nixon in 1973 and brushed off the allegations against him. But as the evidence of wrongdoing grew, Nixon faced an independent and intellectually honest legislative branch. Many Republicans set aside partisanship to check the excesses of his presidency. Is such a concerted, bipartisan effort to contain an abusive presidency even possible today? The early response of the GOP was not encouraging. *Slate*'s Jamelle Bouie noted that for Trump to fire Comey "in the midst of a consequential inquiry into his own inner circle" was "to violate every norm and expectation we have of White House conduct." Yet the reaction from Republicans was muted, leading Bouie to ask: "What will pull the GOP away from Trump? Nothing, it seems."

The question of whether Trump will eventually face a genuinely bipartisan challenge is urgent, not only because of the scandals that have dominated the news but also because of Trump's autocratic instincts.[25]

FOUR

A Penchant for Authoritarianism

How Trump Intimidates Opponents,
Promotes Kleptocracy, and Challenges the Rule of Law

Donald Trump called jurists who ruled against his administration "so-called" judges. He publicly browbeat companies
that did not do his bidding. He claimed that he lost the popular
vote because of "millions of people who voted illegally." He praised
Vladimir Putin as a strong leader and lauded his "great move" of
not retaliating against the sanctions imposed on Russia by President Obama for the country's interference in the 2016 election. He
lavished early and favorable attention on other notorious strongmen around the world, including Turkey's Recep Tayyip Erdoğan,
the Philippines' Rodrigo Duterte, and Egypt's Abdel Fattah el-Sisi.
He continued to denounce his predecessor and his 2016 opponent.
And, as we have seen, he labeled the media "enemies of the people,"
a phrase so dangerous that Soviet premier Nikita Khrushchev ordered that it not be used in the USSR because it could encourage
murder.[1]

A newly elected leader of a free, complex, and disputatious republic usually attempts to calm the country, to reassure the public

and Congress about his intentions, trying to move them through persuasion in the direction he desires. Trump's rhetoric is the barking of an autocrat intent on imposing his will. His attacks on his political adversaries, his contempt for truth-telling, and his shattering of norms brought forth more than the normal discontent of a political opposition dispirited about losing an election. They aroused widespread alarm that he was a clear and present threat to a free and open society.

Many Americans tried to comfort themselves that our constitutional safeguards, a widespread respect for the rule of law, and political institutions built to withstand despotic challenges would inevitably temper his illiberal tendencies and protect our democratic way of life. But the erosion of liberal democracy around the world in recent decades is a sobering reminder that established regimes have no guarantees of permanence.

Fareed Zakaria described the looming danger in a 1997 essay in *Foreign Affairs* entitled "The Rise of Illiberal Democracy." Zakaria noted that across the globe, "democratically elected regimes, often ones that have been reelected or reaffirmed through referenda, are routinely ignoring constitutional limits on their power and depriving their citizens of basic rights." In his recent book on increasingly illiberal regimes in Turkey and India, Basharat Peer built on Zakaria's prophecy:

> Strongmen are revisionists who share a preference for rewriting school textbooks, retelling tales of ancient glories, and reviving old wounds. They are united by their promises to make their countries great again. And they master the art of converting the fears and insecurities of citizens into electoral support. They position themselves as saviors on white horses, big-chested men who alone can rescue their nations from peril.

Zakaria and Peer are among scores of scholars and journalists who have described widespread democratic breakdown since the 1980s—besides Turkey and to some degree India, examples include Poland, Hungary, Venezuela, and Russia—and the risk that this contagion could spread to the United States. Essays by Masha Gessen, Timothy Snyder, and David Frum have rightly received wide attention for sketching illustrative comparisons between the rise of authoritarianism abroad and the potential future of Trumpism in America.[2]

Jeff Colgan's comprehensive guide to the vast scholarship on the risk of democratic decline includes a list of warning signs for those trying to make sense of what is now happening in the wake of Trump's election. They include media intimidation, the identification and even manufacture of crises or political paralysis to justify emergency measures, attacks on minorities, the scapegoating of foreigners, closing off space for civil society, the rhetorical rejection of the current political system, the weakening of the legislature and the intimidation of its members, the silencing of political opposition, and significant increases in internal security forces. Colgan notes, hopefully for Americans, that most cases of democratic erosion involve nations structurally different from the United States. The threat is especially great in poor and only recently democratized countries with weak institutions and weak economies. Yet he cautions that democratic erosion is a more general threat to countries that are highly polarized and have presidential systems. Sound familiar?

> The erosion of liberal democracy around the world is a sobering reminder that established regimes have no guarantees of permanence.

The United States is better positioned than other nations to repel a serious threat to its democracy and republican institutions. It has a long history of constitutional stability, countervailing political institutions at the national, state, and local levels, and competitive elections with relatively frequent rotation in party control. It also enjoys a free press, a vibrant civil society, and a long tradition of resilience in responding to political and economic crises. But in light of the danger signs, it would be foolish to ignore the risks. Decades of polarization, increasingly rancorous partisan warfare, and systematic campaigns to delegitimize government itself have eroded the ability of our formal institutions to check executive abuses. In previous chapters, we assessed the pressures on a free press and the denigration of our political norms. Now we examine how well our system of rule of law and our governmental institutions are positioned to resist challenges posed by Trump and Trumpism to democratic values and our basic civil liberties.[3]

In the manner of would-be authoritarians everywhere, Trump's denial of facts and his assault on the media appear part of a larger effort to suppress dissent, intimidate opponents, and sow confusion. We can look to modern-day Russia for a recent example of a regime that has done this effectively. As Peter Pomerantsev wrote in *Nothing Is True and Everything Is Possible,* his book about the Russian media and propaganda landscape, "the Kremlin has finally mastered the art of fusing reality TV and authoritarianism to keep the great, 140-million-strong population entertained, distracted, constantly exposed to geopolitical nightmares, which if repeated enough times can become infectious."

Russia is, of course, an extreme case. But Trump's attraction to its strongman leadership, his decades-long (if not yet fully understood) business connections with Russian oligarchs, and Russian interventions in our election to help elect him make the comparison more apt than it might otherwise appear. John Podesta, a top adviser to Hillary and Bill Clinton and to Barack Obama, drew a direct parallel between Putin and Trump and urged Americans to "maintain a heightened vigilance and think more carefully about the veracity of the information they consume." He added that "some of the information pumping through social media is indeed fake and sometimes malicious."[4]

The rule of law, an essential component of a free society and thriving democracy, begins with rights enumerated in the Constitution and elaborated bylaws, but it doesn't work unless those charged with implementing those guarantees act in good faith. From the beginning, Trump treated transparency, due process, and avoidance of ethical conflicts with disdain—mere niceties he could ignore. He demonstrated no appreciation for the integrity and professionalization of courts and public bureaucracies, which are essential components of the rule of law. Several episodes during the transition and his presidency confirmed that the behavior patterns established in his business and TV-celebrity careers would not be tempered by the responsibilities and expectations of the presidency.

As we saw in chapter 3, it began with his contempt for rules and norms related to conflicts of interest that all of his recent predecessors had followed. The general worry with such conflicts is that a president should not allow his public decisions to be influenced by private advantage. This is a common problem in autocracies, where public officials, their families, and their friends often amass vast private fortunes. And it imposes enormous costs on both the financial well-being of the citizenry and the strategic interests of the countries involved. Trump entered office with a large fortune and used his wealth to claim he was incorruptible. But his actual financial situation was opaque with respect to his net worth, debt owed to unknown investors, and public subsidies to his extensive and active business interests in the United States and around the world. Trump was certainly aware that the value of his business interests could be directly affected by public policy decisions, and he refused to dispose of his assets or release his tax returns.

Trump made a sweeping claim: that as president, he had near-absolute power to decide what was and was not a conflict. All other officials would have to deal with such ethical concerns. He would not. "The law is totally on my side," he said during the transition, "meaning, the president can't have a conflict of interest." It came very close to *"L'etat, c'est moi."* Trump elaborated: "In theory I could run my business perfectly and then run the country perfectly."

It's true that federal conflict of interest laws exempt the president (and vice president), but the reality of what's required is much more complicated. In addition to federal laws against bribery and fraud, which do apply to the president, there is also the emoluments clause in article 1, section 9 of the Constitution. Its language is a trifle archaic, but its meaning is clear enough: "No Title of Nobility shall be granted by the United States: And no Person holding any Office of Profit or Trust under them, shall, without the Consent of the Congress, accept of any present, Emolument, Office, or Title, of any kind whatever, from any King, Prince, or foreign State."[5]

As Norman Eisen, Richard Painter, and Lawrence Tribe noted:

Rather than worry only about *quid pro quo* bribery, the Framers recognized the subtle, varied, and even unthinking ways in which a federal officeholder's judgment could be clouded by private concerns and improper dependencies. Their anxiety encompassed the gift-giving habits of corrupt European diplomats, but also reached even the most virtuous domestic officials. And given the impossibility of effectively addressing this kind of corruption through bribery laws, or other statutes that criminalize particular transactions by reference to improper intent, the Framers decided instead to write a broad prophylactic rule into Article I.

The Framers were obviously not thinking of Donald Trump, but they were pondering the very sorts of complexities his situation presented. The global interests of the Trump Organization have almost certainly profited from his standing as president of the United States. Foreign countries and businesses will inevitably see the opportunities for influence that helping a company from which Trump has refused to divest could offer them.

Eisen, Painter, and Tribe offered a long list of actions by Trump during the transition and after his inauguration that sounded alarms about how his public actions might serve his private interests. Conversations related to his business ventures in, among other places, Turkey, India, Britain, the United Arab Emirates, and Saudi Arabia have been documented by an array of public interest groups and widely reported.

And Trump appears to have violated the emoluments clause at 12:01 p.m. on January 20 with his continued ownership of the Trump International Hotel in D.C. Trump had pledged to donate any profits he made from foreign government patrons at his hotels to the U.S. Treasury, but in March *USA Today* reported that he had made no such contributions. The Trump Organization then announced it would make the donation at the end of the calendar year, though this, of course, was just another promise, and there were repeated questions about how closely the Trump hotel was tracking foreign receipts.

Even as Trump delegated greater authority over his financial interests to his sons Donald Jr. and Eric, they and his daughter Ivanka were clearly involved in shaping their father's administration. Ivanka eventually joined it. Her husband, Jared Kushner, was already there and assumed a far-reaching White House portfolio, including responsibility over policy toward some countries in which he maintained active business interests.[6]

If the Constitution's main emoluments clause presented problems for Trump, so did a second one, in article 2, section 1, which provides that beyond his salary, the president should not receive during his time in office "any other Emolument from the United States, or any of them." The Associated Press reported in March, for example, that Trump's "executive order calling for a review of a rule protecting small bodies of water from pollution and development is strongly supported by golf course owners who are wary of being forced into expensive cleanups on their fairways." The AP added: "It just so happens that Trump's business holdings include a dozen golf courses in the United States, and critics say his executive order is par for the course: yet another unseemly conflict of interest that would result in a benefit to Trump properties if it goes through."

Similarly, any economic concession to any Trump entities by state governments (states typically provide a broad array of incentives for economic development projects) could violate the second emoluments clause. Trump has already acknowledged that winning the presidency has made his brand "hotter," and he has not been shy about advancing his business interests since his election as president, including his many well-publicized weekends at Mar-a-Lago, his Palm Beach resort—which doubled its membership fee to $200,000 after the election.

Trump's refusal to release his tax returns aggravates all of his conflict problems, and the importance of tax information as a constraint on corruption is why demands for the release of tax returns from presidents and would-be presidents led to consistent, voluntary compliance starting in the early 1970s. The post-Watergate Ethics in Government Act of 1978 required all presidential candidates to file a Public Financial Disclosure Report with the Federal Election Commission but did not mandate the release of tax returns. Nonetheless, presidential candidates assumed that such disclosure was part of the price of running for president—until Trump.[7]

The revelations that Russia intervened in the 2016 presidential election campaign to boost Trump's prospects heightened the importance of the release of his tax information, and his financial dealings with Russia were destined to become an important part of the various investigations into Trump and his 2016 campaign. After all, Donald Trump Jr. had said in 2008 that "Russians make up a pretty disproportionate cross-section of a lot of our assets" and that "we see a lot of money pouring in from Russia." What role, exactly, did Russia and Russians play in the Trump financial empire? Without disclosure, there was no way of knowing.

This is why Citizens for Responsibility and Ethics in Washington (CREW) brought suit against Trump under the emoluments clause two days after the inauguration in the hope of blocking him from receiving any benefits from foreign governments, including government-owned foreign businesses. Other suits on the emoluments issue followed, one from 196 members of Congress. Not a single Republican joined it. Another was filed by the Maryland and District of Columbia attorneys general. They argued that the Constitution demands a president "disentangle his private finances from those of domestic and foreign powers" and that "never before has a President acted with such disregard for this constitutional prescription."[8]

In June, the Trump Department of Justice responded to the CREW lawsuit by arguing that the president's business dealings were not, in fact, violations of the emoluments clause. A 70-page legal brief from the department cited George Washington's selling of crops to foreign countries as evidence that "neither the text nor the history of the Clauses shows that they were intended to reach benefits arising from a President's private business pursuits having nothing to do with his office or personal service to a foreign power."

But that Trump incited such litigation at all—and had to reach back so far for an example so removed from the complexity of his own business dealings with foreign governments—speaks to his indifference to long-standing ethical understandings. He is willing to use sweeping claims of presidential power to avoid steps that all his recent predecessors regarded as appropriate. Thus did he invite comparisons with kleptocratic strongmen around the world—and diminish the United States' moral standing to hold them to account.

Trump's experiences appear to have had another impact on his behavior as president. As a real estate developer and brand marketer, Trump was notorious for using lawsuits to gain advantage over disgruntled investors, suppliers, contractors, customers, and taxing authorities. His approach was entirely transactional. He sought a better deal: one that would save him money, remove a liability, or silence a critic. So we should not be surprised to see Trump's open contempt for an independent judiciary. Many other presidents, up to and including Obama, have expressed unhappiness over court decisions. But few went as far as Trump in expressing his disdain.

When a Seattle federal judge issued a restraining order blocking the nationwide implementation of the first and then-week-old executive order to temporarily bar refugees and nationals from seven countries from entering the United States—the de facto

Muslim ban discussed earlier—Trump's initial reaction was to attack the judge on Twitter: "The opinion of this so-called judge, which essentially takes law-enforcement away from our country, is ridiculous and will be overturned!" A follow-up tweet was more ominous, evoking memories of other countries shutting down their judiciary under martial law: "Just cannot believe a judge would put our country in such peril. If something happens blame him and court system. People pouring in. Bad!"[9]

Facing either a long trial on the merits in the Seattle judge's courtroom or the possibility of another defeat in an appeal to the Supreme Court, the administration withdrew its original order and issued a new one on March 6. It narrowed the scope of the first but still involved a ban on six countries (Iraq was dropped from its restrictions).

Judges in Hawaii and Maryland knocked that version down, too. Trump was incensed and lashed out in a campaign-style rally in Nashville on March 15: "We're talking about the safety of our nation, the safety and security of our people. . . . You don't think this was done by a judge for political reasons, do you? No. The ruling makes us look weak, which, by the way, we no longer are. Believe me. Just look at our borders. We're going to fight this terrible ruling."

Trump attacked his own Justice Department for trying to make his proposal more constitutionally acceptable—and even contradicted his own spinmeisters by insisting, against their claims, that it really was a "Travel Ban." On June 5, he tweeted: "The Justice Dept. should have stayed with the original Travel Ban, not the watered down, politically correct version they submitted to S.C." The "S.C." was the Supreme Court. He did not mention that the "watered down" ban was the revised executive order he had issued himself.

Later that month, a three-judge panel of the Ninth Circuit Court of Appeals ruled that, in issuing the ban, Trump had overstepped the authority granted to him by Congress to regulate immigration for national security reasons. Once again, Trump took to Twitter to express his frustration, writing: "Well, as predicted, the 9th Circuit did it again—Ruled against the TRAVEL BAN at such a dangerous time in the history of our country. S.C."

Trump's "again" referred to another assault he had launched at the Ninth Circuit in late April, when a federal district judge in San Francisco ruled against a Trump executive order that threatened to withhold funding from "sanctuary cities." At the time, Trump said that he was "absolutely" considering proposals to break up the Ninth Circuit. He called the circuit, 18 of whose 25 judges were appointed by Democratic presidents, "outrageous." Again, a president was not simply complaining about a ruling and pledging to appeal it. He was threatening punitive action against judges whose rulings he didn't like.

Trump's cabinet also joined in the verbal attacks. A month after the judge in Hawaii blocked the second travel ban, Attorney General Jeff Sessions vented his frustration publicly. In a comment that would be much mocked (but also represented a form of intimidation from the highest law enforcement officer in the country), Sessions told conservative talk show host Mark Levin: "I really am amazed that a judge sitting on an island in the Pacific can issue an order that stops the president of the United States from what appears to be clearly his statutory and constitutional power." The statement raised many questions, not the least being that the "island in the Pacific" happened to be a sovereign American state, and that the judge was a federal magistrate, not a state official. It was as if he had no right to rule because of where his court was located.[10]

Despite Trump's many public outbursts, his administration continued to follow the law and filed the appropriate legal appeals. But few judges will forget his attacks on the judicial branch or underestimate the likelihood of more efforts to intimidate those who stand in his way.

Trump offered a comparable response to the intelligence community when he disputed allegations of Russian involvement in the 2016 election. At times, he appeared to concede that Russia was likely responsible for the hacking of DNC files and the personal emails of Clinton campaign chairman John Podesta, which were publicly released by WikiLeaks during the closing weeks of the campaign. But he was not at all consistent in accepting the reality of the Russian intervention, reverting during his May interview with Lester Holt to language stressing the word "if" when referring to "a problem with an election having to do with Russia." He then muddled matters further by adding, "or, by the way, anybody else." And Trump repeatedly denied that Russian interference in the election was directed at boosting his prospects of winning, even though all the nation's intelligence agencies agreed that this was its purpose.

In the week before the inauguration, CNN reported that a dossier of mostly raw, unverified intelligence on Trump's alleged ties to Russia prepared by a former British intelligence agent had been shared (in a two-page synopsis) with the president-elect. The dossier was then published in its entirety by *BuzzFeed*. In response, Trump lashed out at the intelligence community on Twitter. "Intelligence agencies should never have allowed this fake news to 'leak' into the public. One last shot at me. Are we living in Nazi Germany?"

Trump's penchant for attacking those making any allegation or charge against him without addressing the underlying issue—and always with a flair for outrageous hyperbole—was deeply ironic in the case of leaks. Trump had, after all, built his career on sharing information with the press. During the campaign, he celebrated WikiLeaks for its exposures about Hillary Clinton's team. The irony was compounded when Trump aides condemned leaks from anonymous sources—but insisted on doing so anonymously.[11]

Moreover, Trump did not merely denounce leaks. He challenged the credibility and legitimacy of our entire intelligence community. The assault on leaks served a double purpose: to contain and discredit his critics inside the government, and to deflect attention from reports on his own behavior and the behavior of his lieutenants. His groundless and astonishingly reckless charge that Obama had his "wires tapped" had a similar purpose.

Trump borrowed other aspects of the authoritarian playbook as well. He singled out individual reporters for harsh criticism when he was unhappy with their stories, often lacing his comments with bigotry and threats of physical violence. One particularly egregious example was Trump's targeting of NBC reporter Katy Tur for abuse at a mass rally late in his campaign. In June 2017, Trump attacked MSNBC host Mika Brzezinski, tweeting that "low I.Q. Crazy Mika" had been "bleeding badly from a face-lift" when she visited Trump at Mar-a-Lago the previous winter. (Brzezinski noted that she had not had a facelift and was not "bleeding.") Mark Kornblau, a spokesman for the network, responded archly: "Never imagined a day when I would think to myself, 'it is beneath my dignity to respond to the President of the United States.'"[12]

> Trump challenged the credibility and legitimacy of our entire intelligence community.

He also pressured individual companies to alter their investment decisions to "save American jobs" (which often involved only

minor shifts on corporate strategy but gained Trump good publicity). And then there was his ongoing effort—often based on distorting reality—to amplify fears of terrorism, allegedly "open borders,"
and urban crime in order to justify extraordinary measures that
impinged on the rights and well-being of many Americans. He
returned to this approach again in his remarkable tweetstorm after
the London terror attack in June, declaring: "We must stop being
politically correct and get down to the business of security for our
people. If we don't get smart it will only get worse."

If there was a limiting factor to Trump's authoritarian bent,
it was perhaps his sheer incompetence in fulfilling the basic functions of his office. Whether tweeting positions at odds with his
legal team's argument in the travel ban case or demanding that
the House vote on an Obamacare repeal bill before GOP leadership had whipped enough votes, Trump repeatedly undercut his
own agenda and hobbled his administration with his brash boasts
and his utter lack of policy knowledge. Ezra Klein, editor-in-chief
of *Vox*, smartly contrasted Trump's ineptitude with his campaign
promise that his business success would translate to success as president. "It has long been a trope in American politics that the government needs to be run more like a business," Klein wrote, "but
no board of directors would allow a business to be run like this."[13]

But Trump would not be the first leader to combine incompetence with autocratic instincts. Both are threats to constitutional
government.

Can the institutions of American democracy resist Trump's attacks
on dissent and opposition? As we have already seen, a free press and
a Congress that fulfills its institutional responsibility to check and
balance the other branches have, throughout our history, played

key roles in maintaining appropriate limits on executive authority and supporting the rule of law. While the media generally rose to the challenge early in the Trump administration, the Republican-led Congress was much less willing to take Trump on. But two other political institutions, the courts and the public bureaucracies, are also essential safeguards, and they were both under stress even before Trump's presidency.

The founders recognized the importance of an independent judiciary by granting life tenure for federal judges following their appointment and confirmation. Their goal was to empower the third branch of government to police unconstitutional actions and statutory violations with some independence from the day-to-day push and pull of politics.

American history is filled with cases in which courts have intervened to protect and enhance individual rights and defend the essential features of our republic. In the landmark 1954 case of *Brown v. Board of Education of Topeka,* the Supreme Court held that "separate but equal" facilities were inherently unequal and violated the equal protection clause of the Fourteenth Amendment. This case helped spark the civil rights movement, which eventually dismantled a racial caste system. And in a 1974 case directly relevant to Trump's authoritarian aspirations, a unanimous Court ruled that President Nixon could not invoke "executive privilege" to prevent release of tapes pertinent to the Watergate investigation. This decision curbed the power of the executive branch to stifle inquiries into its own malfeasance.

But the sharp polarization of the political parties has politicized the appointment and confirmation of Supreme Court justices as well as district and circuit court judges to an unprecedented degree. This raises the question of whether today's Supreme Court, with a majority of its members appointed by

Republican presidents, would act as decisively as the Court did in 1974 if it faced a comparable abuse of executive power. The Garland blockade and Trump's appointment of Justice Gorsuch, a candidate endorsed beforehand by leading conservative organizations, are not encouraging signs.

Presidents now routinely apply informal ideological tests when choosing their nominees. This, in turn, colors the responses of the opposition party during the confirmation process. Norms and processes that encouraged more interbranch negotiation and compromise on judicial appointments have been weakened if not entirely swept away. While most of the cases that come before district and appellate courts do not evoke ideological responses, the positions of justices and judges on both social and economic issues increasingly align with the well-established positions of the party of the president who appointed them. Those partisan/ideological divides have arisen in cases central to the machinery of democracy, such as *Bush v. Gore* (which ultimately decided the outcome of the 2000 presidential election), *Citizens United* (which weakened Congress's power to regulate the financing of campaigns), and *Shelby County v. Holder* (which gutted key provisions of the Voting Rights Act).

The skirmishes over Trump's de facto Muslim ban were reassuring because—initially, at least—they suggested that a concern for the law and basic rights would breach the thickening walls of partisanship. When the full Ninth Circuit ruled in mid-March to maintain the nationwide injunction on Trump's initial travel ban, Judge Jay Bybee, one of the most conservative judges in the country, voted with Trump and against the court's majority. But he also issued a surprisingly sharp critique of the president:

> The personal attacks on the distinguished district judge and our colleagues were out of all bounds of civic and persuasive

discourse—particularly when they came from the parties. It does no credit to the arguments of the parties to impugn the motives or the competence of the members of this court; ad hominem attacks are not a substitute for effective advocacy. Such personal attacks treat the court as though it were merely a political forum in which bargaining, compromise, and even intimidation are acceptable principles. The courts of law must be more than that, or we are not governed by law at all.

In late June, a plainly fractured Supreme Court temporarily reinstated a part of Trump's travel ban but held off on a broad ruling on the core issues of the case until further hearings. It was at once heartening—the Court did not divide cleanly along ideological lines—but also a warning, since the three most conservative justices, including Neil Gorsuch, Trump's nominee, had been prepared to lift the injunction against the ban altogether.

The Supreme Court and the circuit courts get the most attention, but other courts will also be critical to the rule of law. Federal immigration courts decide whether noncitizens charged with violating immigration laws should be allowed to stay in the United States. Overseen by the Department of Justice's Executive Office for Immigration Review, these courts currently have over a half million cases pending before 300 judges. A recent national study of access to counsel in immigration courts found that only 37 percent of all immigrants, and 14 percent of detained immigrants, secured representation for deportation proceedings. Not surprisingly, the study found that "immigrants with attorneys fared far better: among similarly situated removal respondents, the odds were fifteen times greater that immigrants with representation, as compared to those without, sought relief, and five-and-a-half times greater that they obtained relief from removal."

Trump and Secretary of Homeland Security John Kelly have demonstrated a willingness to round up those among the undocumented with no violent criminal records. And in June 2017, *The Guardian* reported that new judicial facilities, separate from immigration courts and lacking the resources to provide even a semblance of due process, are "part of Donald Trump's attempts to ramp up deportations by vastly expanding the arrest powers of federal immigration enforcement and prioritising more vulnerable groups of detained migrants in new court locations around the country." Will immigration judges stand up to protect the rights of immigrants, or will they give the Trump administration free rein to enforce inhumane policies?[14]

Trashing government is common in American politics. For decades, politicians have run for offices in the government by running against the government itself. Most Americans are critical of the government and find it untrustworthy, yet value its services and benefits as public goods to which they feel a genuine entitlement. But it is one thing to run against government as a tactic to insulate oneself from public skepticism. It is another to trash government for the sake of advancing a radical agenda to destroy programs, delegitimize bureaucrats, and consolidate one's own power.

In recent decades, the Republican Party has successfully pursued the explicit strategy of undermining trust in government in order to win majority control over the levers of power of government. What began with Newt Gingrich leading an insurgency against a seemingly permanent House Democratic majority in the 1980s has now been transformed into a quest for what Trump's chief strategist, Steve Bannon, has called the "deconstruction of the administrative state." It reflects a long-standing critique on the right of the entire thrust of American government since the Progressive Era and the New Deal. Critics of the administrative state—"the vast administrative apparatus that does so much to dictate the way we live now," as Scott Johnson, a conservative lawyer and cofounder of the *Power Line* blog, put it in 2014—see it as unconstitutional because regulatory agencies make and enforce rules based on authority they claim was illegitimately ceded by Congress.[15]

Whatever its failings, the public bureaucracy is essential for securing the rule of law in our democracy and resisting the misuse of public authority to punish opponents and quash dissent. When the Justice Department intervenes to protect the voting rights of minority citizens from local or state efforts to block their access to the ballot, it is affirming the rule of law and the rights of citizenship. When the Office of Government Ethics uncovers a violation of ethics or disclosure, it is ensuring that elected officials act in accordance with the law and do not put their own interests before those of their constituents. And when the Environmental Protection Agency fines corporations for illegally polluting the air or waterways, it is demanding that the private sector be accountable to the limitations imposed on it by democratic lawmaking in the name of the public good.

It should be said that not all bureaucracies or bureaucrats are opposed to Trump. He has intense support from the members of the federal public safety unions like the National Border Patrol Council, the association of Border Patrol agents that broke years of precedent by endorsing Trump during the 2016 election.

Trump has taken unprecedented steps to destabilize the civil service, appointing people to lead federal departments and agencies who in many cases are outspoken opponents of their central missions. The list includes Jeff Sessions at the Department of Justice, Scott Pruitt at the Environmental Protection Agency, Rick

Perry at the Department of Energy, and Betsy DeVos at the Department of Education.

Trump's already stormy relationship with the intelligence community is a special cause for concern. His regular attacks on the CIA, the NSA, and the FBI have made national security issues much more challenging and have sowed distrust between the United States and its allies around the world. Thus did the British government shockingly announce after the Manchester bombing in May that it would no longer share vital intelligence with the United States. Witness also the deep anger from Israeli and Jordanian intelligence services after Trump, without much apparent thought, gave critical classified information to the Russians.

The turbulence with the intelligence community was further aggravated by the ongoing FBI and congressional investigations around Russia and the Trump entourage's relationships with the Putin regime.

The Trump administration's efforts to weaken federal intelligence agencies and make them obedient to the White House have been advanced by the pro-Trump media's embrace of a conspiratorial conception of a "Deep State." This idea, drawn from authoritarian societies, sees current and former intelligence and security professionals colluding with the press and Trump's political enemies to delegitimize his election and undermine his ambitious agenda.

There is, of course, no evidence of this. The leaks Trump has faced since his inauguration are largely of his own making. As *New York Times* writer Max Fisher argued, Trump's persistent undermining of the bureaucracy "has forced civil servants into an impossible dilemma: acquiesce, allowing their institution to be sidelined, or mount a defense." Trump has created a vicious cycle whereby civil servants use leaks to counter what they see as delusional thinking and dangerous behavior. Trump then seizes on the leaks to further undermine the agencies. "The problem in Washington is not a Deep State," David Remnick wrote in *The New Yorker;* "the problem is a shallow man—an untruthful, vain, vindictive, alarmingly erratic President."

But the Deep State fantasy conjured by the Trump White House and the pundits allied with it has real consequences. The claim delegitimizes government institutions and stymies their ability to function effectively, feeding Bannon's designs for their "deconstruction." It can be used to discredit anyone who opposes the president, and even legally sanctioned inquiries into his actions. Thus did Trump defender Newt Gingrich tweet that special counsel Robert Mueller represented "the tip of the deep state spear" aimed at Trump. It can also implicitly serve as an argument in favor of what *Washington Post* columnist and former Bush administration speechwriter Michael Gerson called "extraconstitutional thinking." As Gerson noted, "If this [Deep State] is more than a metaphor," then "an existential threat to democracy has been raised. And an administration actually believing this might go beyond leak investigations and feel justified in scarier, Nixonian remedies."[16]

President Nixon did have similar suspicions of enemies within and was not hesitant to misuse the powers of his office to wage war on them. In Nixon's case (as we have begun to see with Trump), many members of the executive branch acted, through leaks or resignation, to prevent abuses of public authority. Acting under the pseudonym "Deep Throat," FBI Associate Director Mark Felt provided *Washington Post* reporters Bob Woodward and Carl Bernstein with critical information about the Nixon administration's involvement in the Watergate cover-up.

This has often been the case in American history: civil servants resist an overreaching president through substantive or symbolic acts of defiance. During George W. Bush's presidency, for example, a leak from within the government supplied the press with a copy of one of the administration's "torture memos," sparking a national conversation about the constitutionality of interrogation practices used in the War on Terror. In the Obama years, Edward Snowden's controversial leaking of troves of classified documents revealed information about a previously unknown government surveillance apparatus (even as it may have put American agents abroad at risk). And in June 2017, a government contractor was charged with leaking a National Security Agency report showing that a Russian military intelligence unit had, as *The Intercept* reported, "executed a cyberattack on at least one U.S. voting software supplier and sent spear-phishing emails to more than 100 local election officials" just before the 2016 election.[17]

The conflicts and tensions within the parts of government charged with protecting us could undermine their very purposes while also threatening rights and liberties. Many civil servants fear this—and it is precisely why they will continue leaking.

Trump's actions suggest that fears of a slow erosion of rights and of a presidency characterized by autocratic habits are not the fanciful inventions of the politically hyperactive. Trump's opponents adopted the language of resistance for a reason: they knew that this was not an ordinary time and that Trump was not an ordinary president. If citizens choose opposition against policies they dislike, they opt for resistance when they see threats to the very system that guarantees them redress.

There is good reason to hope that the worst abuses of Trumpism can be contained. The response to Trump from the moment he took office pointed to the power of the democratic antibodies in American public life. Many Americans availed themselves of the openings our constitutional arrangements provide and our republican tradition lifts up.

The next months will bring a great contest between Trump and the forces that opposed him from the beginning. But another great battle will take place for the consciences of those within his own party who sense the threat he poses but fear giving aid and comfort to their traditional adversaries. Trump attacked the parties when it served his purposes, but he also mobilized partisan feeling as a way of blunting accountability from Congress and the courts. There is thus a second struggle in American politics among Republicans and conservatives over whether Trump's tendency toward autocratic behavior and his threats to our institutions will ultimately lead them to set aside partisan concerns.

Donald Trump defends all of his actions, particularly the most controversial, by insisting that he speaks for "the forgotten men and women of our country." This claim has been key to the narrative of his political ascendancy. But for whom does he actually speak?

FIVE

Phony Friend of the Working Class

Trump, "Populism," and the New Politics of the Far Right

In March of 2017, Donald Trump traveled to Nashville to visit the plantation of former president Andrew Jackson in commemoration of Jackson's 250th birthday. "It was during the Revolution that Jackson first confronted and defied an arrogant elite. Does that sound familiar to you?" he asked reporters, adding: "Oh, I know the feeling, Andrew." Trump underscored his admiration for the controversial seventh president by having a portrait of Jackson hung in the Oval Office.

Team Trump's desire to resurrect the Jacksonian legacy signaled how much Trump's aides counted on voters seeing shades of Old Hickory in their new president. In their conception, Jackson was the populist who democratized and revolutionized American politics in the 1830s, shifting the locus of political power away from the wealthy and toward ordinary citizens. But there was another side of Jackson, the unapologetic slaveholder and brutal persecutor of Native Americans who championed a democracy for white men. It's possible to imagine that at least some of Trump's advisers (and many in the ranks of his more extreme supporters) were in no way turned off by this aspect of the Jacksonian inheritance. In any case, the embrace of Jackson reinforced the idea that Trump would bring about a dramatic realignment of the political system to empower (white) working-class Americans left behind by globalization and cultural change. This certainly was the promise of his inaugural address, in which he declared that "the forgotten men and women of our country will be forgotten no longer."[1]

The idea of Trump as the "populist" successor to Jackson is not entirely outlandish. Both men came to office by eschewing the attitudes and policy preferences of the political mainstream of their time while arguing that they were representatives of ordinary Americans. Both were rich men who cast themselves as tribunes of the people. And there was the politics of race, on which Jackson was decidedly on history's wrong side.

But there are important differences: while Jackson was an orphan who grew up in difficult economic circumstances, was a hero of the War of 1812, and had a long career in public service, Trump's background was privileged, and he had no experience in government or the military before running for president. Jackson and his vice president, Martin Van Buren, contributed in important ways to the democratization of American politics through the creation of the mass political party, which gave the growing working class a powerful means of achieving representation in government. Trump, at least rhetorically, ran against political parties, even if he needed to take control of one of them to become president. And while history (and many economists) might judge Jackson's decision to veto the rechartering of the Bank of the United States as misguided—and also a way of simply empowering a different set of elites—it was a battle with authentically populist resonance during which Jackson really did take on the northeastern power centers of his day.

Trump, on the other hand, immediately and frequently contradicted his past words. As was often noted, his cabinet and a large part of his inner circle could be seen as a coalition of generals and Goldman Sachs bankers. His embrace (later walked back) of the Republican House's bill to repeal the Affordable Care Act that would throw 23 million Americans off their health coverage directly contradicted his promise to provide quality health coverage for all Americans. So did his support of an early Senate version of repeal. His tax proposals were similarly at odds with his egalitarian rhetoric. According to the nonpartisan Tax Policy Center, they would provide the largest benefits, in dollar and percentage terms, to the highest-income households.[2]

The future of Trumpism will thus hang in part on the question: Is Trump a true friend of the working class, or a phony? The evidence is quite clear.

While Trump's specific positions were often in flux during the campaign (he sometimes altered his course in the middle of a speech) and the details at best ambiguous, his core arguments were remarkably consistent. Make America Great Again. America First. Defeat radical Islamic terrorism. End the scourge of slow growth, sluggish wages, too few good jobs. Repair a ravaged economy in the industrial heartland. Bludgeon businesses to keep jobs from going to Mexico or China, and punish those that send them offshore. Stop the spiral of crime and end the "carnage" in our inner cities. Regain control of our borders. Build a Big Wall separating the United States from Mexico. Deport illegal immigrants and reduce the flow of new legal immigrants. Tear up bad trade agreements like NAFTA and make better deals. Make a trillion-dollar investment in infrastructure (even if it turned out that what he had in mind was mostly tax breaks for privatizing public assets). Lessen the burden on the United States as the world's policeman. Force other countries, including our NATO allies, to pay their own way. Do away with political correctness. Lift up ordinary Americans condescended to and mocked by liberal academics, cosmopolitans, the media, and globalists. Appoint Scalia-like justices to the Supreme Court who espouse the "original" meaning of the Constitution and are pro-life. "Drain the swamp" of Washington, D.C., with its ethically challenged politicians and well-connected lobbyist-fundraisers.

Trump was less forthright about two key issues, both of major importance to the Republican Party but at odds with the rest of his pitch. He offered strong rhetorical support to the party's commitment to "repeal and replace" Obamacare, which was the GOP's central mission during seven years of opposition to President Obama. But he linked this standard-issue Republican pledge to an insistence that his plan would provide everyone with insurance and "great" benefits at much lower cost. He pointedly separated himself from his GOP primary foes on the big issues of the welfare state. As Trump tweeted in 2015, "I was the first & only potential GOP candidate to state there will be no cuts to Social Security, Medicare & Medicaid." Where Medicaid and Social Security disability benefits were concerned, this was a promise soon to be broken—and, to use a Trump turn of phrase, broken "big league."

During his campaign, Trump also finessed the issue of taxes, a matter of quasi-theological concern to Republicans since the Reagan era—and especially so after President George H. W. Bush broke with his party's right in 1990 by negotiating with Democrats to raise them to balance the budget. "No new taxes—ever" was the Republican battle cry.

Yes, Trump favored corporate tax reform and tax cuts for individuals, and his actual plan pleased many of the party's supply-side conservatives. But during his campaign, he often distanced himself from supply-side rationales for what he was proposing and spoke critically of tax breaks for the wealthy, particularly the carried interest loophole for hedge fund professionals. He strongly suggested—even though this was at odds with his own plan—that he wanted to provide tax relief to struggling middle-class families, not to billionaires like himself. As we shall see, his initial foray into tax reform as president left that hint far behind.[3]

Thus, the ideological package Trump presented was *populist,* at least in the sense that he rhetorically championed the interests of ordinary people exploited by a privileged elite; *nativist,* in promising to advance the interests of native-born Americans against those of immigrants; *nationalist,* in both an economic and foreign policy sense, and with national identity often defined in ethnic, racial, and religious terms; and *protectionist,* in proposing to shield the country's domestic industries from foreign competition by taxing imports and pressuring employers not to move their plants abroad.

How did this blend of promises fare after he was sworn in as president?

Trump was most true to his nativist promises, pushed by his top aides Steve Bannon and Stephen Miller. Without the commitment of a single peso from Mexico, he forged ahead with his "big, beautiful wall" at our southern border. He sought start-up funds from Congress and charged the Department of Homeland Security (DHS) with letting contracts on the initial stages of the wall. Many in his own party as well as virtually all Democrats saw the wall as a fool's errand, but Trump did not budge. He did, however, stress less and less that Mexico would foot the bill, a rare concession to reality. Requiring American taxpayers to cover the $20–$40 billion costs of his massive building project was destined to be problematic. And, indeed, Trump failed to get funding for the wall included in the omnibus appropriations bill approved by Congress to cover much of 2017. Trump's initial 2018 budget proposal sought to make a modest down payment on the wall by cutting funding to the Coast Guard and the Transportation Security Administration (TSA). This prompted Michael Chertoff, who led DHS under President Bush, to observe: "It's a little bit like putting an extra lock on the front door and none on the back door. You are not really protecting the house." Trump also directed DHS to intensify the arrest and deportation of undocumented immigrants, hiring additional agents and broadening the category of those eligible for immediate deportation to include individuals who have resided and worked in the country for years with no evidence of criminal activity.[4]

Trump's travel and resettlement ban on immigrants and refugees from seven (and then six) Islamic-majority nations raised, as we have already seen, profound legal and administrative problems. But its specific character demonstrated that it was less about security and more about Trump's determination to send a message about who could and who could not come to the United States, about which groups were and weren't welcome. A leaked DHS report concluded that the order would do virtually nothing to protect Americans from terrorism, and some government officials saw it as enlarging the danger by playing into the hands of ISIS propagandists. Still, it would block the flow of a significant number of Muslims to the United States, both directly and by its indirect effects. This was the point.

Trump advanced his protectionist agenda symbolically by formally withdrawing the United States from the Trans-Pacific Partnership trade deal, which Congress had previously failed to ratify (and Clinton had backed away from during the campaign). He indicated a preference for bilateral rather than multilateral trade agreements, and he threatened import taxes on goods produced by American firms manufactured overseas. But Trump sent a mixed message by appointing a staff sharply divided in its approach to trade. Peter Navarro, director of the National Trade Council, and Bannon are outright economic nationalists. Robert Lighthizer, the U.S. trade representative, is a Reagan administration veteran known as a trade hawk. Meanwhile, Gary Cohn, the director of the National Economic Council, is seen as more of a free trader, as is Treasury Secretary Steve Mnuchin, though Mnuchin sent unclear signals early on about which camp he would side with.

Trump offered particularly mixed messages on NAFTA. An early draft of the administration's NAFTA proposals was described as "mostly modest" by *The Wall Street Journal* and as a "compromise" between "trade hawks" and "moderates" by *Axios*. They were a long way from living up to the changes Trump promised when he described the agreement as a "disaster." It was an early sign of the contrast between Trump's campaign bombast and actual policies.[5]

Then, over a bizarre few days in late April, administration officials suggested that Trump was preparing to sign an executive order to withdraw from NAFTA, but the president later announced he would seek to renegotiate it instead. "I was all set to terminate," Trump said in an interview with *The Washington Post*. But when pro-business aides who opposed ripping up the treaty showed him a map and pointed out how many farming communities that had voted for him could be hurt by the decision, Trump changed his mind. With Trump, all politics is about him and about the immediate. "It shows that I do have a very big farmer base, which is good. They like Trump, but I like them, and I'm going to help them," he said. Trump also issued what might be the quintessentially Trumpian statement, oily and utterly meaningless. "Hey, I'm a nationalist and a globalist," he told *The Wall Street Journal*. "I'm both."

Trump's nationalism was reinforced every time he recited his "America First" slogan (which was often), and he played to the far right's traditional skepticism of international organizations by proposing to reduce or eliminate American contributions to them. During the campaign, the transition, and the first months of his presidency, Trump regularly referred to NATO allies as not paying their dues (his critics said he made a defense pact sound like a country club), even as Vice President Mike Pence and Defense Secretary James Mattis made strong pro-NATO statements. But Trump made a total about-face in April 2017, when in a press conference with the NATO secretary general he told reporters : "I said it [NATO] was obsolete. It's no longer obsolete." Like many of his other promises, Trump's anti-alliance nationalism could be abandoned and resurrected on a whim.[6]

Still, Trump and Bannon continued to signal their skepticism of the European Union and international partnerships, whether through Trump's visits with Nigel Farage, at the time the leader of the far-right United Kingdom Independence Party (UKIP) and one of the chief architects of the Brexit campaign, or through his implicit endorsement of Marine Le Pen, the leader of the far-right National Front, for the French presidency. In late May, Trump visited Europe for NATO and G-7 summits, and his behavior there suggested that the United States would abdicate its 70-year role as an indispensable leader of the Western alliance. He declined to give his endorsement to NATO's Article 5 principle of mutual defense, blindsiding his national security team and shocking European leaders. Shortly after Trump's trip, German chancellor Angela Merkel said that Europe now "really must take our fate into our own hands." It took Trump 15 days to declare, at a White House news conference, that "I'm committing the United States to Article 5."

On June 1, Trump announced that the United States would withdraw from the multilateral Paris Agreement on climate change that had been entered into by President Obama. He justified his decision with the argument that he was "elected to represent the citizens of Pittsburgh, not Paris." (Pittsburgh actually voted for Clinton.) But, of course, climate change does not only threaten those beyond our borders; Americans, too, are at tremendous risk from rising temperatures and sea levels. As a result of Trump's shortsighted decision, the United States joined Syria and Nicaragua as the only countries in the world not party to the accords.[7]

And one of the clearest signs of Trump's skepticism of global engagement was his proposed 37 percent budget cut for the State Department—strongly opposed, as it happened, by Secretary of Defense Mattis, even though his agency was one of the few winners in Trump's spending plan. The exceptionally modest public role of Secretary of State Rex Tillerson during his early months was partly the result of internal administration politics and his own inexperience. Still, this, too, suggested a break from substantial diplomatic engagement around the globe.

But what of Trump the populist? Even setting aside the chaos, disruption, and deflection in the early going—along with the administration's obsessive efforts to distract attention from investigations into his campaign's alleged collusion with Russia during the 2016 campaign—Trump regularly demonstrated the hollowness of his populist rhetoric, though more so on some issues than others.

Where money was concerned, his populism was bankrupt.

In a December 2016 column in *The New York Times,* Paul Krugman wrote that "all indications are that we're looking at huge windfalls for billionaires combined with savage cuts in programs that serve not just the poor but also the middle class. And the white working class, which provided much of the 46 percent Trump vote share, is shaping up as the biggest loser." He added: "Trumpist populism is turning out to be entirely fake, a scam sold to working-class voters who are in for a rude awakening."

The influence of Trump's personal reference group was obvious when he assembled his government. During the campaign, he had regularly assailed Clinton's coziness with Wall Street. During the primaries, he charged that Goldman Sachs would have "total, total control" over his GOP primary opponent Ted Cruz, whose wife, Heidi, works for the finance giant. Trump then filled his government with Wall Street veterans. And as of early spring, six of his appointees had ties to Goldman Sachs. Goldman alumni included Treasury Secretary Mnuchin, Bannon, and Gary Cohn. Goldman Sachs stock rose 33 percent following the election.

Many of his advisers were, like Trump, inclined to see little distinction between their private interests and their public duties. Carl Icahn, the pioneer corporate raider and asset stripper worth an estimated $16 billion, was appointed by Trump as an unpaid special adviser on regulatory matters. *Bloomberg Businessweek* disclosed that as part of his work, Icahn pushed for an arcane change in the way renewable fuel credits work that would benefit CVR Energy Inc., his refinery company. As the magazine reported, just the possibility that Icahn might be able to engineer the regulatory shift substantially increased his wealth. The magazine reported that as of mid-March, CVR's share price had "climbed more than 58 percent, boosting the value of Icahn's majority stake by more than $500 million." Concern for ordinary Americans this was not.[8]

It was often said that Trump ran against his party and imposed himself on it as an outsider. That was true in the sense that most Republican politicians favored someone else as their party's 2016 nominee, but Trump's distance from his party has been vastly exaggerated. Once in office, Trump happily cooperated with much of the GOP's corporate agenda. This is evidenced particularly by his position on regulatory reform. Trump campaigned in support of a long-standing Republican proposal to cut sharply the number of regulations allegedly burdening small businesses and diminishing economic growth—including expanded overtime pay and workplace safety regulations. In his early months in office, slashing the rules governing business, often to the detriment of workers, may well have been his most substantive achievement.

Only two weeks into his term, Trump signed an executive order to review a Department of Labor rule aimed at combating conflicts of interest on the part of investment advisers to Americans with 401(k) and other retirement savings plans. Known as the "fiduciary rule," it required that financial advisers work in the best interest of their clients, which limited their ability to push investments favored by their firms. Its repeal had been on the wish list of many such companies. He also pledged to repeal the Dodd-Frank Wall Street reforms and joined his party's effort to gut the Consumer Financial Protection Bureau, whose task is to protect credit card holders and loan recipients from being misled and exploited.

In February, Trump signed one bill repealing a Securities and Exchange Commission rule requiring the oil, gas, and mining industries to report details of payments made to foreign governments and another weakening the rules regulating the coal industry's ability to pollute sources of drinking water. And, walking away from Obama's climate policies, Trump's team targeted the previous administration's clean power regulations as well as the Paris Agreement, claiming that doing so would restore coal jobs. But given the state of the energy market (and shifts in how coal is mined), his moves were likely to do far more to pump carbon into the atmosphere and accelerate climate change than to keep his extravagant promises to coal country.

In April, with little fanfare, he signed a bill passed on a party-line vote to eliminate an Obama administration rule on online privacy protection. Under the law, as *The Washington Post*'s Brian Fung reported, Verizon, AT&T, Comcast, and others "will be able to monitor their customers' behavior online and, without their permission, use their personal and financial information to sell highly targeted ads." This was not the sort of legislation that voters in the old mill towns who had backed Trump were yearning for.

Trump also backed away from many of his populist and protectionist proposals for international trade and finance. During the campaign, he promised to label China a currency manipulator on his first day in office, even though economists broadly agree that China is not currently engaged in the practice. But after meeting with President Xi Jinping in April, he told *The Wall Street Journal* in an interview that "they're not currency manipulators." Trump subsequently tweeted his justification for changing his position on China: "Why would I call China a currency manipulator when they are working with us on the North Korean problem? We will see what happens!"[9]

Especially revealing of Trump's faux concern for the interests of working-class Americans was his embrace of House Speaker Paul Ryan's bill to repeal and replace Obamacare. In his opportunistic health care dance during the campaign, Trump had occasionally (as when he praised the health care system in Scotland) sounded like a fan of single-payer, government-provided insurance. He channeled Bernie Sanders more than he did Ryan when he told *The Washington Post* in January: "We're going to have insurance for everybody. There was a philosophy in some circles that if you can't pay for it, you don't get it. That's not going to happen with us."

But this is exactly what did happen with Trump. Once in office, faced with having to take a stand, he fought for a bill that, according to the Congressional Budget Office (CBO), would initially have thrown 14 million Americans off health insurance in 2018, 24 million by 2026. The first iteration of the House bill failed for many reasons, but the underlying cause was the fact that neither Trump nor Republicans in Congress—despite years of promising to replace the Affordable Care Act—had a coherent proposal capable of keeping their repeal promises to the party's right wing while also continuing to help their party's core supporters who now had coverage because of the ACA. According to an analysis by Nate Cohn in *The New York Times,* Trump supporters were more likely to lose coverage under the Republican bill than Clinton voters were. This view was backed up by an Urban Institute study showing that the states that would suffer the largest coverage losses from Obamacare's repeal included the Trump strongholds of West Virginia, Arkansas, Kentucky, and Louisiana.[10]

Nevertheless, House Republicans continued to try to reach an agreement on an Obamacare repeal bill that would appease both far-right members of the House Freedom Caucus and more pragmatic conservatives. A slightly revised version of the American Health Care Act (AHCA) finally passed the House on May 4. An ebullient President Trump held a triumphant ceremony at the White House with gleeful House Republicans to celebrate the "victory"—even though no bill becomes law until passed in identical form by both houses. He lavished praise on a measure that would be a catastrophe for health care. It would strip coverage from 23 million people, threaten the coverage of millions more with preexisting conditions, and promise to gut Medicaid. As Krugman summarized the matter: "It's a miserably designed law, full of unintended consequences. It's a moral disaster, snatching health care from tens of millions mainly to give the very wealthy a near-trillion-dollar tax cut."

And it was deeply unpopular, even with Trump's base. A Quinnipiac poll released on May 11 found that 56 percent of Americans, including 48 percent of white Americans without college degrees, disapproved of the House legislation. An analysis for *The New York Times' Upshot* blog by two political scientists found that in not one of the 50 states did the AHCA enjoy majority support.[11]

Perhaps Trump was paying attention to the polling. Meeting in mid-June with a group of Republican senators working on an alternative bill, Trump—never one to be tied to his own past positions—called the House bill he had extolled a little over a month earlier "mean." The Senate Republicans, as we saw in chapter 3, initially guarded their bill as closely as the nuclear codes. What eventually emerged from their secret sessions was based in large part on the House bill, including its large tax cuts for the wealthy, and was less "mean" only in that it threw recipients off the insurance rolls a bit more slowly.

"Nobody knew health care could be so complicated," Trump declared after the House's first, failed attempt to pass the AHCA. It was a statement that underscored the emptiness of virtually every promise Trump made to American workers. The kudos, attention, and positions close to the Oval Office went to those with whom he had forged the strongest relationships: his friends in the world of business and finance. There were no labor leaders or working-class champions in Trump's orbit. The most rhetorically outspoken "populist" was Bannon, the Goldman Sachs veteran who listed his net worth as between $9.5 million and $48 million.[12]

Trump's advisers seemed aware that he needed to offer an occasional nod to populism, so in mid-April, he signed an executive order tightening up the rules on the H1-B visa program for highly skilled workers and giving preference to American bidders and American steel in federal projects. "We're going to protect our workers, defend our jobs, and finally put America first," he declared.

But even this move was more symbol than substance. *The New York Times* noted that the H1-B reforms were "relatively modest steps" that came as a relief to Silicon Valley after Trump's hardline rhetoric and actually represented "a small win for bigger tech companies." And Trump's "Buy American" proposals brought forth reminders from the media of how many of the products of Trump's own companies were manufactured overseas.[13]

Trump's indifference to working-class interests emerged again in late April when he announced his plan to overhaul the tax code. "Plan" is a strong word, since what the administration issued was a single page with no estimates of its effect on low-, middle-, and high-income households, federal revenues, or deficits. But its central pillars—cutting corporate tax rates by more than 50 percent, collapsing seven tax brackets into three, and eliminating the alternative minimum tax and estate taxes—promised enormous benefits for the wealthiest taxpayers. Trump would likely benefit himself, although no one could know for certain in the absence of his income tax returns. Senator Ron Wyden, the ranking Democratic member on the Finance Committee, summarized the reaction of Democrats and many independent tax policy analysts: "This is an unprincipled tax plan," Wyden said, "that will result in cuts for the one percent, conflicts for the president, crippling debt for America and crumbs for the working people."

The would-be populist had fully morphed into a supply-side conservative, embracing the long-discredited idea that big tax cuts for the wealthy would spur economic growth and thereby benefit the rest of us. Conservative *New York Times* columnist Ross Douthat declared Trump's populist war on the establishment stillborn: "As a populist he's a paper tiger, too lazy to figure out what policies he should champion and too incompetent and self-absorbed to fight for them."

Richard Trumka, the president of the AFL-CIO, used colorful language to warn of Trump's "bait and switch" approach to working people. "When the president says, 'I'm for you,' and then does the old switcheroozy and he pulls a health or safety regulation that hurts us, we'll let him know," Trumka said.

For Trump's working-class supporters, "the old switcheroozy" became the rule.[14]

Might Trump plausibly lay claim to the moniker of populism while championing the economic interests of the wealthy over the working class? Populism *is* a philosophically slippery concept. Politicians of diverse ideological persuasions and levels of attachment to liberal democracy have long denounced established economic, cultural, and political elites while portraying themselves as champions of the people. Scholars and political commentators have struggled to define when this behavior constitutes "populism" and when it does not. They have also sought to apply the term beyond its American origins in the (largely) left-of-center agrarian People's Party in the late nineteenth century to explain the modern phenomenon whereby populist leaders with widely varying political ideologies have come to power in countries around the world. The historian Michael Kazin underscored how broadly the term could be applied in his 1995 book *The Populist Persuasion* by citing a comedian who said in 1992, "To be populist, all you have to be is popular." Kazin got at the capaciousness and complexity of the term when he urged advocates of change "to stress the harmonious, hopeful, and pragmatic aspects of populist language and to disparage the meaner ones." You can take populism in many directions.

Because the meaner aspects of populism have come to the fore in movements of the European far right like France's National Front, "populism" is more a term of opprobrium in Europe than it has been in the United States. Yet for decades, there has been a rich American debate about populism as well. Richard Hofstadter and other historians and social scientists inspired by his approach stressed the anti-immigrant feelings and anti-Semitism within the movement and often cast it as a revolt against modernity. But a later generation of historians, notably Lawrence Goodwyn and more recently Charles Postel, emphasized the deeply democratic character of American populism, pointing to examples of its effort to build coalitions across racial lines and of the intellectual depth and curiosity of many of populism's grassroots supporters. In *The Populist Vision*, published in 2007, Postel insisted that the original American populists were not "Don Quixotes tilting at the windmills of modernity and commercial change," but were rather seeking "fair access to the benefits of modernity."[15]

In his influential *The Populist Explosion*, published in 2016, John Judis argues that populism should be thought of as a "political logic," that is, as an attack on elites in the name of the masses rather than a coherent policy program or belief system. Judis draws a helpful distinction between right-wing and left-wing populists. Right-wing populists such as Trump define the people's enemy as foreigners, racial minorities, and other outsiders, who are said to be the beneficiaries of coddling by an out-of-touch establishment. Left-wing populists like Bernie Sanders champion the interests of ordinary people against an economic and political elite, but without scapegoating marginalized communities.

The Australian political scientist Benjamin Moffitt, like Judis, argues that populism should be understood as a "political style" because it encompasses a range of performative behaviors that can overlay a wide variety of policies or ideologies. In his view, populism has three distinct features: appeals to "the people" versus "the elite"; the performance of "bad manners" or political incorrectness; and "the perception of crisis, breakdown or threat" in society. And as we saw is the case with Trump in chapter 2, Moffitt specifically points to the increased role of mass media in politics as a key contributor to the rise of populist leaders.

The near obsession with the upsurge of populism in the West led the political scientist Larry Bartels to offer an important caveat: contrary to the scaremongering, populist views across the developed countries have been rather constant over the last 15 years. The success or failure of populist movements, he argued, depended in significant part on the behavior of elites. "Where populist entrepreneurs have succeeded, they have done so by tapping a reservoir of populist sentiment that existed all along," he wrote. "Conversely, where mainstream politicians have managed to marginalize right-wing populist parties, they have done so despite substantial public support for the main ingredients of populism."

In France, for example, mainstream center-right leaders opposed the far-right candidacy of Marine Le Pen. In the second round of the French presidential election in May 2017, these established conservative politicians helped elect centrist Emmanuel Macron, even though doing so had a high short-term political cost for their own party. By contrast, most mainstream Republican politicians helped elect Trump after he took over their party, and have largely stuck with him. Bartels rightly lays a great deal of responsibility at the feet of the political establishment. "Populist views were there long before the current populist 'wave' made them salient," he wrote. "What happens next will depend on the ability and willingness of political elites to exploit or defuse them."[16]

Whether populism is good or bad for democracy, Judis argues that it can be a useful warning sign that "the prevailing political ideology isn't working and needs repair." But Jan-Werner Müller, a political scientist at Princeton who is particularly interested in European and Latin American examples of populism, has argued that the label should be reserved for a much less benign force in modern democracies. It is not sufficient for a political actor to be critical of elites to count as a populist, in Müller's telling. All politicians want to appeal to "the people" and to speak of how sensitive they are to the thoughts and feelings of the common men and women. And many have authentic ambitions to speak up on behalf of those who have been ill represented and left behind. But, he writes, only "populists claim that they, and they alone, represent the people." Or, as Trump has put it: "I alone can fix it." Müller sees populism as an exclusionary form of identity politics and a danger to democracy. In his book *What is Populism?*, he concludes:

> For democracy requires pluralism and the recognition that we need to find fair terms of living together as free, equal, but also irreducibly diverse citizens. The idea of the single, homogeneous, authentic people is a fantasy. . . . And it's a dangerous fantasy, because populists do not just thrive on conflict and encourage polarization; they also treat their political opponents as "enemies of the people" and seek to exclude them altogether.

By some of these definitions, Trump possesses the characteristics of a populist, and Bannon would insist that he is one. At times, he seems close to authoritarian forms of populism represented by Viktor Orbán in Hungary and Recep Tayyip Erdoğan in Turkey. Both have sought to undermine countervailing powers such as courts, media, political parties, and civil society actors, through what the Dutch political scientist Cas Mudde called "a variety of mostly legal means, but not classic repression." Trump continues to signal his sympathy for such leaders. In April, he called Erdoğan to congratulate the Turkish president after he won a voter referendum that dramatically expanded his political power. Friends of democracy around the world were far less sanguine about Erdoğan's victory.[17]

_____

For Trump, populism is more a marketing strategy than any set of deeply rooted beliefs. Steve Bannon, on the other hand, is a true believer. He was an early Trump supporter and had won Trump's trust long before he joined his campaign in the summer of 2016. Bannon helped direct it toward its unlikely success and has come to represent one pole of the Trump administration, embodying ideas and beliefs now associated with "alt-right" populism. Looking at his core views offers insight into the ideology and worldview of this wing of the Trump team, which also includes Stephen Miller and Attorney General Jeff Sessions.

Bannon now generally avoids writing in his own name or giving public interviews, but he made his views clear in his work as editor of the right-wing nationalist *Breitbart* website, where he often wrote and also hosted a radio show.

Through a close reading of articles published on *Breitbart*, Daniel Kreiss found a coherent ideological framework and a clear point of view on American democracy. "For Bannon and Trump's core group of supporters, the president's victory was a rejection of multiculturalism, cosmopolitanism, and globalization and the triumph of white, Christian populist nationalism," Kreiss wrote. The site's articles embraced a common refrain of "taking back our country," the battle cry of the Tea Party. They foresaw "'middle

America,' 'real America,' 'deplorables,' and 'fly over country' standing up, asserting themselves and their values, and rejecting those
who would repudiate them." Their targets included "Democrats,
the socialist left, the media, people of color, women, immigrants,
establishment Republicans, free traders, Wall Street, and Washington, D.C. insiders."

Kreiss also found that *Breitbart's* writers "explicitly rejected
immigrant *incorporation,* particularly for Muslims, into multicultural democracy." They argued that
"Islam is incompatible with democracy, freedom of speech, and the
peaceful and law-bound resolution
of conflict." And their critique extended to contemporary immigrants
in general, casting them as unlike

> For Trump, populism is more a marketing strategy than any set of deeply rooted beliefs.

their predecessors because of what these writers saw as a failure to
affirm American values and embrace American ways.

The critique of globalism on *Breitbart,* Kreiss wrote, "offers an
assault on global financial flows and international financial capitalism and free trade in favor of protectionism." One contributor
captured this disdain for globalism by describing it as "a curious
combination of socialism and capitalism—that is, bureaucrats
and bankers, working together to flatten national boundaries and,
indeed to flatten the nation-state itself. . . . [J]ust about all the
peoples of the world are instinctive nationalists; it's globalism that
is the strange mutation, afflicting mostly the West."[18]

Breitbart's positions closely tracked Trump's rhetoric during
the campaign. In effect, even before Bannon joined Trump's campaign team in August 2016, *Breitbart* provided the ideology for a
Trump candidacy. Or it may be just as accurate to say that Trump's
instincts about what many on the Republican right were looking

for coincided with *Breitbart*'s line and Bannon's hopes. Trump, after all, sensed a market long ago for birtherism, for an identification with the economic and cultural disaffection of white working-class Americans, and for a rejection of "political correctness." He had long been given to broadsides against corrupt political and business elites, as well as the immigrants and refugees they were seen as coddling—or employing in preference to the native-born. Bannon spent his years at *Breitbart* preparing the ideological ground and building an online political community for just such a candidacy.

Bannon himself was especially revealing in a speech broadcast through Skype to a Rome meeting of the Human Dignity Institute, a right-wing Catholic group that often finds itself at odds with Pope Francis. (A recording and transcript were published by *BuzzFeed* after the 2016 election.) His apocalyptic "clash of civilizations" worldview emerged clearly:

> I believe we've come partly offtrack in the years since the fall
> of the Soviet Union and we're starting now in the 21st century,
> which I believe, strongly, is a crisis both of our church, a crisis
> of our faith, a crisis of the West, a crisis of capitalism. And we're
> at the very beginning stages of a very brutal and bloody conflict,
> of which if the people in this room, the people in the church,
> do not bind together and really form what I feel is an aspect of
> the church militant, to really be able to not just stand with our
> beliefs, but to fight for our beliefs against this new barbarity
> that's starting, that will completely eradicate everything we've
> been bequeathed over the last 2,000, 2,500 years.

Bannon said that he found it disturbing that the "enlightened capitalism" of the Judeo-Christian West had been displaced by what he saw as two decidedly inferior forms. One was the sort of state-sponsored capitalism that prevailed in China, Russia, and elsewhere, marked by a crony capitalism in which a small number of people privileged by the state emerged with great wealth. He associated the other with Ayn Rand's objectivist ideology and libertarianism more generally. This version, he argued, turned people into commodities to create great wealth, again for the few. Here, Bannon certainly was channeling a form of populism, and, were his views not drenched with both nationalism and *Breitbart*-style racial animus, they might be seen as in line with a variety of Catholic criticisms of capitalism, including more progressive versions.

A second, not unrelated, trend identified by Bannon was the rampant secularization of the West, strikingly evident among the young. This converged, dangerously in his view, with the unpleasant reality that "we are in outright war against jihadist Islamic fascism." His declaration that "the Judeo-Christian West" is "in a crisis" reflected his overriding concern with securing a Western, Christian bulwark against Islam. And he reached all the way back to the eighth century to praise the "forefathers" who defeated Islam on the battlefield and "kept it out of the world, whether it was at Vienna, or Tours, or other places." It was difficult to get more apocalyptic, or more backward looking.

Bannon identified *Breitbart* as the third-largest conservative news site, behind only *Fox News* and the *Drudge Report,* and with a larger global reach than *Fox.* "We believe—strongly—that there is a global tea party movement," he said. This included the UK Independence Party in Britain, which fought for Brexit, and the National Front in France, as well as similar movements in other countries in Europe, Latin America, and Asia. Many of these groups brought ethnic and cultural baggage, he acknowledged, "but we think that will all be worked through with time." What bound these groups together was a "center-right populist movement of really the middle class, the working men and women in the world who are just tired of being dictated to by what we call the party of Davos."

Finally, Bannon expressed interestingly mixed views on Vladimir Putin. According to Bannon, Putin is the "state capitalist of kleptocracy," but he also embraces a traditionalism and nationalism that many in his so-called global tea party movement find attractive. As Bannon put it, "I think strong countries and strong nationalist movements in countries make strong neighbors." It was one of many signs of Putin's success in establishing himself as an ally of traditionalist right-wing movements around the world (and a hint of what was to come in the 2016 election).[19]

These remarks were made well before the Brexit vote and the launch of Trump's candidacy, and a year or so after the 2013 Conservative Political Action Conference (CPAC). As *The New Yorker*'s Ryan Lizza noted, Bannon had been something of an outcast at this important gathering for activists, politicians, and media professionals on the right. Following Romney's loss in the 2012 election, many conservatives were looking to emphasize diversity and tolerance to broaden the movement's appeal to young and nonwhite Americans who had been key to Obama's victory. Bannon organized an evening of counterprogramming to highlight what he viewed as the real issues on the right: the threat of Islam, illegal immigration, and corporate influence on politics. Several days after the conference, Reince Priebus, then chairman of the Republican National Committee, released what became known as the "autopsy" of the Republicans' defeat, which stressed the need for Republicans to reach out to nonwhite groups, to use more tolerant language, and to "embrace and champion comprehensive immigration reform." It was the exact opposite of the strategy pursued by the president whom Priebus would eventually serve.

Fast-forward to the February 2017 CPAC gathering. The highlight was a joint appearance by Priebus, by then chief of staff, and Bannon. In describing Priebus's half of the presentation, Lizza called him "milquetoast." "In bureaucratic fights," Lizza observed, noting Bannon's dominance of the conversation, "a White House staffer with strong and clear ideas, even ones that are bad, will beat a rival with no ideas every time."

Bannon now spoke for the president and the Republican Party, not just a right-wing website, but his presentation was true to his *Breitbart* legacy, including an obligatory attack on the "corporatist, globalist media." Bannon crisply divided the Trump agenda into "three verticals" or "three buckets." The first entailed "national security and sovereignty," the second "economic nationalism," and the third "deconstruction of the administrative state." Lizza captured the moment with his headline: "How Steve Bannon Conquered CPAC—and the Republican Party."

CPAC was once seen as a young and heavily libertarian redoubt. The ease with which it adapted to Trumpism was another signpost on the party's long journey. Yet the staying power of Trump's nationalist and populist turn will be measured by Bannon's own staying power inside Trump's inner circle. Trump certainly showed great affinity for the populist style during his rise to power. On immigration especially, as *The Washington Post* reported in April when the White House battle between Bannon and Trump son-in-law Jared Kushner was in full swing, Trump and Bannon had a kind of "mind meld." And absent an appeal tinged with populism, Trump would not have been able to assemble the coalition that allowed him to carry Pennsylvania, Michigan, and Wisconsin.[20]

Bannon's position waxed and waned within a Trump White House that became known for rather vicious forms of backstabbing.

For a while, he seemed to lose ground to Kushner and economic adviser Gary Cohn, who pushed more conventional policies. But with Trump's decision to leave the Paris climate accord (and particularly with the rhetoric the president deployed to defend it), Bannon-style nationalism seemed on the ascendancy again. And whenever Trump spoke about immigration and terrorism, his rhetoric was clearly shaped by Bannon and Miller.

Trump used populism, the Bannonites, and the nationalist right to win the election. They used him to get to power. In the meantime, on so many questions of direct concern to workers, Trump continued to govern in a way more responsive to the interests of those who patronized his Mar-a-Lago resort than to his voters in Appalachia or the struggling communities of the Midwest.

If Trump's populism is primarily opportunism, he seems most faithful to its "alt-right" version, involving aspects of Islamophobia, anti-Semitism, and xenophobia.

Consider his campaign's closing ad, a remarkable pastiche of images redolent of old anti-Semitic tropes. It was described well by Matthew Rozsa in *Salon:*

> Titled "Donald Trump's Argument for America," the ad depicts Trump as a populist outsider determined to free Americans from the corrupt insiders ruining this country.
>
> "The establishment has trillions of dollars at stake in this election," Trump asserts. "For those who control the levers of power in Washington," he intones (as an image of philanthropist George Soros appears), "and for the global special interests," he adds (while an image of Federal Reserve chair Janet Yellen appears), "they partner with these people that don't have

your good in mind." At his utterance of the last phrase an image of Democratic nominee Hillary Clinton appears.

Later the ad shows video footage of Goldman Sachs CEO Lloyd Blankfein as Trump declares, "It's a global power structure that is responsible for the economic decisions that have robbed our working class, stripped our country of its wealth and put that money into the pockets of a handful of large corporations and political entities."

As Rozsa noted, while "this footage may seem innocuous, anti-Semites watching the ad will immediately pick up on the fact that—aside from Hillary Clinton—every insider mentioned in the campaign spot is Jewish." And except for their Jewishness, he added, "they don't have very much in common. . . . Yet the ad evokes the stereotype that Jews are corrupt and secretive and aspire to control the world, a longstanding prejudice that has fueled anti-Semitic persecutions."

It was not the only time Trump trafficked in such stereotypes. In October 2016, Trump had claimed that "Hillary Clinton meets in secret with international banks to plot the destruction of U.S. sovereignty in order to enrich these global financial powers, her special interest friends, and her donors." The term "international banks," as Rozsa noted, "has also been long used as a code word to refer to Jews and suggest that they combine internationally to discuss secret plots to destroy national sovereignty."[21]

> Trump used the Bannonites and the populist nationalist right to win the election. They used him to get to power.

Trump would regularly fend off charges of anti-Semitism by noting the extraordinary faith he put in his Jewish son-in-law, his warm ties with Israeli prime minister Benjamin Netanyahu, and the presence of many Jews in his administration. In May 2017, Trump tried to put these charges to rest for good with a forceful denunciation of anti-Semitism at the U.S. Holocaust Memorial Museum's remembrance ceremony. There was nothing hedged about Trump's condemnation of "the hatred and evil that sought to extinguish human life, dignity and freedom," his criticism of those "who want to forget the past," and his call "to bear witness, to make sure that humanity never, ever forgets." It was one of the few speeches of his presidency that received warm reviews across ideological divides.

So let us assume that there is not an ounce of anti-Semitism in Trump. It is nonetheless true that his approach to politics clearly courts and exploits prejudice whenever it can be useful. As a candidate, he inspired white supremacist and anti-Semitic groups, including remnants of the Ku Klux Klan. They embraced him with enthusiasm and without reservation—and he avoided nearly every opening to criticize their behavior and their corrosive rhetoric. His closing ad would have been an embarrassment to any previous major party candidate for president. His comments about women, about immigrants, about Mexican Americans, and about Muslims would in the past have disqualified him as a nominee. The moves of Attorney General Jeff Sessions against civil rights enforcement and the administration's efforts to shut down or curtail civil rights bureaus in various cabinet departments, including Labor, the Environmental Protection Agency, and Education, sent another message congenial to Trump's alt-right enthusiasts.

There are many ways, as we have seen, in which Trump's populism is almost certainly more a means than an end, more a style than any sort of philosophical orientation. But to the extent that Trump is a populist, he is the sort Müller described, one who imagines a "single, homogeneous, authentic people" and treats his political opponents as "enemies of the people," a concept, as we have seen, that Trump himself has invoked.[22]

Populist or not, Trump clearly appealed to two broad, overlapping streams of discontent. One was animated by race, immigration, religion, and culture. The other was inspired by economic discontent, the flight of well-paying jobs overseas, and the hollowing out of many of our communities. But which was dominant? And how do they relate to each other?

SIX

Race, Immigration, Culture, or Economics?

The Complicated Motivations of the Trump Voter

Donald Trump's "Make America Great Again" slogan proved to be a work of political genius. It was not simply the open-ended nature of its promise. Many slogans have that quality. And who could oppose the idea of greatness? "Great" also happened to be a word that Trump rather liked, especially as it applied to himself and his projects.

The key was the nostalgic "again." It was the all-purpose word for Trump. It appealed broadly to Republicans and conservatives who believed devoutly that President Obama had squandered the country's greatness. "Again" implied that America's greatness lay in its past and that it was something to be regained. This contrasted with Obama's view that America grew greater with time, that it "perfected" itself as it changed. For those whose votes Trump sought, the changes of recent years were jarring and negative, sources of unhappiness and insecurity.

And by keeping matters vague, Trump's "again" could refer to a variety of pasts. For some, it was a more homogeneous America with fewer immigrants and less pressure to be "politically correct."

For others, it was an America of humming factories and productive coal mines where wages were good, Chinese competition was unheard of, unions were strong, and a cottage on a lake was within reach of the average working man. The word "man" here is not an oversight. The costs of economic change were felt especially keenly by men who once relied on industrial work for a living wage. For a share of Trump's voters, these two visions of a more congenial yesterday came together in a longing for so much they felt they had lost.

In light of the dangers that Trump clearly posed to the country and of personal flaws that were entirely obvious before the election, understanding why tens of millions of Americans backed him anyway is crucial to charting the future. Thus, before turning to a vision of the country after Trump, we explore the critical question of whether voters were drawn to him primarily because of issues related to race, culture, and immigration or because of his promises to lift up Americans battered by deindustrialization, trade, and economic change. In truth, as we will argue, these two factors cannot be entirely separated. By examining a series of detailed studies of why Trump's supporters decided as they did, we try to illuminate paths to political change and to a less divisive approach to our politics.

―――――――――――

Liberals and pro-Trump conservatives each have characteristic blind spots in analyzing the Trump upsurge. Conservatives who support Trump focus on his role as a spokesman for legitimate discontent. They often dismiss any attention to the strong racist and nativist strains within the Trump movement as "elitism," usually with some reference to Hillary Clinton's use of the word "deplorables."

Liberals (as is so often the case) are divided. Some on the left end of the Democratic Party, including many who rallied to Senator Bernie Sanders's presidential campaign, focus on economic discontent as the main driver of Trump's support. This analysis fits well with the issues they would emphasize anyway: the problems created by free trade, the decline of the labor movement, and the concentration of economic power. If Trump supporters are mostly angry at the behavior of Wall Street and corporate titans and dismayed by their own economic circumstances at a time of rising inequality, the obvious solution is a far stronger dose of populist economics and less coddling of the Democratic Party's donor class.

Another faction of liberals questions the idea that Trump supporters can be won over at all. This camp understands support for him as motivated primarily by racial reaction or outright racism, hostility to immigrants, and extreme social conservatism. These mainly social liberals see a long-term progressive majority emerging from rising groups in the electorate: Americans of color, younger voters who are more socially liberal, and a professional middle and upper-middle class that favors a more open society. Such an analysis points to a strategy based more on mobilizing groups already sympathetic to Democratic and progressive goals than on converting Trump voters.

> No one who reveres the New Deal tradition can accept writing off a white working class that has a legitimate claim to a greater share of the nation's prosperity.

There is something to each of these views, but each misses important aspects of the political distemper ailing the country that led to Trump. Conservatives are certainly right to insist that Trump supporters cannot be dismissed as a solid phalanx of racists. Trump supporters were obviously motivated by a mix of discontents. A large share of the Trump vote, as the exit polls show, came from reliably Republican and conservative voters. The Democratic left is correct to see that for many voters, particularly in the Rust Belt swing states, Trump's views on trade and his emphasis on manufacturing were genuinely persuasive. As John Judis wrote in the *New Republic,* "Trump's victory was not merely a sign of an electorate gone mad; it was also a cry of dissatisfaction with the way that Democrats, as well as Republicans, responded to the Great Recession and its brutal aftermath."

The social liberals thus need to concede that this aspect of Trump's appeal is genuine and not simply a cover for racism. They also need to accept, as we saw in chapter 1, that winning a decent share of the white working-class vote is essential for building a progressive coalition, particularly in the swing states in the Midwest. And as a moral matter, no one who reveres the New Deal tradition can accept writing off a white working class that has a legitimate claim to a greater share of the nation's prosperity.

Nonetheless, these critics of Trumpism are right to insist that nativism and racial feeling, including outright racism, cannot be ignored and were indeed a decisive part of Trump's appeal. It's significant that in the exit polls, voters who listed the economy as their most important issue voted narrowly for Clinton, 52 percent to 41 percent, while those who listed immigration voted overwhelmingly for Trump, 64 percent to 33 percent. But it is also true that voters who said that trade with other countries took away American jobs voted for Trump by a comparable margin, 64 percent to 32 percent.[1]

The debate over the nature of the Trump constituency often leads to dead ends because it is usually binary—race versus class, culture versus economics—whereas actual human beings are complicated. It is perfectly possible to be culturally conservative, racially motivated, and also deeply class-conscious about economic changes that have greatly harmed well-paid industrial workers. This is not new. Studies showed that race-conscious voters for George Wallace in 1968 were also among the most class-conscious voters in the electorate. It is possible to identify, as we have seen, with both aspects of what others might write off as nostalgia for the 1950s: a belief in unionized workforces and employers with long-term loyalties to their employees on the one hand, and old-fashioned, intact families with strong religious values on the other.

And it's impossible to separate entirely the upsurge of economic discontent from the rise of racism and nativism. It's true that racism has survived during good times and bad. But historically, times of widely shared prosperity are associated with greater social generosity. It is probably not an accident that the great gains in civil rights, a far more open immigration policy, and new efforts to alleviate poverty occurred in the 1960s, when the great post–World War II period of prosperity was at its zenith. As the economist Benjamin Friedman has argued, "a rising standard of living makes a society more open and tolerant and democratic, and perhaps also more prudent on behalf of generations to come." The corollary is also true: it is not surprising that Trumpism arose after three decades of rising inequality aggravated by a sharp decline in manufacturing employment and then the Great Recession. Among the white and native-born, attitudes toward racial minorities, and particularly toward immigrants, often grow harsher and more hostile in hard times.

Finally, it is no less important to note for being obvious that sharp increases in immigration have always been associated with a resurgence of anti-immigration politics. The Know Nothing movement in the 1850s was a response to large-scale Irish immigration after the Great Famine. The rise of a new Ku Klux Klan in the 1920s and other forms of agitation that led to the exclusionary 1924 Immigration Act were a response to the great wave of Eastern and Southern European immigration from the 1880s to the early 1920s. Over the last half century, we have seen another great wave of immigration, and its composition was changed by the 1965 Immigration Act, a vast liberalization of immigration law. In our time, the percentage of Americans who are foreign born has risen from just 4.7 percent in 1970 to 13.5 percent in 2015, a proportion roughly equal to the foreign-born share of our population at the peak of the great immigration wave in the early twentieth century.[2]

The long rise of inequality, the decline of manufacturing, the Great Recession, and the new wave of immigration would, by themselves, have created enormous political turmoil. But they were accompanied by new fears of terrorism after September 11, 2001, and frightening incidents of terror in both the United States and Europe in 2016. Public impatience with two long and, at best, inconclusive wars in Iraq and Afghanistan created widespread distaste for American intervention abroad. And older, more religious, and more traditional Americans were jarred and angered by vast cultural changes. These were sometimes overlaid with feelings about race and ethnicity, but also involved new issues such as gay marriage and transgender rights. Many traditional voters saw a country transforming itself in ways they never anticipated. (It was another way in which the Trumpian "again" resonated.) Robert Jones, a pollster and social scientist, described the fears of many who rallied to Trump with the title of his recent book *The End of White Christian America*. Jones showed that white Christians were already a minority in 2016 and were destined to constitute an ever-smaller share of the population over time.

If the financial collapse and the subsequent bailout helped give birth to the Tea Party movement, a combination of fear, anger, and unease over cultural change fueled it and eventually led most of its supporters into the Trump orbit. In the Tea Party's heyday, Vin Weber, a former Republican congressman, said that many of its supporters reflected their alarm with variations on the statement: "This change taking place in the country is really scary to me." Haley Barbour, the former Republican governor of Mississippi, said that 2009 and 2010, the years after the financial crash, were the first years in which he heard voters regularly say, "I'm afraid my children and grandchildren are not going to inherit the same country I inherited."[3]

After the fact, the unexpected can often be described, with a kind of false all-knowingness, as having been inevitable. Trump's election was certainly not inevitable. But a retrospective view does allow us to see more clearly how many forces came together to create his movement.

Which were the most important, and how did they interact?

———————

Brexit, Trump's success, and the growing popularity of ultra-nationalist movements in many countries in Europe have brought forth a rich trove of scholarship and thoughtful journalism aimed at explaining the rise of a new far right and the collapse of a middle-of-the-road consensus that seemed dominant before the economic troubles of 2008.

Ronald Inglehart and Pippa Norris are among the many scholars who see cultural backlash as more important than economic discontent in determining support for right-wing populists. In "Trump, Brexit, and the Rise of Populism: Economic Have-Nots and Cultural Backlash," they argued that the strength of populist parties in Europe was "largely due to ideological appeals to traditional values" and was "concentrated among the older generation, men, the religious, ethnic majorities, and less educated sectors of society . . . groups most likely to feel that they have become strangers from the predominant values in their own country, left behind by progressive tides of cultural change which they do not share."

Their paper was published before the 2016 election, but Inglehart and Norris offered preliminary data suggesting that the dominance of culture over economics would apply to support for Trump as well. Other scholars found evidence for this view after the election. In a paper published in January 2017, "Explaining White Polarization in the 2016 Vote for President: The Sobering Role of Racism and Sexism," Brian F. Schaffner, Matthew MacWilliams, and Tatishe Nteta concluded that while "the 2016 campaign witnessed a dramatic polarization in the vote choices of whites based on education . . . very little of this gap can be explained by the economic difficulties faced by less educated whites." Instead, "most of the divide appears to be the result of racism and sexism in the electorate, especially among whites without college degrees." They write:

> Sexism and racism were powerful forces in structuring the 2016 presidential vote, even after controlling for partisanship and ideology. Of course, it would be misguided to seek an understanding of Trump's success in the 2016 presidential election through any single lens. Yet, in a campaign that was marked by exceptionally explicit rhetoric on race and gender, it is perhaps unsurprising to find that voters' attitudes on race and sex were so important in determining their vote choices.

Michael Tesler, a political scientist at the University of California at Irvine, found that racial attitudes played a strong role in explaining support for Trump in the Republican primaries as well. "Republicans who scored highest on racial resentment were about 30 percentage points more likely to support Trump than their more moderate counterparts in the bottom quartile of the party in racial conservatism," Tesler wrote. He found that on racial matters, Trump's voters contrasted sharply with supporters of both of the party's previous nominees, Mitt Romney and John McCain, and also that "Republicans with very unfavorable views of Muslims were substantially more likely than their fellow partisans to support Trump."[4]

Philip Klinkner, a professor of government at Hamilton College, reached a similar conclusion in an analysis of the 2016 American National Election Studies pilot survey. Klinkner found that moving from the lowest to the highest measure of resentment against African Americans increased Trump's support over Clinton by 44 points, while affirmative responses on the question of whether President Obama was a Muslim pushed Trump's advantage up by 24 points. By contrast, attitudes toward free trade had an effect of only 11 points, and views on whether the economy was better or worse moved voters toward Trump by 23 points— less than racial attitudes, about equal to the Muslim question. But when Klinkner controlled for attitudes toward President Obama, the effects of both trade and economics were washed away, suggesting, as many other analysts have found, that views of how healthy the economy is depend more on a respondent's partisan preferences than on an assessment of the economy itself. Those who like the incumbent president or support his party offer a sunnier view of the economy, even when they are not necessarily doing well themselves, while those who are prospering will nonetheless give the economy low grades if they don't like the incumbent. Klinkner concluded that "attitudes about race, religion, and immigration trump (pun intended) economics."

Those who stress the role of economics in the election typically point to communities where there was a significant swing of 2012 Obama voters to Trump. A white voter who had backed Obama is presumed not to be racially motivated. But in March 2017, Sean McElwee, a policy analyst at the liberal think tank Demos, and Jason McDaniel, a political scientist at San Francisco State University, published a careful analysis in *The Nation* that cast doubt on this assumption.

Using data from the Cooperative Congressional Analysis Project, they found that 9 percent of Obama's 2012 voters switched to Trump in 2016, while 5 percent of Mitt Romney's 2012 voters defected from Trump to Hillary Clinton, and another 6 percent went to third-party candidates. What is striking is that racial attitudes explained the swings both ways. McElwee and McDaniel found that "individuals with high levels of racial resentment were more likely to switch from Obama to Trump," while Romney voters "with low racial resentment and more positive views about rising diversity" moved to Clinton or third-party candidates.

Intriguingly, McElwee and McDaniel found that "seeing diversity as a threat had a particularly strong effect on white Republican identifiers who switched from Obama to Trump, but a comparatively modest effect on white Democratic switchers." Additionally, "racial resentment towards blacks had a stronger impact on the probability of Obama-to-Trump vote switching for white Republicans compared to white Democrats." This points to Obama's success in nurturing a racial identity that made him acceptable even to some white voters clearly sensitive to race. It also suggests that Obama's sharp class-based attacks on Romney moved some racially sensitive voters to vote their class rather than their racial identity.

The fact that racial politics moved Republicans even more than Democrats toward Trump underlines what virtually all studies of the election found: the importance of Republican identification in explaining support for Trump. And it suggests that Trump reached back, consciously and successfully, to a backlash politics that had been helpful to Richard Nixon and also to Ronald Reagan and George H. W. Bush (in 1988 if not 1992).

It may seem odd that race played a larger role in an election in which an African American candidate was *not* on the ballot. *But Trump consciously made race and culture central to his campaign in a way that George W. Bush, Mitt Romney, and John McCain did not.* As Perry Bacon Jr. wrote at *FiveThirtyEight:* "Trump campaigned on a kind of white identity politics, highlighting black crime, Latino immigration and Islamic terrorism as defining issues for the nation. This was not just a break from Obama's approach, but also a shift from the last Republican president." Clearly, Trump increased the saliency of race.

"Our analysis," McElwee and McDaniel wrote, "indicates that Donald Trump successfully leveraged existing resentment towards African Americans in combination with emerging fears of increased racial diversity in America to reshape the presidential electorate."[5]

There is, finally, a set of attitudes common among Tea Party and Trump supporters that can be interpreted in racial terms but are not necessarily seen as racial by those who hold them. In their seminal book *The Tea Party and the Remaking of Republican Conservatism,* Theda Skocpol and Vanessa Williamson noted that Tea Partiers strongly supported Medicare and Social Security, in many cases because they were at or near retirement age but also because they saw them as earned benefits. By contrast, they opposed programs they perceived as going to "freeloaders" and were angry at "being stuck with the tax tab to pay for 'unearned' entitlements handed out to unworthy categories of people." These attitudes suggest that Trump was shrewd in insisting that whatever else he cut, Social Security and Medicare would not be on his list.

This view of "freeloaders" is not necessarily racial, and in his sensitive reporting in eastern Kentucky, Alec MacGillis noted that the backlash among voters against "undeserving benefit-recipients" was not confined to race but was often directed against "rising dependency they see among their own neighbors, even their own families." But the term certainly does carry racial connotations. Skocpol and Williamson, who went out of their way to avoid blanket charges of racism against the Tea Party, observed that some of this resentment does fall along "racial and ethnic fault lines." This research points to the challenge progressives face in making the case for programs that do not have universal application.

> Trump reached back, consciously and successfully, to a backlash politics that helped Richard Nixon.

All of these studies suggest that to ignore or downplay the role of race and immigration in creating the Trump coalition is to be willfully blind to the obvious. It is to ignore the content of Trump's campaign and the roots of his quest for the presidency in anti-Obama birtherism. It also requires ignoring strong racial undercurrents on the websites of the far right, including an increasingly open embrace of white supremacy. And it means dismissing the extent to which older conservative media trafficked in racially tinged messages during the Obama administration. (Rush Limbaugh did this often, once putting the words "Barack the Magic Negro" to the tune of "Puff the Magic Dragon." This passed for humor.) Being honest about the role of prejudice in the rise of Trump is not the same as accusing all or most of his voters of racism. It is simply to recognize that Trump played on prejudice, and that doing so helped him win over voters who had rejected both Romney and McCain.[6]

A May 2017 survey by PRRI for *The Atlantic* added useful detail to a cultural explanation for Trump's white working-class showing. As the magazine's Emma Green wrote, "anxiety about cultural change" was one key to Trump's strength. The survey found that 68 percent of white working-class voters said the American way of life needed to be protected against foreign influence, and nearly half agreed with the statement "Things have changed so much that I often feel like a stranger in my own country." Among white working-class voters who had these anxieties, 79 percent voted for Trump. He received the votes of only 43 percent of those who did not.

Immigration was also important. While only 27 percent of white working-class voters favored a policy of identifying and deporting immigrants, almost all of them—87 percent—voted for Trump.

Intriguingly, Green reported, the survey found that white working-class voters who said "their finances are only in fair or poor shape were nearly twice as likely to support Clinton compared to those who feel more economically secure." Trump, in other words, did *not* do best among the most financially stressed white working-class voters.

Further underscoring the power of a cultural analysis was the striking age split in the electorate. The exit poll found that voters 18 to 44 years old gave Clinton a 53 percent to 39 percent advantage over Trump. But voters 45 and older backed Trump, 52 percent to 44 percent. One of Trump's strongest groups in the electorate: whites aged 45 to 64, who gave him 62 percent of their ballots.

Trump did carry whites aged 18 to 29, but his margin among them was narrow, 47 to 43 percent, with about a tenth of young white voters defecting to third-party choices. The 15-point gap in Trump support between whites under 30 and those aged 45 to 64 points to the long-term problem he could create for the Republican Party in appealing to the new generation. A study by the Pew Research Center found that 23 percent of its 18-to-29-year-old respondents who identified as Republicans in December 2015 had left the party by March 2017. Over the same period, only 9 percent of 18-to-29-year-old Democrats had defected.[7]

Consistent with Trump's emphasis on the war against "radical Islam," fear of terrorism was another noneconomic component of the Trump backlash. The contrast between voters who said that foreign policy was their motivating issue and those who listed terrorism was striking. Those who decided on the basis of foreign policy backed Clinton by 60 percent to 33 percent. Those who named terrorism as their voting issue supported Trump, 57 percent to 40 percent.

One of the most important stories in the campaign was Trump's success in winning the votes of white evangelical Christians, despite the many obvious ways in which Trump violated the personal values they upheld.

The campaign represented something of a moral showdown within the white evangelical world. Many important evangelical voices, led by Russell Moore, the president of the Ethics and Religious Liberty Commission of the Southern Baptist Convention, were scathing in taking on Trump. "His personal morality is clear, not because of tabloid exposés but because of his own boasts," Moore wrote in *The New York Times*. "His attitude toward women is that of a Bronze Age warlord. He tells us in one of his books that he revels in the fact that he gets to sleep with some of the 'top women in the world.' He has divorced two wives (so far) for other women."

Moore did not limit his criticism to Trump's personal life. "In a time when racial tensions run high across the country, Mr. Trump incites division, with slurs against Hispanic immigrants and with protectionist jargon that preys on turning economic insecurity into ugly 'us versus them' identity politics," Moore said. "When evangelicals should be leading the way on racial reconciliation, as the Bible tells us to, are we really ready to trade unity with our black and brown brothers and sisters for this angry politician?"

And he told an audience of Baptist pastors: "If you lose an election you can live to fight another day and move on, but if you lose an election while giving up your very soul then you have really lost it all."[8]

But Moore turned out to be a minority voice within his religious community and came under attack from many on the Christian right for his consistent witness against Trump. In the end, a different moral calculus prevailed among white evangelicals. Their sense that the broader culture had become hostile to them and that a strong hand was required to push back against their enemies fed substantial support for Trump. A PRRI survey in June 2016 asked voters if they agreed or disagreed with this statement: "Because things have gotten so off-track in this country, we need a leader who is willing to break some rules if that's what it takes to set things right." Trump was viewed favorably by 59 percent of white evangelicals who wanted such a leader, but by only 33 percent among those who didn't.

"Frankly, I want the meanest, toughest son of a gun I can find," said Robert Jeffress, the pastor of the First Baptist Church in Dallas and an early Trump supporter, in an interview with the *Dallas Observer*. "And I think that's the feeling of a lot of evangelicals. They don't want a Casper Milquetoast as the leader of the free world." Jeffress was talking specifically about dealing with ISIS, but the desire for strong pushback in the culture wars was part of the story, too. "He has said that be believes that Christians and Christianity are being marginalized," Jeffress observed. "He always gets a laugh when he says, 'We're gonna start saying "Merry Christmas" in America again.' We all know what he's talking about."

They did. As the campaign went on, Trump, once upon a time pro-choice, offered steadily stronger statements in opposition to abortion—he hit the issue especially hard in the final debate—and offered a list of conservative judges he would name to the Supreme Court who met the religious right's specifications. Together with intense dislike of the Clintons among evangelicals, Trump's moves led to the most unlikely achievement of his campaign: Trump won the largest margin among white evangelicals of any Republican presidential candidate since exit polling began, defeating Clinton 81 percent to 16 percent.

Trump's landslide among white evangelicals ought to cause genuine (and literal) soul-searching in the movement, not just because of who Trump is but also because evangelicals proved willing to alter some of their basic commitments to rationalize supporting him. They should not necessarily be singled out for this. There is evidence that members of many other religious groups conformed their religious and moral judgments to politics. (One example: white Catholics voted by almost exactly the same margin for Trump as all other whites; Latino Catholics backed Clinton by the same margin as Latinos generally.)[9]

But the shift in the moral standards of white evangelicals was genuinely breathtaking. An October 2016 survey by PRRI asked:

"Do you think an elected official who commits an immoral act in their private life can still behave ethically and fulfill their duties in their public and professional life?" In 2011, only 44 percent of all respondents answered yes; in 2016, 61 percent said yes.

Where did this movement come from? Not from those without any religious affiliation. Their views hardly changed, going from 63 percent yes in 2011 to 60 percent in 2016. Catholics moved roughly in tandem with the population as a whole, going from 42 percent to 58 percent. Similarly, white mainline Protestants went from 38 percent to 60 percent.

But among white evangelicals, there was what can only be called a moral revolution: only 30 percent of them said in 2011 that a politician who committed an immoral act could fulfill his or her public duties; in 2016, 72 percent said yes. White evangelicals went from being far less inclined than the country as a whole to separate a politician's personal life from his or her professional life to being more insistent than almost any other group in doing so. It is hard to escape the conclusion that whatever else was going on, white evangelicals changed their views on what had once been a matter of deep conviction to justify supporting a presidential candidate they knew to be, by their own moral reckoning, personally immoral. It was one of the most dramatic examples of how Trump debased so many aspects of American public life.

The flocking of evangelicals to Trump was not simply motivated by a fear of secularism or the traditional religious issues. It was a reminder, as the journalist Sarah Posner noted in an insightful article in the *New Republic,* that white southern evangelicals had moved to the Republican Party and political conservatism in the 1960s—long before there was a religious right—in reaction to the passage of civil rights laws under Lyndon Johnson. She noted a galvanizing event in the history of the religious right: the Internal

Revenue Service's decision to revoke the tax-exempt status of Bob Jones University and other religious schools that discriminated against nonwhites. The slogan of "religious liberty" was linked to segregation. Historian Randall Balmer noted that the bloc's support of Trump suggested the movement had come "full circle," and Richard Spencer, a leading alt-right figure and unapologetic white supremacist, told Posner that many white evangelicals were motivated not by religious concerns but by racial anxieties. "Trump has shown the hand of the GOP," Spencer said. "The GOP is a white person's populist party."

No doubt many religious conservatives really were motivated, primarily or even exclusively, by their opposition to abortion and their desire for conservative judges. But as Posner suggests, Trump's implicit and at times explicit racial narrative likely contributed to his white evangelical landslide. The Rev. Rob Schenck, a conservative evangelical who joined Russell Moore in opposing Trump, offered this coda on his victory: "This could be the undoing of American evangelicalism. We could just become a political operation in the guise of a church."[10]

But if race and culture mattered a great deal in 2016, there is significant evidence that swing voters who went for Trump (as against solid Republicans and voters who constituted his base in the GOP primaries) may have been more motivated by economics than other parts of his constituency. These include some who had voted for Obama, and others who skipped the 2008 or 2012 elections but rejoined the electorate to vote for Trump.

There is a fascinating disjunction between studies that focused on opinion data, which largely point to a cultural explanation for the election, and those that looked primarily to the geography of

Trump support. It's clear that Trump, on the whole, posted large gains over earlier GOP candidates in the parts of the country (and in the regions within states) where economic anxiety was high.

An analysis by the sociologist Richard Florida, for example, found that Trump gained votes over Romney in more than half of the country's metropolitan areas (202 of 381). Most of them were in smaller and medium-sized metros, but he did pick up support in 10 of the 53 large ones. His top five in this group were revealing. They were the areas around Buffalo; Providence; Detroit; Cleveland; and St. Louis. All had suffered from deindustrialization. Trump's gains in smaller metros were concentrated in the Rust Belt and the Sunbelt, with particularly big gains in metropolitan jurisdictions in West Virginia, Ohio, Pennsylvania, Michigan, and Indiana. Something economic was happening here.

Ben Casselman, the chief economics editor for *FiveThirtyEight*, pushed back hard against what he called "it's all culture or race" explanations of the election in a useful essay whose title made his point: "Stop Saying Trump's Win Had Nothing to Do with Economics."

Casselman found that "the slower a county's job growth has been since 2007, the more it shifted toward Trump. (The same is true looking back to 2000.)" And he argued that "the role of economic anxiety becomes even clearer in the data once you control for race." Casselman continued:

> Factoring in the strong opposition to Trump among most racial and ethnic minorities, Trump significantly outperformed Romney in counties where residents had lower credit scores and in counties where more men have stopped working.

"Where more men have stopped working" refers to the change since 2000 in the share of men ages 25 to 54 who are employed, according to data from the American Community Survey.

The list goes on: More subprime loans? More Trump support. More residents receiving disability payments? More Trump support. Lower earnings among full-time workers? More Trump support. "Trump Country," as my colleague Andrew Flowers described it shortly after the election, *isn't the part of America where people are in the worst financial shape; it's the part of America where their economic prospects are on the steepest decline* [emphasis added].[11]

Jed Kolko, the chief economist at Indeed.com, an employment search site, added another layer to the economic story. Certain economic measures, he said, were not particularly helpful in explaining Trump's vote. For example, places with higher rates of unemployment were no more likely to vote for Trump than those with less unemployment.

But economic anxiety, Kolko posited, is "about the future, not just the present." And sure enough, he found that "Trump beat Clinton in counties where more jobs are at risk because of technology or globalization." He went on: "Specifically, counties with the most 'routine' jobs—those in manufacturing, sales, clerical work and related occupations that are easier to automate or send offshore—were far more likely to vote for Trump."

"It is clear," Kolko concluded, "that the places that voted for Trump are under greater economic stress, and the places that swung most toward Trump are those where jobs are most under threat."

On the other side of the economic divide, Brookings Institution researchers Mark Muro and Sifan Liu provided evidence of Trump's weakness in areas most tied to the modern economy.

They found that the 472 counties that Clinton carried accounted for 64 percent of the nation's GDP; Trump's 2,584 counties generated just 36 percent of the nation's output. By contrast, Al Gore carried 187 more counties in 2000 than Clinton did, but his counties represented only 54 percent of the GDP. "This is a picture of a very polarized and increasingly concentrated economy, with the Democratic base aligning more to that more concentrated modern economy," Muro told *The Washington Post*'s Jim Tankersley. "In the rest of the country," Muro added, there were a lot of votes and a great deal of anger.

Finally, Trump succeeded because on economics, he managed to separate himself from the Republican brand among white working-class swing voters, even as he persuaded rank-and-file Republicans he was one of them (at least compared with Clinton). His persistent attacks on Washington Democrats and Republicans alike clearly paid dividends among the voters he needed to reach.

A 2017 survey of Wisconsin and Michigan voters who defected from Obama to Trump conducted by Priorities USA, a Democratic super PAC, found that 42 percent of Obama-to-Trump voters said that the congressional Democrats' economic policies favored the wealthy, with roughly the same proportion (40 percent) saying this of congressional Republicans. By contrast, only 21 percent of them said this of Trump. However phony Trump's populism might be, his message reached its target. And whatever their cultural views, these defectors to Trump also brought economic grievances to the polls: 50 percent of Obama-to-Trump voters said their incomes were falling behind the cost of living, while another 31 percent said their incomes were merely keeping pace.

"If you felt like your life wasn't getting better over eight years, then you might draw a conclusion that Democrats don't care about you," Guy Cecil, chairman of Priorities USA, told *Washington Post* blogger Greg Sargent. "Certainly a subset of these voters were responsive to what Trump was selling them on immigration. But you had a lot of consistency with the Obama-Trump voters . . . in terms of the severe economic anxiety they face."[12]

Taken together, the various postelection studies and surveys point to the dangers of two different forms of denial. To underplay the large role of race, immigration, and cultural conservatism in building the Trump constituency is to be blind to how he ran his campaign and to why so many were drawn to him. But to overlook the economic backdrop of 2016 and the desire of many of his supporters to strike back against their sense of material deprivation is to ignore social injustices that our country needs to confront. Rolling back Trumpism requires being unafraid to acknowledge and to condemn racism, sexism, nativism, and religious prejudice where they exist. But it also demands an empathetic ear for the genuine pain and unease that led many voters to Trump.

Contrary to the notion that most journalists failed to predict Trump's victory because they live inside a "bubble," reporters spent a great deal of time talking to Trump voters during the 2016 campaign. To move from the data and immerse yourself in the stories Trump supporters tell is to understand how many different reasons they had for making a profoundly radical choice. Some spoke of Trump's personal qualities, with a heavy emphasis on his outspokenness, his willingness to "tell it like it is," and his business experience. Others expressed their distrust of politics in Washington. Many said they liked that Trump was not "politically correct," and others offered catalogs of Hillary Clinton's shortcomings. Religious and traditionalist conservatives spoke often of their opposition to abortion. Such conversations are a reminder that there is no single reason that explains why Trump is our president.

A particularly fascinating set of portraits of Trump voters came from Sam Altman, who runs a Silicon Valley start-up incubator. A liberal who opposed Trump, Altman spent months traveling the country interviewing Trump supporters in a quest to understand their motivations. He published his findings on his personal blog and shared some postelection interviews with *Business Insider* in February 2017.

Two were especially revealing of the difficulties in disentangling the racial, the economic, and the personal. One of Altman's interlocutors told him: "I'm so tired of hearing about white privilege. I'm white but way less privileged than a black person from your world. I have no hope my life will ever get any better."

Another said: "I'd love to see one-tenth of the outrage about the state of our lives out here that you have for Muslims from another country. You have no idea what our lives are like."[13]

A nation so deeply divided by race and culture and divided again by regional disparities and economic inequalities is in need of remedy. American history has taught that our country has a gift for reform and self-correction. We are in urgent need of both.

PART TWO

The Way Forward

SEVEN

With Opportunity and Justice for All

Building a New Economy

Our account so far has largely focused on the dangers of Trump's rise. But his election ought to jar those who make up our nation's governing class. They now know that Americans in large numbers were so disaffected that they embraced a candidate whose temperament and behavior were plainly ill suited to the requirements of the nation's highest office.

Turning back Trumpism requires sustained opposition to his abuses, but also something more: a commitment to addressing the economic, social, and cultural challenges we would confront even if Trump had been satisfied remaining a reality television star without the White House as his set.

The social crisis we face—and "crisis" is not too strong a word—should call forth the same spirit of innovation that our country has demonstrated in the technological, cultural, and financial spheres. The United States has shown that it knows how to create wealth. By so many measures, we remain the strongest and most prosperous country in the world. The task of the next generation is to show again that we know how to create wealth in ways that allow it to be broadly shared across classes, races, and regions.

The promise of American life should be available to all Americans. Right now, it is not.

But as we saw in the last chapter, our crisis (like the reasons why Trump won support) extends beyond economics. In the forthcoming pages, we thus also offer proposals for a new patriotism, a new civil society, and a new democracy. Building one nation after Trump requires a vision of patriotism that celebrates our nation's diversity as a great asset but is also rooted in a set of shared understandings and purposes that bring us together. It also demands a view of America's role in the world that is at once realistic and committed to democratic ideals. We focus on civil society because the nation's economic troubles have eroded the ties that bind Americans together in local communities. This has weakened our ability to act in common while threatening the country's social cohesion. And a new democracy is essential not only to respond to the resonance of Trump's charges that "the system is rigged" but also to battle against efforts to narrow participation, restrict access to the ballot, and flood the political system with campaign money raised from a small and privileged group of Americans. In many ways, the system *is* rigged—although, as we have argued, some of the rigging actually benefited Trump. A new democracy would draw citizens to the task of self-government and provide them with the tools and opportunities to make their participation effective.

We turn first to the challenge of shared prosperity, because creating a just and growing economy is essential to achieving our other national purposes.

Historically, the United States has been seen as a model for the world in offering upward economic and social mobility, even if we have often fallen short of this ideal. There have been surges in anti-immigrant feeling at many points in our history, and opportunities have not been universal. African Americans, whose ancestors were brought to our shores in bondage, were oppressed for centuries by a vicious racial caste system whose effects are still felt today. Native Americans have faced extreme mistreatment and isolation throughout our history.

But to the extent that our promises of mobility did, indeed, hold over many decades, they are being broken now. Social mobility in the United States has declined sharply since the 1980s and now ranks significantly lower than in Finland, Norway, Denmark, Sweden, Germany, Canada, and France. The economist Alan Krueger coined the term "The Great Gatsby Curve" to describe a degree of inequality and entrenched economic status that now mirrors that of Jay Gatsby's era in the 1920s. Voters experiencing a sense of dislocation are not delusional.[1]

Our economic debate is trapped by our inability to accept a truth about American history: that our national dynamism has always entailed vigorous partnerships between the public and the private, between government at various levels and workers and entrepreneurs. There has never been a period of pure laissez-faire in the United States, even when we thought we had one. We view the Gilded Age, for example, as a time when government stayed out of the way of the robber barons. And in many ways it did. But the enterprises so many of them ran were protected by thick tariff walls. The great railroads were built through government grants—and, sometimes, wholesale corruption. Before that, the roads and canals that were the product of Henry Clay's American System allowed the country to grow and industry to thrive. The Homestead Act gave away 10 percent of U.S. land to settlers who, according to the National Park Service, made 4 million claims. Some 93 million Americans descend from homesteaders.[2]

We think of the period beginning with the Progressive Era and reaching its culmination in the New Deal and Great Society as entailing a highly unusual degree of government involvement in the economy. It's certainly true that the regulatory state took hold in this period, that far-reaching government social insurance programs were established, and that the federal government—through the Federal Reserve, budget policy, and countercyclical programs such as unemployment insurance—took responsibility for easing the cycles of boom and bust.

But the period from 1940 through the early 1970s was also a time of unparalleled private-sector economic growth. If some of life's risks were socialized in this period, we had nothing resembling a state socialist economy.

The major change in our national approach involved government tailoring its policies more to the needs of workers and consumers than to those of economic elites. Through the Wagner Act of 1935, which guaranteed the right to organize and bargain collectively, government consciously took the side of workers and encouraged the formation of unions. Through the GI Bill, one of the greatest investment projects in American history, millions of veterans were empowered to pursue higher education, start businesses, and buy their own homes. Continuing in this spirit, President Dwight Eisenhower championed two great investment programs, building the interstate highway system and financing access to higher education through the loans made available by the National Defense Education Act.

We thus need to recover the very old American idea that government, working in partnership with the private market, can foster both growth and equity. As the political scientists Jacob S. Hacker and Paul Pierson argue persuasively in their book *American Amnesia,* "if advanced democratic capitalism won the twentieth century, the mixed economy deserves to stand atop the podium." And this shared prosperity was key to the success of our democracy. "If we start using government successfully again to enhance prosperity," Hacker and Pierson conclude, "we can fix our broken politics."

There is another difference between the great postwar period of shared prosperity and the current day: American corporations then understood that they had larger purposes and obligations than simply "maximizing shareholder value." In an important Brookings Institution paper and in other writings, Steven Pearlstein, a professor at George Mason University, a *Washington Post* columnist, and a staunch defender of the market system, argues that until the 1970s, corporations understood that a return to shareholders was only one aspect of their purpose. Corporations, he notes, "were generally chartered not for private but for public purposes," and "well into the 1960s, corporations were widely viewed as owing something in return to the community that provided them with special legal protections and the economic ecosystem in which they could grow and thrive."

The rise of the shareholder-value standard, Pearlstein writes, shortened the time horizons of CEOs and boards of directors, discouraging long-term investment. Short-termism also loosened the bonds of loyalty between corporations and their employees, their consumers, and the communities in which they operated. Investment in workers' training and skill enhancement was less rational in a less loyal world. The shift was not just ideological, though Pearlstein is shrewd in showing how an ideology that served the interests of investors was bolstered over time by political and legal support. The same forces that have upended so many other aspects of the economy reinforced the shareholder-value standard—"globalization, deregulation and rapid technological change."

What's been lost, Pearlstein argues, is the understanding that physical capital alone does not make capitalism successful. What is also required is "social capital," which "provides the necessary grease for the increasingly complex machinery of capitalism, and for the increasingly contentious machinery of democracy. Without it, democratic capitalism cannot survive."

Thus, the sense that something has gone wrong with the American economic system, reflected on the left as well as among many of the voters who swung to Trump, is not the invention of demagogues but the product of real change. If Trump's "solutions," such as they were, were deeply flawed—and if he had little interest in following through on them anyway—he was responding to that change with at least a feigned urgency that many voters related to.

It's certainly true that some of the magic of the American economic system from the late 1940s until the 1970s was due to unparalleled American dominance after World War II, which left the economies of so many of our competitors in shambles. Many aspects of that era simply cannot be re-created. The entry of more than a billion new workers into the global labor market, particularly in China and India, is another brute fact destined to put the least-advantaged workers in the richest economies at even greater risk in the international bidding war for wages.[3]

But we have also lost aspects of the American economy and the social system surrounding it that we need to reclaim. The first is the confidence we once had that government can work in partnership with the private market to achieve broadly shared economic growth. The long American tradition of using public action to spur innovation and investment while also enhancing the bargaining power, skills, education, and wealth of average citizens no longer animates the public imagination. Partly, this is the product of actual government failure, and reforming government to work in the twenty-first century is an imperative for creating a post-Trump world. But this loss of confidence is also the product of a political and ideological project to demean government's essential role. We need to restore our sense of pragmatism, realism, and inventiveness about what government can be asked to achieve.

And we need to restore the social capital Pearlstein describes by taking steps to reduce corporate short-termism and to restore a sense that corporations have responsibilities to the public and to stakeholders, including their employees, in addition to shareholders.

These imperatives—for responsive government and responsible corporate behavior—are an alternative to Trumpist pro-corporate policies with a populist sheen and also a response to the legitimate economic discontent that Trump exploited.

We organize what needs to be done around the idea of a *Charter for American Working Families*. As part of that framework, we propose a *GI Bill for American Workers* and a *Contract for American Social Responsibility* for our companies. The former would focus on providing greater protection for workers, along with robust job training and education. The latter would offer a new set of standards for corporate governance, pushing away from short-term profits and encouraging deeper social responsibility.

Those who support an open and pluralistic America must be very clear that they are not content with a country divided between affluent metropolitan enclaves and declining regions, cities, and towns. They must find the ideas, the language, and the passion to convey that this is a matter of political urgency. However manipulative and ultimately empty his agenda was, Trump persuaded voters that he was making them a big offer. His opponents must make a big offer of their own.

There is a desperate desire on the part of most Americans to move past the divisions reflected in the 2016 campaign—both the internecine progressive struggle between supporters of Hillary Clinton and Bernie Sanders in the Democratic primaries, and the sharp racial, ethnic, regional, cultural, and class divisions of the general election. The approach we suggest is designed to draw on the insights of different parts of the broad progressive and moderate movement that finds Trumpist politics so offensive, and to persuade those not yet part of it that there are better options than Trumpism.

It is aimed at combining Sanders's strong calls for labor rights and worker empowerment and his critique of corporate excess with Clinton's practical and incremental policy proposals that, had they been enacted together, promised substantial improvements in the lives of struggling Americans. Clinton's failure owed less to the merits (or demerits) of her particular policies than to her campaign's lack of focus on the depth of the economic difficulties so many Americans face. As should be clear from our earlier chapters, we believe that a significant number of white working-class Americans who voted for Trump are open to alternatives to his approach—and will be all the more so as his claims to being an economic "populist" prove empty.

There is one other key component of the anti-Trump coalition— the moderate Independents and Republicans, many of them well-off professionals. They share with progressives a desire to defend an open and tolerant society and view capitalism as a dynamic and innovative force even as they also seek more social responsibility from corporations. In an earlier generation, they would likely have been Eisenhower Republicans. A broad movement against Trumpism would, in effect, unite Clinton and Sanders Democrats with the modern-day equivalent of Eisenhower Republicans and Independents, as well as conservatives who are seeking an alternative to Trump's divisiveness. As we will note later, the anti-Trump conservatives, while largely confined to the ranks of writers and policy specialists, are increasingly unhappy with the path the conservative movement and the Republican Party have taken. Their restiveness could be the harbinger of political realignment.

Our framework is also designed to address two other forms of coalition building that are essential.

One is between voters of color, who arrayed themselves solidly against Trump, and white working-class voters, who will be looking for alternatives to Trumpism as the president and his party fail to deliver on his populist promises. A politics that divides along racial lines obscures the extent to which working-class Americans across backgrounds share common problems with similar causes. As *Washington Post* blogger Greg Sargent wrote in a very perceptive analysis of the 2016 outcome, much of the postelection debate was "framed around a false choice" that pitted "the need to minister to the Obama coalition versus the need for economic appeals to working-class whites." Sargent was right to observe that many of the problems faced by both groups "are, at bottom, about the need for reforms that make the economy fairer and render prosperity more inclusive." Writing in *The American Prospect,* Robert Griffin, John Halpin, and Ruy Teixeira succinctly described the imperative in partisan terms: "Democrats need to be the party of and for working people—of all races."

The other alliance that must be nurtured is between younger and older voters. The young (who are the most progressive electoral cohort since the New Dealers of the Greatest Generation) seek social justice within a context of economic growth, dynamism, and opportunity. Many find themselves on the left end of politics, frustrated, as Sarah Leonard wrote in the journal *Democracy,* with liberals "who are unable to inspire Americans with their vision of the future and are simultaneously strongly resistant to change." Older voters, in the meantime, are threatened by the decline of economic security over the last three decades. Healing our divisions requires economic policies sensitive to the challenges facing the young and old alike, and also attentive to the cultural rifts we address in the next chapter. But if the broad center left cannot find ways of addressing economic injustices, it will never get a hearing on other matters.

We stress that we are sketching out broad approaches and calling for a larger vision. This chapter does not pretend to be the final word, but is instead an invitation to bold and creative thinking about how to restore economics to its central place in progressive politics. The political scientist Lynn Vavreck found that while only 9 percent of Clinton's television advertisements were about jobs or the economy, more than one-third of Trump's ads focused on economic issues, including taxes, jobs, and trade. As a result, many voters were unaware of what Clinton was offering as an alternative to Trumpism.[4]

We also do not pretend that a brief chapter is sufficient to working out the problems of a complex economy, for we are deeply aware of something that came as a surprise to Trump: public policy is difficult. Unintended consequences of even good ideas are inevitable. Details matter. Expertise is to be celebrated, not denigrated, and many who are belittled as "technocrats" often have the virtue of understanding how complicated systems work. Trade-offs are the stuff not only of political compromise but also of careful policy analysis.

Finally, we emphasize that we are building on much good work that has been done in this area over the last decade. Before the 2016 election, for example, two detailed economic agendas were put forward that included many ideas that would be helpful in advancing broadly shared prosperity. One report, from the Center for American Progress, was offered by a working group (with which one of the authors of this book was involved) headed by former treasury secretary Larry Summers and the British Labour Party's Ed Balls. The other, from the Roosevelt Institute, was principally authored by the Nobel Prize–winning economist Joseph Stiglitz. The ideas in each—from profit-sharing with employees to new approaches to job training, from reform of the financial system to promote long-term time horizons on investment to more progressive taxes and large-scale infrastructure investment— would help create a more just economy.

> Progressivism without a robust economic agenda will be neither attractive nor credible.

Yet neither study got the attention it deserved. More generally, counterideas to Trump's demagogic bromides were barely discussed during the general election campaign. There is a lesson here, partly for the media but particularly for Democratic strategists who believed that Trump's manifest shortcomings would be enough to elect Clinton.

If the 2016 campaign teaches nothing else, it is that progressivism without a robust economic agenda will be neither attractive nor credible to a large share of the electorate. It won't convert white working-class voters back from their support for Trump, as the democratic pollster Stanley Greenberg observed, and it won't mobilize turnout among African Americans, Latinos, and the young who are already opposed to him. Absent compelling offers for opportunity, mobility, and fairness, bold-sounding bad ideas will often triumph over better ideas that seem hedged and timid—or aren't even discussed.[5]

A Charter for American Working Families would respond to the practical struggles faced by all families. It is a statement of rights and principles reflecting how families would answer the question: What are the basics of a decent life in the United States in the twenty-first century?

The outlines of such a charter should be clear enough. Family members have a moral claim to jobs with decent incomes; health care coverage; education for themselves and their children; working hours that achieve a balance between work, family, and community responsibilities; decent housing in thriving neighborhoods with low crime rates; confidence in the fairness and efficiency of local law enforcement; freedom from discrimination on the grounds of race, gender, religion, and sexual orientation; access to treatment for addictions and mental health challenges; a chance to better themselves in midcareer and to seize new opportunities; an ability to build up savings and wealth; and retirement security.

This might be seen as a wish list for a comfortable material life, and that is the point. Far too much in our politics is rooted in abstract argument—big government versus small government, traditionalism versus modernity, religion versus secularism, state versus market, and family values versus, well, whatever those who talk about them see as the dreadful alternative. Far too little in our debate is about how to enable and empower individuals and families to secure the economic stability necessary to achieving their other ends, including those rooted in family, community, and both spiritual and moral purposes. Government can do a far better job of creating the circumstances in which family values flourish than it can of providing an exact and enforceable list of how family values should be defined.

What we suggest might fairly be seen as a new form of traditional bread-and-butter politics. It is aimed at encouraging what Arthur Schlesinger Jr. saw as one of the noblest purposes of democratic politics: "the search for remedy." Politics should be about solving problems and resolving disputes, not aggravating divisions and hoping that conflicts between different groups of Americans can be exploited, election after election, for immediate political gain. Trumpian politics depends upon fanning grievance, not responding to it. A focus on practical responses to particular problems is the antidote to a politics of perpetual resentment.

> A focus on practical responses to particular problems is the antidote to a politics of perpetual resentment.

The policies that could keep these promises vary in complexity. We will touch on several illustratively.

The most basic pledge, heard in every electoral contest, is for "good jobs at good wages," to use the much maligned but, after the 2016 election, more relevant than ever mantra of former Massachusetts governor Michael Dukakis. Promises of jobs are used to justify a broad range of policies—usually policies a candidate already favors for other reasons—from tax cuts to major infrastructure investments, from less to more regulation.[6]

But at this moment, more than generalized, all-purpose policies are required because of the disappearance of well-paying (often unionized) manufacturing work, the potential loss of even more jobs through the decline of retail, the long-term decline in employment rates among prime-working-age men, and the spread of robotization and other forms of advanced manufacturing. These are leading to increasingly large gaps between the incomes of the better educated and better trained and those of Americans with less formal education and fewer skills.

Free-trade advocates need to acknowledge that they oversold the broad benefits of trade deals and underestimated how trade would interact with technological change to produce major job losses—particularly after the admission of China to the World Trade Organization. They regularly failed to deliver the relief promised to those displaced by trade. As Dennis Snower, president of the Kiel Institute for the World Economy, noted, the United States spends "a ludicrous 0.1 percent of GDP" on training measures, less than one-sixth of what rich countries spend on average for what economists call "active labor market policies." Is it any wonder that Trump drew such a powerful response when he spoke of the millions of American jobs lost to China—even if he abruptly reversed his China policies upon taking office?[7]

Opponents of free trade need to acknowledge, in turn, that technological change is an even greater threat to jobs than trade itself and that radical restrictions on the international trading system are both unlikely and potentially counterproductive. Promises of a return to an earlier era can't be kept (as Trump himself showed when he broke one trade promise after another). The focus must instead be on trade deals that take far better account of the interests of workers.

But what free traders and their critics ought to agree on is that a large share of American workers have ample grounds for feeling that the deal they thought they had been promised—of a decent standard of living in exchange for hard work—never materialized.

The speed of economic change has created new interest in ideas that had long been off the policy agenda. Fears that technology could, over time, wipe out many more jobs as machines and robots do what workers once did have revived interest, for the first time since the Nixon administration, in a guaranteed national income (now generally referred to as Universal Basic Income, or UBI) and also in variations on proposals that would have the government serve as an employer of last resort.

Both ideas take many forms. Progressives such as Andy Stern, former president of the Service Employees International Union (SEIU), see UBI as a way of strengthening and supplementing existing safety net programs. More conservative versions of the UBI proposal (like the one put forward by Charles Murray from the American Enterprise Institute) see it as replacing a variety of welfare programs.

Government job guarantees would begin with a robust commitment to rebuilding the nation's infrastructure, which should in any event be a high national priority. Until conservatives extended their attack on government to include opposition to federal investments in what Henry Clay accurately called "internal improvements"—roads, bridges, airports, and the other basics of a thriving economy—infrastructure spending won broad bipartisan support. We must renew this shared commitment to the public underpinnings of growth (while remaining deeply wary of Trump's proposals to use tax breaks for the wealthy to encourage privatization of public works). Beyond infrastructure, job guarantees could take the form of updated versions of the New Deal's WPA, subsidies for employers, assistance to localities in creating jobs, or combinations of all of these. A robust national service program, which we discuss later, should also be part of any plan of this sort.

This is a debate the country should welcome. Our own sympathies generally run toward an emphasis on job creation linked with training, apprenticeships, and service. As the progressive writer Jeff

Spross noted in an essay proposing the job guarantee, "the vast majority of people really do feel better about themselves when they're contributing to the social project in some way" and resonate to the idea that society and employers bear "a moral duty to provide good, dignified work to all."

We are also deeply skeptical that any universal income guarantee could be large enough to replace existing safety net and social insurance programs. Moreover, as *Vox*'s Matthew Yglesias has cautioned, there is a danger in focusing too much on UBI in the current political environment. The immediate priority must be to protect food stamps, Medicare, Medicaid, and other vital social services from dramatic cuts proposed by the Trump administration.

Additionally, the jobs guarantee could be combined with aspects of the UBI. The economist Jared Bernstein, for example, has suggested a child allowance of $250 a month per child and an expansion of the earned-income tax credit to cover not only the poor, whom it has already helped immensely, but also working-class Americans.

A long period of rapid economic change has left large numbers of Americans out of the workforce altogether, underemployed, or working for far lower wages. Rising interest in universal programs focusing on either jobs or incomes reflects the fact that we need more adventurous social policy thinking that matches the size of our problems.[8]

Overlapping proposals by three senators also get at economic reforms that we see as necessary to achieve the principles laid out in the Charter. Senator Sherrod Brown of Ohio has put forward "A Plan for Restoring the Value of Work in America." Its components include a minimum wage increase to $15 an hour, guaranteed sick leave, stronger rules on overtime pay, cracking down on employers who misclassify workers as independent contractors, a variety of measures to make it easier for workers (including independent contractors) to save and to make retirement and savings plans portable, ending wage theft, expanding collective bargaining rights, and creating a "Corporate Freeloader Fee" that would apply "to all corporations whose pay is so low that taxpayers are forced to subsidize their workers."

Senator Kirsten Gillibrand of New York has introduced a package of benefits she calls the "American Opportunity Agenda." Her proposals include paid family leave, a minimum wage increase, affordable child care, universal pre-kindergarten, and equal pay for equal work. Her leave program—cosponsored with Representative Rosa DeLauro, a Connecticut Democrat—would provide 12 weeks' leave at partial pay for new parents, financed as an insurance program paid for through income-based premiums ranging from about $75 to $225 annually.

And responding to one of the most radical sets of changes in the organization of work, Senator Elizabeth Warren of Massachusetts has advanced a policy agenda focused on the "gig economy"—encompassing those workers who fall somewhere between the traditional "employee" classification and the formal "independent contractor" status, like Uber drivers or people providing at-home services. Some of her proposals are highly specific, such as guaranteeing that gig workers could pay into Social Security so they could draw on its benefits, including disability insurance; providing catastrophic insurance for all workers, even those who had not been able to build up credits for traditional disability and worker's compensation plans; and covering sick leave and paid medical leave even for workers who have multiple employers.

Warren has also advocated building on the Affordable Care Act to enhance its portability (an idea that, in principle at least, conservatives also support), finding new ways to help gig workers save for retirement, and streamlining labor laws to make them more applicable to an economy in which the boundaries between regular employees, contract workers, and gig workers are not always clear. Like Brown, she calls for promoting the right of workers to organize, and argues for cutting student college debt and guaranteeing access to "affordable lifelong learning and retooling for future jobs."[9]

With somewhat different starting points, Brown, Gillibrand, and Warren have reached broad common ground on the problems that need solving and the steps that should be taken to ease the discontents of work. All three Democrats provide what might be seen as useful opening bids for a comprehensive program that reaches across many of our social, racial, and ethnic divides.

Importantly, conservative intellectuals such as Michael Strain of the American Enterprise Institute (AEI) have proposed constructive ideas for promoting a more innovative, equitable economy. These include relocation vouchers for unemployed people who might find better opportunities in another city or state but cannot afford to move or pay a deposit to rent an apartment or home. Strain and his colleague Kevin Hassett have also proposed job-sharing plans like those that have been effective in Germany in keeping workers from being laid off during recessions. More generally, the "flexisecurity" policies pursued in many northern European countries have sought to combine market dynamism with social protection.

Another promising avenue for innovative economic policy is a 2015 consensus report from the Brookings Institution and AEI, *Opportunity, Responsibility, and Security,* focusing on education, work, training, and family policies that could reduce poverty. And in June 2017, Aparna Mathur of AEI and Isabel Sawhill of Brookings offered a plan to create and finance eight weeks of paid parental leave designed to win support across the philosophical divides.

It may be too much to hope for in the short term, but over the long run, the nexus of liberal and conservative economic proposals might provide openings for bipartisan action.

Fulfilling the pledges in the Charter involves other direct policy choices as well. The most obvious: Does the country build on the achievements of Obamacare by fixing its flaws and extending insurance to the roughly 28 million Americans still not covered? Achieving universal coverage will almost certainly require some sort of public option—a government-administered plan available for purchase on the insurance exchanges—as well as an ability for those between the ages of 55 and 65 who cannot get private insurance to buy into Medicare. Many progressives favor a single-payer system, where the government pays citizens' medical bills as Medicare currently does for seniors. Our view is that defending one of the central achievements of the last decade and then building on it should take priority. A debate about next steps—including single-payer and other alternatives—can take place after everyone is covered. Walking away from the coverage problem, which is what repealing Obamacare entails, should not be an option. And Republicans should realize, as Ezra Klein has argued, that the end of Obamacare would only build support for the single-payer option, their least-favored outcome. Scrapping an approach that sought balance between market and government, Klein noted, would show that "including private insurers and conservative ideas in a health reform plan doesn't offer a scintilla of political protection, much less Republican support."[10]

The Charter also suggests that economic security implicitly demands both the right to live in low-crime neighborhoods and the right to fair treatment from the police. We include this issue in a chapter devoted to economics not only because crime is itself a deterrent to economic development in many communities across our nation, but also because of the relationship between crime and upward mobility. The cycle here is genuinely vicious: a shortage of economic opportunity contributes to higher crime rates, and crime in turn leads to further financial and communal divestment from already impoverished neighborhoods. Children who grow up in deprived, high-crime communities are less likely to succeed. Crime must be dealt with as an economic and social problem to be solved, not as an opportunity for deepening ideological and racial divisions.

Trump and Attorney General Jeff Sessions regularly cast the goals of safer neighborhoods and better community-police relationships as contradictory. They argue that "supporting the police" is antithetical to responding to the concerns of Black Lives Matter and other groups about the killing of young, unarmed African Americans as well as mass incarceration. On the contrary, fighting crime, supporting the police, respecting the rights of the people the police serve, and criminal justice reform should be seen as overlapping and reinforcing goals. Ending the National Rifle Association's veto power over our gun laws would make our communities and our police officers safer. And the problem of drug addiction, which is tearing apart minority and white communities alike, must be addressed with compassion and a commitment to healing and opportunity, not with slogans about a "war on drugs" or with harsh penalties in the place of rehabilitation.

We are not naïve, and we know that the politics of these issues are difficult. But we would insist that a new politics of rights and a new politics of crime prevention must be pursued in tandem as part of a politics of remedy.

Finally, individuals and families live in places, in communities. The economic deterioration of many parts of our country has created grave problems for family life and undercut the vibrancy of neighborhoods and civil society, as we explore in chapter 9. There, we make a case for place-based economic strategies designed not only to improve the material circumstances of our fellow citizens but also to reweave the country's social fabric.[11]

The GI Bill for American Workers would be a comprehensive effort to reinforce the Charter for American Working Families. In calling for a new GI Bill, we look back consciously to one of the most successful pieces of social legislation in American history. The extraordinary investment in people that the GI Bill represented is often overlooked as a major source of growth in the post–World War II era. More than that, as Suzanne Mettler argued in *Soldiers to Citizens: The G.I. Bill and the Making of the Greatest Generation*, it created the civic generation that built not only our nation's economy but also a more vibrant public life. Mettler, a professor of government at Cornell University, found that veterans who used GI Bill benefits became more active citizens than those who did not.

The GI Bill's scope was staggering by the standards of today's more cramped social vision. As Mettler notes, among men born in the United States in the 1920s, "fully 80 percent were military veterans." This was an inclusive program—for men. A champion of the GI Bill, Mettler is nonetheless alive to the problem of gender exclusion, since women constituted only 2 percent of the armed forces in World War II. Ironically, she notes, the GI Bill thus "widened the gender divide in educational attainment." But for those whom the GI Bill did serve, it decidedly equalized both economic and civic opportunity:

> Prior to the war, advanced education had been restricted predominantly to the privileged, especially to white, native-born, elite Protestants. The social rights offered by the G.I. Bill

broadened educational opportunity to veterans who were Jewish or Catholic, African American, and immigrants as well as to those whose families had struggled in the American working class for generations. Once G.I. Bill beneficiaries became active citizens, they altered the civic landscape of the United States, helping to make the political system yet more inclusive and egalitarian during the middle decades of the twentieth century.

By 1947, veterans accounted for 49 percent of students enrolled in American colleges. Ten years after World War II, Mettler writes, 2.2 million veterans had attended college under the GI Bill, and 5.6 million more were able to "acquire training below the college level." In addition, 4.3 million purchased homes at low interest rates, and 200,000 purchased farms or businesses.[12]

The particular moment that gave rise to the GI Bill—the mass mobilization for World War II, which followed the New Deal era, when confidence in government was especially high—cannot be replicated. And the sense of indebtedness the country felt toward those who had served in the armed forces made the GI Bill's generosity possible. It was the quintessential "earned benefit." Nonetheless, the crisis of mobility, income, and opportunity the country is experiencing now demands social inventiveness on the same scale. If no one, as the cliché goes, is entitled to a living, citizens of the world's wealthiest country are certainly entitled to the chance to *earn* one.

A GI Bill for American Workers would focus on opportunities for education, training, and advancement; a degree of income security; opportunities to save and build wealth; and paths to finding balance among work, family, and community obligations. Components could include wage insurance, profit sharing, additional federal support for retirement accounts, a training insurance plan alongside unemployment insurance (which would be reformed and linked to wage insurance), universal access to postsecondary education (including not only four-year college but also one or two years of training), and a large-scale expansion of apprenticeships linked to the availability of good jobs. The great mismatch between skills and opportunities is harmful to individuals, to businesses, and to the economy as a whole.

Finally, achieving economic security for all American families will require reforming corporate practice and culture. A Contract for American Social Responsibility would respond to Pearlstein's important critique of the modern corporation and its embrace of the shareholder-value standard. Its purpose would be to create new rules and incentives for corporations to emphasize a longer view rather than short-termism, and to embrace responsibilities that encompass more than attentiveness to fluctuating share prices.

His suggestions include recalibrating the capital gains tax "so that short-term trading profits are taxed the same as wages and salary, while gains from investments held for long periods are taxed more lightly than they are now or not at all." A small transactions tax, he argues, could "dampen enthusiasm for short-term trading."

The Securities and Exchange Commission, Pearlstein says, could "adopt rules that discourage corporations from giving quarterly earnings projections or guidance, while accounting regulators could insist that corporate financial reports better reflect long-term costs and benefits and measure long-term value creation." Additionally, states "could make it easier for corporations to adopt governance rules that give long-term shareholders more power in selecting directors, approving mergers and takeovers and setting executive compensation."

The need to promote a long-term perspective in the corporate world was also a central theme of a 2015 Brookings Institution paper, "More Builders and Fewer Traders: A Growth Strategy for the American Economy," by Elaine Kamarck and William Galston. "We need . . . more Warren Buffetts and fewer Carl Icahns," they write. "To get them, we cannot rely on cultural change or the collective conversion of CEOs and hedge fund leaders on the road to Damascus. Instead, we must change the laws and rules that shape corporate and investor behavior."

Their proposals parallel Pearlstein's: limits on company stock buybacks, capital gains tax reform that encourages long-term holdings, reporting rules that focus on a company's "sustainability" and not just financial information, and executive compensation rules that encourage a commitment to a company's long-term success.[13]

What Pearlstein, Kamarck, and Galston all encourage is a view of corporate behavior that accepts what capitalism can accomplish but acknowledges the holes in our system that have aroused legitimate populist backlash on both the left and the right. At times of crisis in the past, often pushed by popular movements, business leaders accepted that reform was the only way to restore confidence in the system's workings. As we have argued, Trump's populism is a cover for an approach that would, if anything, deepen the problems our current brand of capitalism already creates. His opponents must expose the phoniness of his approach, but they must also offer practical proposals for change that would make the system advance the interests of the many and not just the few.

There is one obvious political objection to the agenda we have outlined here: Hillary Clinton's program in 2016 included a plethora of specific and detailed ideas that in many cases parallel those we have outlined. She was often criticized for having a "laundry list" without a "vision" or a "message." How is what we are suggesting any different?

In the first instance, it should be acknowledged that, in some cases pushed by Bernie Sanders, Clinton had a far more progressive program than she was credited with offering. It is worth reexamining because she did put forward an array of constructive ideas that got little attention.

But this also underscores the problem she had. The Clinton campaign, as we have seen, was persuaded that Trump's personal shortcomings were so extreme that focusing on them would secure her election. This approach was enough for her to win a solid popular vote victory, but not enough to withstand Russia's interference or James Comey's intervention at the end of the campaign, and not enough for her to prevail in three heavily blue-collar states in the Electoral College. Shortchanging economics is a mistake Trump's opponents should never make again.

It's also true that Democrats throughout President Obama's two terms had difficulty in addressing economic issues, and ended up with a muddled message. On the one hand, many (particularly in his administration) wanted to hail Obama's success in pulling the nation out of the worst economic collapse since the Great Depression and establishing an enviable record of job growth. On the other hand, 30 years of rising inequality and then the crash of 2008 deepened the economic problems in the heartland and left many Americans behind. In the end, Democrats had the worst of both worlds: they neither defended Obama's achievements adequately (because they feared looking out of touch with those still suffering) nor conveyed sufficient urgency about the situation of those left behind. This was a Clinton problem, to be sure, but also a problem for the Democratic Party as a whole. It should not have been as hard as it proved to be to defend Obama's achievements while also acknowledging the work that still needed to be done. And Democrats, including the president, would have done well to try to use their majorities during the first two Obama years to move more boldly on behalf of those, in inner cities as well as the old factory towns, who faced long-term economic dislocation.

Trump's victory solves part of this problem, if only because those out of power no longer have to defend an incumbent's record. And Trump has made such sweeping promises to working-class voters that his failure to live up to them will be especially obvious.

But Trump's foes must use the freedom that opposition affords to make clear what Clinton did not, and perhaps could not. Obama's record shows that progressives can manage the economy effectively. Pushing the nation's unemployment rate to below 5 percent after it had gone above 10 percent at the bottom of the Great Recession is an enormous achievement in which all progressives should take pride. But if growth has been restored, genuinely equitable growth still eludes us.[14]

Obama faced the problem of reviving a collapsed economy with determination and pragmatism. Those who would offer an alternative to Trumpism now need to bring the same virtues to the task of lifting up those left out of the nation's prosperity. Economic growth is essential to solving other problems. But only widely shared economic growth will begin to heal our social divisions. We offer an economic charter, a GI Bill for workers, and a contract for corporate social responsibility as one approach to underscoring the urgency of the progressive commitment to economic change. Moving from anger and division to hope and confidence in the future requires a vision of a just and productive economy that is both credible and inspiring. It also demands a set of policies at once sophisticated enough to do the job and straightforward enough to engage widespread support. The New Deal was certainly complicated, but Americans knew instinctively where Roosevelt wanted the country to go.

Another important characteristic of the New Deal was its emphasis on solidarity, a belief in the obligation of all of us to lift up each of us. The sense that we have a stake in each other's success and that we all owe a debt to our nation's democratic tradition should be the spirit that gives birth to a new patriotism.

EIGHT

Yearning to Breathe Free

Discovering a New Patriotism

Patriots' Day is formally celebrated only in Massachusetts and Maine (which was part of the Bay State until 1820), though Wisconsin and Florida pay it some honor as well. The holiday commemorates the rebels at Lexington and Concord who fired the shot heard 'round the world on April 19, 1775.

For tragic reasons, the holiday commanded the nation's attention on April 15, 2013. Two homemade bombs exploded 12 seconds apart at 2:49 p.m. near the finish line of the Boston Marathon, killing three people and injuring nearly 300.

Boston will never forget the dead and severely hurt. And it will always remember the heroism of its citizens, including the first responders and medical professionals who saved countless lives. A sense of solidarity arising from the love of a place and its people gave birth to the slogan "Boston Strong." The worst Patriots' Day in history produced an outpouring of local patriotism.

But in the Trump era, another impulse jostles with patriotism as the definition of dedication to country. Nationalism, it's true, runs deep in American history, as the brilliant and ideologically idiosyncratic writer Michael Lind often reminds us. It's not just a President Trump or Steve Bannon import. It was, after all, Theodore Roosevelt, a hero to many progressives, whose forward-looking program was memorialized as the New Nationalism. As Lind's work has reminded us, Alexander Hamilton, Henry Clay, and Abraham Lincoln can all, in a sense, be seen as nationalists as well as patriots, since all believed in the idea of the United States as one nation.

Yet nationalism rankles, partly because of its association with the evils of Nazism and fascism, and partly because its claims are so sweeping. As George Orwell wrote, patriotism stems from "devotion to a particular place and a particular way of life." Nationalism, by contrast, "is inseparable from the desire for power."[1]

Even patriotism makes some people uncomfortable. They see it in the same light as chauvinism, which is defined as "excessive or prejudiced loyalty or support for one's own cause, group or gender." They worry as well that patriotism is an excuse to sweep the less wholesome parts of our past and present under the rug.

It's a mistake, however, to view patriotism as nothing but chauvinism in bright colors. American patriotism is special not only because the United States has proven itself to be a nation with an exceptional capacity for self-correction—from slavery to freedom, from segregation to equal rights, from the Gilded Age to the New Deal—but also because ours is not a loyalty to blood or soil. It is an embrace of a series of powerful propositions, beginning with "all men are created equal" and a Constitution that opens with the words "We the People." At a foreign policy conference in April 2017, the gifted young political theorist Yascha Mounk told his audience of recently becoming a U.S. citizen. He did not discount his new country's problems, particularly the costs of a "racial hierarchy." But he saw the United States as genuinely different because it rejected a "mono-ethnic and mono-cultural" definition of nationality. "In America," he said, "there is an idea that you can have an accent and be American, you can have immigrated and be American." He could be an American, he said, in a way he could not be part of any other nation.[2]

The 2016 campaign was a moment when this special definition of American patriotism was partly lost. Trump, Bannon, and their allies, with their embrace of ideas from the European far right, seemed ready to abandon an American patriotism rooted in ideals and commitments for something linked far more closely to ethnicity and, in the case of the Trumpian far right, to race. There was certainly pushback against this, most powerfully from the Gold Star Khan family. Hillary Clinton's Democratic National Convention was draped in the symbols of traditional patriotism. But Democrats and progressives are often uneasy with arguments about national identity, and this problem also affects the left and center left elsewhere. It is an uneasiness that can prevent them from effectively defending an inclusive and democratic patriotism.

Franklin D. Roosevelt understood what this larger vision required, rhetorically and substantively. On April 21, 1938, he spoke to the Daughters of the American Revolution (DAR), a group known for its conservatism and whose members could (and often did) distinguish themselves from new immigrants by tracing their backgrounds to the founding generation—or before. It is commonly remembered that Roosevelt addressed his audience as "fellow immigrants." He didn't say that.

In fact, Roosevelt made a point of observing that "through no fault of my own, . . . I am descended from a number of people who came over in the Mayflower. More than that, every one of my ancestors on both sides . . . every single one of them, without exception, was in this land in 1776. And there was only one Tory among them."

It was only after this buildup that Roosevelt got to challenging the ancestry-mavens. His actual words are even more powerful than the misremembered version. "Remember," he said, "remember always that all of us, and you and I especially, are descended from immigrants and revolutionists."[3]

Reminding Americans that they are descendants of "immigrants and revolutionists" is a worthy project in every generation, but it is an especially useful thing to do when immigrants feel less than welcome and when the country is feeling less than adventurous. FDR was a gifted politician who always knew when to seize the moment. But he also understood the tensions that surged through his own coalition, which broadly united working-class voters across ethnic divides and, over time, across racial lines as well.

Coalition building of the sort FDR specialized in is the imperative for those who seek to form an alternative and enduring majority to combat Trumpism. The American task in every generation is to stitch together a very diverse nation whose citizens are devoted simultaneously to their own particular cultures and to a broadly shared set of ideas and values.

The Trump ascendancy says to those of us who believe in the value of a diverse immigrant nation that we have failed to offer an adequate account of what both pluralism and solidarity demand. If we would insist, rightly, that patriotism is different from nationalism—particularly a nationalism circumscribed by race and ethnicity—we need to define what our brand of patriotism means and requires. If we would defend the particularism of the United States' mosaic of ethnic and social groups (and this includes not only newcomers but also long-standing residents with traditional religious and social beliefs), we also need to advance ideas about what all Americans have in common. Particularism has always been part of the American story, as Roosevelt's DAR speech reminds us. The German, Irish, Italian, Jewish, and Polish immigrants of his day celebrated their roots, their languages, and their religious commitments no less than do today's newcomers from Latin America, Asia, and Africa. But their rights came to be located within a broad framework that was embraced by everyone. And if earlier waves of immigration stoked fears that newcomers would not share our core values, Americans were disabused of these anxieties by experience time and again. Immigrants embraced being American, and rather quickly at that. In that embrace, they found common ground—despite animosities and differences—with other Americans.

We should take pride in the United States' exceptional ability to absorb newcomers, and also in their own intense desire to be American. American culture is made up of many cultures, regional as well as ethnic, but there is a national culture that all of us share in and shape. Our culture freely absorbs new ways of thinking, talking, making music, playing sports, cracking jokes, and telling stories. But generation after generation, we create and re-create a uniquely American synthesis. The old and the new interact and coexist. To borrow from Walt Whitman, our great national poet, we contain multitudes. We honor our democratic tradition and appeal across all our divisions to a set of founding documents that we revere even as we argue with them. We are raucous, mobile, rebellious, and contentious, reverent but also irreverent, individualistic but also communal. We can be resolutely local in our loyalties but also capaciously national. We're strivers who also come to each other's aid. We love our country not only for its ideals but also for its tensions and contradictions.

Trump's foes need to advance patriotism not simply for its own sake but as the proper alternative to nationalism. This is a view that spans our ideological divide. "Patriotism is enough—it needs no improving or expanding," wrote Mona Charen of the conservative Ethics and Public Policy Center. She labeled nationalism "a demagogue's patriotism" likely to be converted "into something aggressive." Similarly, conservative columnist Jonah Goldberg argued that "because nationalism is ultimately the fire of tribalism, having too much of it tends to melt away important distinctions, from the rule of law to the right to dissent to the sovereignty of the individual." This is precisely the correct concern in the Trump era.[4]

Trump has been challenged for his use of the "America First" slogan primarily because of its association with isolationism in the late 1930s and early 1940s and opposition to American intervention in the war against Nazi Germany. But there is a more fundamental problem with the phrase: it describes an attitude, not a purpose, and it substitutes selfishness for realism.

It implies that nations can go it alone in the world, that we stand for nothing beyond our immediate self-interest, and that we should give no thought to how the rest of the world thinks or lives. It suggests that if a nation is strong enough, it can prosper no matter how much chaos or injustice surrounds it.

To use what has become a loaded word in the Trump era, it reflects the diplomacy of narcissism. And narcissism is as unhealthy for nations as it is for individuals.

Perhaps the best approach to the problem as it affects us both individually and collectively was offered by Rabbi Hillel, who lived in the century before the birth of Christ. In one of the most widely quoted adages in history, Hillel said: "If I am not for myself, who will be for me? If I am only for myself, what am I? And if not now, when?"

All of us have a duty to stand up for ourselves. Where patriotism is concerned, citizens love their own country in a way they can love no other. But the United States exists in a world of more than 7 billion people and nearly 200 other countries. Does our country not stand for something more than its own existence? Can we possibly survive and prosper if we are only for ourselves?

This constricted vision encourages destructive ways of thinking and, paradoxically, actions that harm long-term American interests. Almost as disturbing as the irresponsibility of Trump's decision to abdicate American global leadership on the environment by pulling out of the Paris climate accord was the language he used to justify it. He effectively cast the United States as stupid and easily duped, not as the shaper of its own fate but as the victim of invidious foreign leaders whom he cast as far shrewder than we are.

"The rest of the world applauded when we signed the Paris Agreement—they went wild; they were so happy—for the simple reason that it put our country, the United States of America, which we all love, at a very, very big economic disadvantage," Trump declared. "A cynic would say the obvious reason for economic competitors and their wish to see us remain in the agreement is so that we continue to suffer this self-inflicted major economic wound."

These are astonishing sentiments. They suggest that our very best friends in the world, starting with Canada, were just trying to scam us. They do not allow even the possibility that signers of the accord (every country in the world but two) might actually be concerned about staving off a catastrophe for the planet we all share.

Did Trump really believe that President Obama and business supporters of the pact (including, among others, the leaders of General Electric, Facebook, Apple, Microsoft, Google, IBM, BP, Hewlett-Packard, and Shell) were naïve idiots? Even Trump had to concede the agreement was "non-binding," which raised the question about how it could bring about all the horrors he described.

A diplomacy of narcissism is of a piece, to borrow from Richard Hofstadter, with the paranoid style of this American president. In his statement, Trump spoke of "foreign lobbyists" who "wish to keep our magnificent country tied up and bound down by this agreement." He painted our nation as a pitiful heap of insecurity. "At what point does America get demeaned?" he asked. "At what point do they start laughing at us as a country?"[5]

If anyone laughed after Trump's decision, it was our actual enemies and adversaries in the world. They welcome an American president who wants to rip up or weaken alliances and other forms of collective security that our own practical visionaries, since the days of Harry Truman, Dean Acheson, and George Marshall, put in place to *advance* our interests.

His decision was often described as having been driven partly by political motives. Trump seemed to realize how much trouble he was in from the metastasizing Russia story and wanted to appeal to his political base by reembracing his "nationalist" side. This only reinforced how narrow a definition of self-interest was in play here.

Even for conservatives who did not share the outrage among liberals and environmentalists over Trump's decision on the Paris agreement, his brand of nationalism created a profound unease because of the break it portended with long-standing approaches to collective security and alliances with democratic friends in Europe. His first foreign trip, during which Trump treated the absolute monarchs of Saudi Arabia with deference that neared obsequiousness, and NATO allies with hostility bordering on contempt, heightened the alarm already created by his lavish public praise of Vladimir Putin and the many questions surrounding his campaign's relationship with Russia. His acclaim for Philippine president Rodrigo Duterte's "unbelievable job on the drug prob-lem" raised similar fears about Trump's commitment to democratic and constitutional values (at home as well as abroad) in light of the thousands of extrajudicial killings that have been the centerpiece of Duterte's anti-drug efforts.

A new patriotism begins with an unflinching defense of the United States' commitment to democratic values and a renewal of alliances with other democratic nations. It means unabashedly rejecting what Trump "is needlessly, recklessly, and mindlessly do-ing," as the neoconservative foreign policy scholar Max Boot put it, "to destroy the underpinnings of the American-led international order." The costs of what Boot described were obvious when Trump met the leaders of the world's wealthy nations at the G-20 summit in Hamburg. The lead paragraph of *The Washington Post*'s account on July 7, 2017, told the story: "The growing international isolation of the United States under President Trump was starkly apparent Friday as the leaders of major world economies mounted a nearly united opposition front against Washington on issues ranging from climate to free trade." It was hard to see how isolation and a sharp decline in our influence would make America great or greater.[6]

The United States has every right to defend its own interests, but a new patriotism would also insist that our nation, at its best, has stood for liberty, self-rule, and equal rights. And to succeed, a new patriotism must respond to the forces behind the new na-tionalism. Hillel's third question—"And if not now, when?"—resonates in the face of the global threat to liberal democracy.

Consider these words from Steve Bannon in his speech at the 2017 Conservative Political Action Conference, which we cited in chapter 5: "The center core of what we believe," Bannon said, is "that we're a nation with an economy, not an economy just in some global marketplace with open borders, but we are a nation with a culture and a reason for being."

Progressives agree with the view that the economy exists to serve the interest of people, of citizens; citizens do not exist to serve the economy. And progressives need to acknowledge more than they sometimes do that democracy has up to now largely prospered within the framework of nation-states.

The European Union is the one political entity in the world that has tried over an extended period to make democracy work across national boundaries. It is an admirable effort worthy of more support than those with Bannon's views are willing to offer, and the breakup of the EU would be a calamity not only for the alliance of Western democracies but also because of the economic and social dislocation the collapse would leave in its wake. (Trump's ambivalence on this subject was yet another way in which his recklessness posed great dangers for American foreign policy.) Nonetheless, even the EU's strongest defenders acknowledge what is often called its "democratic deficit," including the extent to which its governance is driven more by technocrats than elected representatives.

As dangerous as so many forms of nationalism are, the current brand of nationalism in Europe and elsewhere is, to a degree at least, an expression of a desire by citizens to subject globalism to democratic discipline. The Brexit slogan, "Take Back Control," was a brilliant articulation of this wish, even if the promises made by advocates of Britain's departure from the EU were in so many cases false.[7]

Where the battle with Trump and Bannon, with the nationalists and nativists, needs to be waged is over the definition of "a culture" and "a reason for being." Bannon's words about the "global marketplace," after all, were not a call for liberal democracy and shared prosperity but the rationale for divisive isolation. As has been the case at other moments when nativism rose in the United States, the idea of the United States as a culture that has absorbed so many other cultures needs defense again. We are, indeed, "one nation," but we have been a nation proudly open to the influence of new people and the traditions they brought with them. Newcomers partially transformed our culture, but were in turn transformed by it—as any American whose family has been in the country for more than a single generation knows. As we noted in the introduction, our credo of "out of many, one" is an embrace of both parts of our country's historical journey.

> We are, indeed, "one nation," but we have been a nation proudly open to the influence of new people and their traditions.

For progressives especially, the economic discontents of angry voters are easy enough to understand. In principle at least, they are amenable to redistributive solutions with which progressives are comfortable. But the backlash against immigration sits uneasily with the left—and also with the libertarian and pro-market right—and properly so.

The response to Trump and Trumpism must include a vigorous defense of immigrants against racism and religious prejudice. It means battling deportations that break up families. It means identifying with those who have embraced the American dream, American values, and the American work ethic with the special commitment of people who struggled to get here. The pronouncements about immigrants by Trump and the far right have often been so vicious that simple decency requires a robust defense of newcomers. Caving in to racism, explicit or implicit, is unacceptable.

And this is about more than common kindness. Pushing back against Trump's hateful rhetoric toward immigrant communities is also about rallying to an American patriotism that enshrines pluralism in all its forms. Across the Western democracies, a war is being waged against pluralism in the name of nationalism. The argument, made by leaders like Trump and France's Marine Le Pen, holds that difference—be it racial, ethnic, or religious—undermines a nation's sense of shared identity and solidarity. This is deeply flawed and misguided, especially in the United States.

Yes, our history holds troubling examples of the consequences of fear and mistrust of the other, from slavery and Jim Crow to the expulsion of Native Americans from their ancestral lands and the persecution of LGBTQ Americans. But it was in those moments when people from all walks of life came together to resist and redress injustice that we saw America at its finest. And no one can doubt the enormous contributions made to our cultural, political, and economic life as a result of the diversity of those who have been able to call themselves Americans. If Hillary Clinton's campaign slogan, "Stronger Together," failed to connect with voters, it did convey an important truth about the American Experiment. The struggle to preserve a pluralist outlook from the dangers of Trumpian xenophobia is a struggle to preserve the very core of American identity itself.

Calling out prejudice, however, should be no barrier to understanding the causes of backlash. In some cases, residents of older communities are shocked by a sudden influx of migrants and experience a genuine sense of displacement and powerlessness in the face of change they cannot control. To say that this is an old story (Italians or Jews moving into neighborhoods of the 1910s generated hostile responses not much different from those generated now by Latinos) does not make the problem go away. In other cases—and this, too, goes back a long way—longtime residents are simply annoyed that newcomers speak a different language.

There are also struggles for power as new groups gain political ascendancy and older groups, once a majority, become minorities. The privileged need to acknowledge that working-class voters are, on the whole, more likely to find themselves in situations of direct competition with immigrants than are members of the well-off and professional classes. Religious differences can heighten the sense of conflict, and racial differences can aggravate them further.

Again, the United States has struggled through other periods of backlash in response to high rates of immigration. We tend to resolve these conflicts over time, often helped by periods of robust economic growth that produce something better than zero-sum games.

Supporters of immigrant rights need to be sensitive to who pays the highest cost for a more open society. They can support— as many progressive immigration advocates already do—specific measures to provide federal funds to communities where there are clear costs to local governments from absorbing large numbers of new residents. They can back policies (a higher minimum wage is one of them) that can lift the living standards of lower-income immigrants and native-born alike. They can point out what nativists usually ignore: that all major immigration reform proposals have linked a path to citizenship for undocumented immigrants to their paying penalties for being in the United States illegally and to requiring immigrants to learn English. And supporters of a path to citizenship for the undocumented can consider whether a new emphasis on skills-based immigration in the future could broaden the alliance for immigration reform. In the meantime, those who rightly support a generous refugee policy can take care to help those fleeing oppression and violence to locate in areas with the capacity to absorb them, and not expect a small number of communities to take an outsized number of those in need.

In truth, none of these measures will abruptly change the politics of immigration. But understanding the legitimate worries of those troubled by immigration is better than dismissing a large share of our fellow citizens as bigots. And, as we have already argued, the best way to fight bigotry itself is to reduce the sources of discontent that aggravate it.

———————

"Cosmopolitanism" is another word that captures an aspect of the reaction that led to Trump. Attacks on "rootless cosmopolitans" are the stuff of old forms of anti-Semitism, and the old anti-Semitism, along with various other forms of bigotry, is not as old as we would wish it to be.

But there is a highly positive sense of the term, offered by Princeton philosopher Kwame Anthony Appiah. "There are two strands that intertwine in the notion of cosmopolitanism," he writes. "One is the idea that we have obligations to others, obligations that stretch beyond those to whom we are related by the ties of kith and kind, or even the more formal ties of a shared citizenship. The other is that we take seriously the value not just of human life but of particular human lives, which means taking an interest in the practices and beliefs that lend them significance."

This should be an aspiration that unites us as Americans. And it means that those who live cosmopolitan lives must themselves go about "taking an interest in the practices and beliefs" of those whom the late Father Andrew Greeley called "neighborhood people." They are the people who do not aspire to being "citizens of the world" and who love the particular patch where they were raised or which they have adopted as their own.

There's evidence that many Brexit voters were neighborhood people, and some evidence that this is true of Trump's supporters as well. Economic change, particularly globalization, is very hard on neighborhood people. It can disrupt and empty out the places they revere, drive young people away, and undermine the economic base a community needs to survive.[8]

Too many liberals and conservatives alike insufficiently appreciate what makes neighborhood people tick and why they deserve our respect. Liberals are instinctive cosmopolitans who often long for the freedom of the big metropolitan areas. Free-market conservatives typically say that if a place can't survive the rigors of market competition, if the factories leave, the people left behind are best off if they simply find another place to live.

Let it be said that there are no simple answers to address the needs of those neighborhood people who believe themselves to be under siege by social, cultural, and economic transformations. But to write them off and to abandon the places they love (as so many of Trump's economic policies, contrary to his rhetoric, threaten to do) is morally unacceptable and politically dangerous. If there are limits on what government can do to help such places help themselves, this does not mean that nothing can be done, as we discuss in the next chapter. Neighborhood people are the forgotten men and women of an integrating planet. Their affections and their loyalties are civic gifts that those who oppose Trump and Trumpism must come to appreciate and admire.

Finally, there is a word that conservatives like much more than progressives do, "tradition." There's good reason for their different reactions: one person's reverence for tradition can be seen by another as a rationalization for prejudice and oppression. Southern whites did, indeed, invoke "tradition" to rationalize the subjugation of African Americans. Opponents of gay rights and gay marriage invoke tradition to explain why they believe that the only valid forms of sexual union are between a man and woman.

But not every tradition is oppressive, and many who, in principle, support gay rights and same-sex marriage live quite "traditional" lives themselves. This, by the way, includes many same-sex couples.

And when those reacting to changes all around them say, "I fear I will not be able to pass the world I grew up in to my children," they are not displaying paranoia, and they are not necessarily being reactionary. Change has come very fast in the last half century, when many traditional markers and boundaries have disappeared. Religious people, especially Christians and Orthodox Jews, have seen both a rising secularism and the growing importance of non-Western faiths in their own societies. For many, the rise of violent forms of Islam has made these changes all the more frightening. New rules and habits in human relationships challenge the ways in which many people have lived for the entirety of their lives. Economic forces have disrupted family life.

We know that we risk lumping many things together here in some sort of traditionalist parade of horribles. Our own view is that modernity has liberated far more than it has oppressed and that our nation should want to continue to move forward to advance the rights of women, African Americans, ethnic minorities, the LGBTQ community, and others who were previously held down by bigotry. Moreover, as police shootings in recent years and the high costs to minority communities of mass incarceration have reminded us, we have much more work to do in achieving genuine racial equality and justice.

But those of a progressive temperament cannot be blind to the ways in which social changes, both positive and negative, have disrupted both the lives and sense of security of millions of our fellow citizens. It was Marx and Engels who wrote: "All that is solid melts into air." This is how the world feels to many millions who have never read the *Communist Manifesto* and have no interest in Marxist doctrines. In such a world, the rise of new and often dangerous forms of right-wing politics should not come as a surprise. These movements must be opposed. But they are more likely to be defeated by progressives and moderates who understand that not all forms of regret over the passing of an earlier age are simply nostalgic or reactionary. There can be loss even in broadly beneficial social changes, and those losses need to be accounted for, even when the changes that create them cannot and should not be reversed.[9]

All this points to why those who would turn back Trumpism must embrace a new patriotism built on a capacity for empathy. Empathy here should not be mistaken with sympathy, defined as "feelings of pity and sorrow for someone else's misfortune." The empathy we propose does not just flow one way, from the elite in a society to the less privileged or from the rich to the poor. Rather, we imagine empathy as a mutual, universal obligation to try to understand the situations in which others find themselves and the complexities of their thoughts and feelings. "Make America Empathetic Again" is a useful counterpoint to Trump's favorite slogan.

We should be honest about how difficult empathy can be. It's far easier to feel empathy for people we see as like us, who agree with us and who live in our own neighborhoods. The challenge is to feel empathy for those who are very different from us, with whom we may disagree on a great many things.

The left and center left must remember that they reject elitism on principle—these movements are, after all, *democratic*. They should stand up for those who are not privileged, who have reason to complain, who suffer from injustice—even if they might not share the current political views of progressives, and even if progressives have an obligation to oppose expressions of those complaints that promote racism or anti-Semitism or homophobia or other forms of prejudice.

"Criticism is most powerful," the philosopher Michael Walzer has said, "when it gives voice to the common complaints of the people or elucidates the values that underlie those complaints."

> Those who would turn back Trumpism must embrace a new patriotism built on a capacity for empathy.

The historian James Kloppenberg made a similar point in channeling St. Paul about one of the central obligations of democratic citizens: that we need to "learn to see through one another's eyes, to think with one another's minds, and to treat each other with charity." Our country desperately needs more of this now.[10]

It comes down to this: progressives are right to ask supporters of Donald Trump to empathize with immigrants and refugees; with African Americans, Latinos, Muslims, and Asian Americans; with LGBTQ Americans. White Americans, whatever their political views, have a moral obligation to understand the anxiety and the anger felt by African American parents who fear that their unarmed sons might be shot in the streets for no reason other than their skin color. It is not unfair or "elitist" to ask Trump's supporters to consider the plight of families that risk being torn apart before voicing their support for harsh immigration enforcement. Among the many lessons to take away from the Trump campaign is how destructive a candidate who capitalizes on and encourages a lack of empathy can be.

And that need for empathy with minority communities is especially pressing now that Trump is president. He and his attorney general, Jeff Sessions, have already signaled their desire to reverse progress made during the Obama presidency on police-community relations in black and immigrant neighborhoods, and on protections for transgender Americans. These policy changes will have human consequences. If we are to overcome the bitter divisiveness of our politics and bring our country back together, Trump voters must be willing to hear the appeals of those who are different from them and try to understand where they are coming from. They may find that the people Trump presented as their enemies in fact share many of their concerns and hopes for our country.

But Trump supporters also have every right to ask progressives, in turn, to stand in their shoes, to see the world as they do from Appalachia or a once thriving and now devastated mill town, to understand that empathy cannot be selective, and to muster the social and moral imaginations to understand their struggles, their hardships, and their hopes. In chapter 6, we quoted a Trump voter who told a member of the Silicon Valley elite: "You have no idea what our lives are like." For many affluent liberals (and conservatives, too), there is truth to his claim. Those who would do battle against prejudice and bigotry must extend their sense of solidarity and respond to his demand for respect. Dietrich Bonhoeffer, the courageous German churchman who was killed by the Nazis shortly before the end of World War II for his participation in the plot against Hitler, taught us that "nothing that we despise in the other man is entirely absent from ourselves. . . . We must learn to regard people less in the light of what they do and omit to do, and more in the light of what they suffer."

We will defend democratic values not through an arrogance that is contrary to the democratic spirit but by embracing that spirit in empathy and grace. We are still seeking the world Martin Luther King Jr. described when he urged us to speed the time when "justice rolls down like waters and righteousness like a mighty stream." We will do this not simply by defeating our adversaries but by converting them, and, in the process, converting ourselves. The path to a new patriotism passes through a new spirit of empathy.[11]

NINE

Our Little Platoons

The Urgency of a New Civil Society

Writing about the devastation of a seemingly indestructible mountain culture in a West Virginia community struck by flooding in 1972, the sociologist Kai Erikson described the human role of community as clearly as anyone has. "It is the *community* that cushions pain, the *community* that provides a context for intimacy, the *community* that represents morality and serves as the repository for old traditions." His classic *Everything in Its Path: Destruction of Community in the Buffalo Creek Flood* underscored how fragile community can be.

How does a society find ways to bind itself together? How do we come to accept, across all of our divides, that there is still such a thing as a "common good"? The Latin root of "common," *communis,* is the same as the root of "community." It evokes "shared," "ordinary," and "public" all at the same time. In civic terms, the common good is the shared welfare of all citizens who have responsibilities to the community, and who in turn look to the community to protect, defend, and uplift them.

What support the communal exchange of responsibility and cooperation are our civic institutions—the fabric of governance but also the less formal organizations of civil society. And the informal institutions matter enormously. "What is written in a constitution can take a nation only so far unless society is willing to act to protect it," wrote Daron Acemoglu, a Turkish-born economist at the Massachusetts Institute of Technology who has watched his native country move toward authoritarianism. "Every constitutional design has its loopholes, and every age brings its new challenges, which even farsighted constitutional designers cannot anticipate." When our institutions are in danger, civil society must step in.[1]

Civil society is an idea so wholesome that it is often not taken seriously. It refers to all the nongovernmental institutions we take for granted, from Little Leagues and service clubs to Boy Scouts and Girl Scouts, churches, synagogues, and mosques, NAACP chapters, local Chambers of Commerce, unions, service clubs, Shriners, and Elks. Yet it is precious and complicated and essential. The decline of civil society helped create the circumstances for Donald Trump's rise, and civil society has been essential in the resistance to Trump since his election. Rebuilding community and civil society across America is vital to dealing with the social and economic problems that Trump exploited and that our nation must begin to solve.

Since the 1970s, the United States has witnessed a steep decline in trust in American institutions and a decay of American civil society. These problems were aggravated by the financial crisis of 2008–9, rising income inequality, and a deepening pessimism about the future of the country.

The numbers are staggering: 65 percent of Americans had confidence in organized religion in 1979, compared to 57 percent in 1996, 52 percent following the financial crisis in 2009, and 41 percent in 2016. Banks were at 60 percent in 1979. Not surprisingly, that number fell to 22 percent in 2009, and was back to only 27 percent in 2016. Trust in public schools fell from 53 percent in 1979 to 30 percent in 2016; in newspapers from 51 percent to 20 percent; in organized labor from 36 percent to 23 percent; and in big business from 32 percent to 18 percent. Only small business, police, and the military have stayed over 50 percent in public confidence.

The collapse of trust in institutions has been matched by a decline in confidence in elites, the result of a widespread sense that elite groups are profiting from economic circumstances and a distribution of power that are damaging the rest of the country. The paradox is that the citizens of democratic societies have an instinctive mistrust of elites, yet also count on elites to defend the institutions they value. As Rob Goodman, a former Capitol Hill speechwriter, put it, "It will be nearly impossible to rebuild democratic norms as long as elites are so distrusted, and they're likely to remain distrusted as long as they're capturing such a massive share of economic growth."

This was a distinct worry of the Framers, as Ganesh Sitaraman argued in his powerful 2017 book *The Crisis of the Middle-Class Constitution*. Sitaraman, a law professor at Vanderbilt, argued persuasively that in the founding period, "there was a robust and strong belief that a truly republican form of government was only possible in a society with relative economic equality." The founding generation, he wrote, "understood that the balance of political power had to mirror the balance of economic power in society." Here again the paradox: elites are trusted most in societies where they do not exercise undue control to advance their own interests.

Most devastating of all is the fact that Americans increasingly lack trust in each other. The University of Chicago's General Social Survey found that while 46 percent of Americans agreed in

1972 that "most people can be trusted," only 32 percent felt this way in 2012.[2]

A steep drop in civic participation has accompanied our diminishing faith in each other and in institutions. Robert Putnam's seminal 2001 book *Bowling Alone* marshaled a broad array of empirical data to show an erosion in community and social capital in America. Measuring such things as the decrease in bowling leagues, PTA participation, and Sunday picnics, Putnam demonstrated a dramatic collapse from the 1970s to the 1990s across many fields—informal socializing, religious participation, philanthropy, political activity, workplace interactions—in sharp contrast to the extraordinary civic creativity and growth fostered by the generation that came out of the Depression and the Second World War.

Bowling Alone received wide attention at the time, and the full costs of what Putnam described continue to emerge. But the consequences of civic decline were predictable. The conservative sociologist Robert Nisbet observed decades earlier, at the beginning of the 1960s, that "behind the spreading sense of insecurity and alienation in Western society" was "a growing realization that the traditional primary relationships of men have become, in certain areas, functionally irrelevant to the larger institutions of society, and sometimes meaningless to the moral aspirations of individuals." He added an observation with deep resonance today:

> A great deal of the character of contemporary social action has come from the efforts of men to find in large scale organizations, especially political ones, those values of status and intellectual security which were formally acquired in church, family, and neighborhood. How else can we explain the success of such movements in the modern world as Communism and Nazism except as mass movements designed to confer on the individual

some sense of that community which has been lost under the impact of modern social changes. The horror and tragedy are that such political movements have been based upon, and dedicated to, force and terror.

Similarly, in his pathbreaking 1959 work *The Politics of Mass Society*, William Kornhauser noted a relationship between "the atomization of social relations" among ordinary citizens and the success of mass (and often totalitarian) political movements. Social exclusion drives radical politics.[3]

Trump's campaign can fairly be seen as a movement that was motivated by the sense of alienation that both Nisbet and Kornhauser observed and was rooted in the forces Putnam described. Writing during the Republican primaries, Yoni Appelbaum, a historian and editor at *The Atlantic,* drew directly on Putnam's insights to argue that Trump supporters were "voting alone," citing the findings of a PRRI/*Atlantic* survey in late March and early April of 2016. Among all Republican-leaning voters at the time, 37 percent supported Trump, while 31 percent favored Senator Ted Cruz. But among civically disengaged Republicans, 50 percent supported Trump, as compared to just 24 percent for Cruz.

No doubt this result was due in part to Cruz's strength among churchgoing Republicans: regular churchgoers, the survey found, were more likely to support Cruz, while Republicans who seldom or never attended church tended to favor Trump. But Appelbaum was right to notice that the Trump-Cruz split was about more than relative religious commitment. Trump's style of campaigning—his willingness to break with the norms of "political correctness," the energy and sense of shared purpose that characterized his mass rallies—brought out Americans who felt disconnected from the political system and from their communities.

Appelbaum wrote: "The modal event for the Trump campaign is a mass rally in a stadium—thousands of voters file in, take their seats, cheer their candidate, jeer at demonstrators, and then depart. But they don't interact all that much with each other; it's politics as spectator sport." Nisbet, whose sociological imagination was shaped by the events of the 1930s, would recognize what Appelbaum described.[4]

The polarization of our politics is both a product and a cause of the decay in civil society and decline in mutual trust. In his 2008 book *The Big Sort,* the journalist Bill Bishop argued that as the old ties of community and faith eroded in the 1960s, new bonds based on lifestyle and political preference supplanted them. Americans congregated in areas where they were surrounded by like-minded people, creating not just red states and blue states, but red communities and blue communities. Democrats and liberals tended to live in and around big cities; Republicans and conservatives preferred suburban, exurban, and rural areas. The country, he suggested more than a decade ago, was balkanizing into a nation of echo chambers, heterogeneity replaced by reinforcing homogeneity.

> The polarization of our politics is both a product and a cause of the decay in civil society and in mutual trust.

When he examined 2016 voting data, *The Cook Political Report*'s David Wasserman confirmed that Purple America was shrinking. More and more counties, large and small, had become bright red and bright blue. Between 1992 and 2016, Wasserman wrote, "the share of voters living in extreme landslide counties quintupled from 4 percent to 21 percent." And in the 2016 election, 60 percent of voters lived in counties where either Clinton or Trump received at least 60 percent of the major-party vote.

These trends have been particularly damaging in areas where the culture is deeply rooted in traditional values about family, work, and community. These were places where Trump did well in the 2016 election. The conservative writer J. D. Vance made this point eloquently in his bestselling *Hillbilly Elegy*. Vance, who grew up in rural Kentucky and working-class Middletown, Ohio, described the high costs of weakening community bonds— poverty, opioid addiction, alcoholism, violence, a diminished sense of self-worth and responsibility, and social insularity. He noted that the legitimate grievances of the people living in these communities created fertile ground for a backlash against government, which had been unable to address their needs. It made them natural constituents for Donald Trump.[5]

The weakening of civic culture, the decline in social participation, and the crumbling of mutual trust thus began long before Trump's rise. But all contributed mightily to his success. And far from healing the breach, Trump's divisive approach to politics only widened it.

If Trumpism can in part be explained by a weakening of civil society, a vibrant civil society will be required to check Trump and his autocratic impulses—and ultimately, to restitch the very social bonds whose weakening contributed to his rise.

The early response to Trump from an array of civil society groups suggested that what the political philosopher Edmund Burke described as "the little platoon we belong to in society" was by no means a thing of the past—even if the mobilization also served to underscore how politicized civil society had become. Indeed, Trump's presidency seemed to infuse many civil society organizations with renewed purpose and vitality.

Religious leaders, for example, were at the forefront in battling Trump's immigration policies. This work was not new for many churches, synagogues, and mosques. In the 1970s and 1980s, religious congregations offered shelter to refugees fleeing violent civil wars in Central America as part of the sanctuary movement. When Trump's incendiary rhetoric and his early immigration orders spawned fear of mass deportations, houses of worship moved quickly to reassert themselves as sanctuaries for immigrants. Longstanding federal policy has been to consider churches and temples as "sensitive locations" off-limits for arresting, detaining, searching, or interviewing people. The Arch Street United Methodist Church of Philadelphia, for example, sheltered Javier Flores, an undocumented Mexican immigrant who feared being deported. Flores, a father of three with no criminal record, wanted to stay in the United States for his children. "Today and every day, if Javier and his family choose to stay with us, they will have a home with us," said the Rev. Robin Hynicka, the senior pastor at the church.[6]

Even religious institutions that were reluctant to provide sanctuary spoke up boldly for immigrants, particularly since Latinos now form such a large segment of both the Catholic and evangelical communities. Christian and Jewish activists have grounded their work to protect immigrants and refugees from harsh Trump policies in a prophetic tradition of caring for the vulnerable and the stranger. As Rabbi Jonathan Roos of Temple Sinai in Washington, D.C., put it in an op-ed in *The Washington Post,* "The teaching from scripture is clear: 'When a stranger sojourns with you in your land, you shall do him no wrong. The stranger who sojourns with you shall be to you as the native among you, and you shall love him as yourself for you were strangers in the land of Egypt.'" Speaking in the spirit of Pope Francis, members of the Catholic hierarchy, including Cardinal Archbishop Blase Cupich of Chicago, Cardinal

Archbishop Joseph Tobin of Newark, and Bishop Robert McElroy of San Diego, were forceful in their criticisms of Trump's policies. On immigration especially, they were joined by many of their more conservative brethren.[7]

Religious leaders mobilized around many other issues as well. The deans of 25 Catholic law schools wrote a public letter to Office of Management and Budget Director Mick Mulvaney objecting to the proposed elimination of the Legal Services Corporation, a publicly funded nonprofit organization that provides legal assistance to low-income people. A wide range of progressive Christian leaders—the Rev. Jim Wallis, the president of Sojourners; the Rev. Gabe Salguero of the National Latino Evangelical Coalition; and Sister Simone Campbell of the organizing group NETWORK—joined a broad movement organized around Jesus's words in Matthew 25 on the urgency of protecting "the least of these." The long-standing Circle of Protection coalition, which includes Catholic bishops and other religious leaders, rededicated itself to opposing Trump's budget cuts that affect programs for low-income Americans, including food stamps, the earned-income tax credit, and Supplemental Security Income.

A variety of American Muslim organizations like the Islamic Society of North America and Muslim Advocates, as well as a wide range of Jewish organizations, including HIAS (the Jewish refugee resettlement agency), the Religious Action Center of Reform Judaism, and Bend the Arc Jewish Action, also played critical roles in the near-instantaneous response to Trump's travel ban. One heartening sign in the Trump presidency: the willingness of American Jews and American Muslims to join together to condemn the rise of both anti-Semitism and anti-Muslim sentiment, and to support each other in local communities when Jewish cemeteries were desecrated or when Muslims faced intimidation. Here again was evidence of the power of the little platoons. At a time of polarization and divisiveness, Muslims and Jews stood up for each other as friends, neighbors, and fellow citizens.

Few American religious leaders have had a greater impact than the Rev. William Barber, whose Moral Monday protests in North Carolina revolutionized state politics and galvanized social action around the country. The witness of Barber, the former president of the North Carolina chapter of the NAACP and the founder of Repairers of the Breach, brings home the importance of the religious voice in American reform movements, and in particular of the power of the African American church in our history. His recovery and adaptation of the language of civil rights Christianity for the twenty-first century raises up ideas quite antithetical to the spirit of the Trump era: that there is such a thing as a common good, that the rights of all are secure only when the rights of the oppressed are restored, and that it is still possible to imagine society as a beloved community.[8]

Our listing here by no means does justice to the full range of religious participation in the pushback to Trump's policies. But the role of religious groups should prompt more secular progressives to a greater appreciation for the importance of people of faith to movements for equality and justice. Hillary Clinton's campaign was widely critiqued by religious progressives for its failure to organize among religious voters (in contrast to both her own and Barack Obama's 2008 campaigns) and to lift up one of the most authentic and important aspects of Clinton's own persona: the role of her deep religious faith in motivating her progressivism. If religious congregations are essential to the reconstruction of civil society, religious voices are indispensable to the progressive movement. Issues such as gay marriage and abortion have driven wedges between more religious and more secular Americans. But social action on behalf of the marginalized, as the cross-ideological acclaim for Pope Francis has shown, has the potential to ease long-standing rifts.

Professional groups were also particularly effective in checking Trump's agenda. During the first Muslim ban, armies of attorneys mobilized to provide legal assistance to the embattled travelers denied entry. As Marcia Tavares Maack, director of pro bono activities at the large Chicago firm Mayer Brown, noted, they used the tools of their profession as instruments of protection. "Law firms," she wrote, "obtained temporary restraining orders against the ban, filed habeas petitions on behalf of individuals who were being held at airports by Customs & Border Protection, and represented legal permanent residents and visa holders who were trapped overseas." Other lawyers and nonprofit legal organizations like the Northwest Immigrant Rights Project volunteered to help when ICE agents illegally or wrongly detained or arrested individuals and charged them with immigration violations.

Many law firms and associations stepped up pro bono efforts to challenge the Trump administration in other areas. As we noted earlier, former presidential ethics advisers Richard Painter and Norm Eisen led an impressive coalition to challenge Trump's violations of the Constitution's two emoluments clauses and to call out other ethical violations in public and in legal proceedings. Lawyers also took advantage of the Internet to provide analysis and insights to a wide audience. These efforts included *Lawfare,* a blog on national security issues run by Brookings Institution scholar Benjamin Wittes and bolstered by insights from Bush administration legal adviser Jack Goldsmith and former National Security Agency lawyer Susan Hennessey, as well as the newer *Take Care,* a forum for writings about the Trump administration from lawyers and legal scholars.[9]

Political scientists and other academics joined in the efforts to call out Trumpian actions that stray from democratic values and behavior. Four astute scholars—John Carey and Brendan Nyhan of Dartmouth College, Gretchen Helmke of the University of Rochester, and Susan Stokes from Yale University—created Bright Line Watch, using their expertise to monitor administration practices. Their first project was a survey of political science experts to create a robust set of benchmarks for measuring the vibrancy of democracy in the United States and other countries over time. They constructed the benchmarks around 29 democratic principles, including the absence of pervasive election fraud or voter manipulation, equal voting rights for all adult citizens, a free press, and a functioning system of checks and balances between branches of government. When there are signs of slippage, the benchmarks will become a valuable tool for assessing the danger.

The nature of Trump's Electoral College victory, the role of dark money in funding campaigns, and the challenges to voting rights also invigorated many public interest groups, some long active and some new. Let America Vote, an organization founded by former Missouri secretary of state Jason Kander, is working to combat voting restriction efforts. The Campaign Legal Center has been one of the premier forces litigating against voter suppression laws, felon disenfranchisement, and discriminatory redistricting. Bruce Freed's Center for Political Accountability has focused on persuading public corporations to disclose their political activities and expenditures in order to monitor the sources of election funds.

Other groups, including the Center for Responsive Politics, the Project on Government Oversight (POGO), Citizens for Responsibility and Ethics in Washington (CREW), Democracy 21, Public Citizen, Common Cause, Issue One, Represent.US, Run for America, and the American Constitution Society, have also focused on ethics issues and the role of political money. They have sought to protect the independence of the Offices of Congressional Ethics and Government Ethics, and POGO has begun to train federal employees across the country about their rights to resist political pressure and intimidation.

As the Trump administration has advanced regressive policies on issues related to civil and voting rights, climate change, women's reproductive health, racial justice, and LGBTQ equality, many organizations have stepped into the fray to mobilize rallies, raise funds, and lobby government officials. These include the American Civil Liberties Union, 350.org, the Sierra Club, Planned Parenthood, NARAL, the Advancement Project, Color of Change, the NAACP, the Leadership Conference on Civil and Human Rights, and the Human Rights Campaign.

We have already discussed the importance of independent media, and civil society has been important in promoting new forms of journalism aimed at vigorous watchdog reporting at all levels of government. Groups such as ProPublica and the Center for Public Integrity have played a central role in ensuring accountability in the Trump presidency. David Cay Johnston, a longtime financial reporter who has tracked and analyzed Donald Trump and his business dealings for decades, has created a blog called *DCReport.org* to focus on Trump—who, of course, has attacked Johnston on Twitter. State and local not-for-profit journalistic outlets, among them *MinnPost* in Minnesota, *The Texas Tribune,* and *WyoFile* in Wyoming, have stepped in where financial challenges have reduced the capacity of local media to offer intensive coverage of various levels of government.

The initiatives we have described here speak to the importance of organizations not directly linked to party politics or government in resisting government abuses and engaging more Americans in public work. (We will have more to say about party politics later.) We have offered a partial accounting of their efforts both to emphasize the vibrancy of civil society's response to Trump and to show how the health of our democracy depends upon the continued engagement of the independent sector.

In the long term, the problems that gave rise to Trumpism can only be countered through innovative strategies to revitalize American communities and rebuild trust, particularly parts of the country where deindustrialization and economic decline have especially damaged social ties. These include new approaches to policymaking and new forms of intervention from outside government that would rekindle the spirit of mutuality and a shared sense of belonging.

Ask the typical economist about place-based (as opposed to individually oriented) policies, and the answer will usually focus on the inefficiency of remedies aimed at redeveloping or renewing local and regional economies. It makes more economic sense, they argue, to give individuals financial help to move to where the jobs are than to try to move jobs to languishing areas. The gains made in areas helped by place-based policies, they say, are often offset by negative effects in other places. And revitalizing particular places can often end up helping the more privileged members of these local communities rather than those most in need of assistance.

These are all reasonable objections, and the shortcomings of policies aimed at reviving areas on a downward trajectory have played out in the disappointments of a variety of federal efforts to help regions grow. But these should be taken as a sign that place-based policymaking is hard, not that it is impossible. Large-scale infrastructure measures—the Tennessee Valley Authority and

rural electrification in the New Deal years are good examples—
have often created new opportunities in places once mistakenly
deemed "backward" by outsiders. Investments in educational institutions have not only helped individuals rise but also reinvigorated
whole states and regions. The Research Triangle in North Carolina
is the product of both private endeavor and the large investments
in education, particularly higher education, undertaken by vision-
ary governors, notably the late Terry Sanford.[10]

And as we have seen throughout our account, large regional
disparities in economic performance (as well as disparities within
states) have had devastating effects not only on individuals but also
on communities and civil society. They have had the same impact
as the flood at the heart of Kai Erikson's work: they devoured everything in their path, creating the social alienation and atomization that contributed to Trump's victory.

At the very least, the federal government should undertake a
national effort to help local communities identify those assets they
can build on. In some cases, it is solid—if old—infrastructure; in
others, ample supplies of clean water; and in still others, a stock
of decent but often abandoned housing. Small amounts of both
federal and philanthropic money can strengthen local institutions
to undertake the work of revival. And both state and federal encouragement of a pooling of resources among neighboring ailing
communities can have a multiplier effect on what those communities can do to help themselves.

The Obama administration experimented with place-based
approaches to federal poverty and education policy. It identified
particular towns or neighborhoods that could especially benefit
from support and then worked closely with local administrators
and community organizations to target grants and technical assistance. The three initial programs—Promise Neighborhoods,

Choice Neighborhoods, and Byrne Criminal Justice Innovation—directed resources at, respectively, strengthening educational opportunities, improving affordable housing, and addressing violent crime through community engagement. By the end of Obama's first term, the federal government had invested more than $365 million in these projects. In 2014, the administration announced the launch of the Promise Zones initiative, which worked with target communities to create jobs, bolster economic security, and increase access to education and housing.

Revisiting how the Obama administration's programs worked and considering how they might be usefully expanded should be part of a community rebuilding agenda. The evidence thus far suggests that these programs, modest in scope, did make substantive improvements to the communities where they operated. San Francisco's Mission Promise Neighborhood, for example, saw high school graduation rates rise by 10 percent and significant decreases in absenteeism and school expulsions. In Indianapolis, designated a Promise Zone in April 2015, millions of public dollars were invested in local businesses and nonprofit organizations to create jobs in areas of high unemployment and to train young people in career skills.[11]

If there is any single national program that is aimed directly at strengthening civil society, it is the collection of voluntary initiatives under the umbrella of the Corporation for National and Community Service, including AmeriCorps. These programs support volunteers—in the case of younger Americans, with small stipends or college scholarships—who work in the heart of civil society through local voluntary groups, including religious institutions. Many Republican governors and conservative policy intellectuals and entrepreneurs (such as John Bridgeland, who directed George W. Bush's Domestic Policy Council, and Leslie Lenkowsky, now a professor at Indiana University) have argued that if there is any federal program that conservatives should embrace, it is national service.

The abolition of the military draft brought many advantages, but it also ended an institution that was effective at breaking down the divides of region, race, and class. Service programs reinforce the idea of a mutual obligation that overrides our differences.

Still, limited funding means that only a small proportion of Americans participate in national service each year. Service Year Alliance, a coalition chaired by retired U.S. Army General Stanley McChrystal, has put forward a compelling proposal to expand opportunities for young people to complete one paid year of national service. The coalition's hope is that a year of service, either in the military or through community organizations, would become an expectation for all Americans; its goal, through not only enhanced federal funding but also substantial private and philanthropic support, is to create 100,000 service slots by 2019, and perhaps as many as 1 million eventually. Economists have also begun to think about service programs as an opportunity to reduce unemployment and to bring those who have dropped out of the labor force back into participation. Service programs have a record of providing forms of training that benefit participants and employers over time. "We've a remarkable opportunity now," McChrystal said in 2013, "to move with the American people away from an easy citizenship that does not ask something from every American yet asks a lot from a tiny few."[12]

The slashing or outright elimination of such programs in Trump's budget proposal was a singularly destructive attack on the

> Service programs reinforce the idea of a mutual obligation that overrides our differences.

nation's social infrastructure. In the short run, preserving existing service programs should be a priority, and states should be ready to step in to fill the gaps. But in the long run, an ambitious expansion of service should be a national objective—and it is a goal that should draw support across our partisan and ideological divides.

It is often forgotten how important the labor movement has been to strengthening civil society in the United States. The economic function of unions is widely recognized, and their decline is an important cause of rising income inequality. The collapse of union membership, driven by federal and state laws that have made it harder for workers to organize and also by the sharp decline in the traditionally unionized manufacturing and extractive industries, has been dramatic. In 1979, among private-sector employees, 34 percent of men and 16 percent of women were union members. By 2013, the shares had fallen to 10 percent and 6 percent, respectively. According to a 2016 report by the Economic Policy Institute, non-union workers would have been making 5 percent more on average in 2013 had union membership remained at 1979 levels.[13]

Beyond economics, unions were also once a primary vehicle of social cohesion and civic engagement, especially in industrial and manufacturing towns. Membership in a union brought with it a shared identity and sense of commitment. Unions provided not only economic benefits but also forms of social organization, education, and leisure-time sociability. Defending unions and battling efforts to destroy them (including so-called right-to-work laws in the states) should remain a progressive priority. And progressives must develop new models of union organizing and other ways to strengthen workers' rights in an era of "gig" jobs like driving for Uber or Lyft.

Local governments are the obvious first responders for reviving community. One promising strategy is to leverage public schools to help build social bonds and address neighborhood problems. Reuben Jacobson of the Institute for Educational Leadership defines "community schools" as "hubs of the community where educators, families, nonprofits, community members, and others unite to create conditions where all children learn and thrive." These schools, which now number nearly 5,000 across the United States, are intended to educate youth during the school day and also to serve as places of activity and learning for the wider community in the evening, on weekends, and over the summer. In some cases, a full-time coordinator and a site-based leadership team work to identify student and community needs and then address them by collaborating with families, local businesses, nonprofit organizations, and religious congregations. When successful, Jacobson writes, community schools "engage families and communities as assets in the lives of their children and youth." In so doing, they strengthen social bonds and invest in the future vitality of their communities.

Our schools should be places where democratic citizenship is taught and where students learn at a young age not only how our government works but also how they can change its course. Educators have discussed the revival of civics education for years, with valuable recommendations coming from the Center for Information & Research on Civic Learning and Engagement (CIRCLE). Civics should be seen as having the same importance as basic literacy, numeracy, and knowledge of science. School systems might also expand existing service requirements and encourage high school students to work on a political campaign or intern in local, state, or federal government.

Community and technical colleges are also important hubs of local engagement. In his travels across the country, *Atlantic* writer James Fallows found that the presence of well-functioning community colleges tended to be associated with stronger, more vibrant cities. In 2010, between 60 and 70 percent of community colleges offered some form of community engagement or service learning to their students. And community colleges often form partnerships with local businesses and organizations, or open their doors to members of the community for public events, low-priced classes, and health screenings. At Montgomery College in Maryland, for example, the Office of Community Engagement offers classes on basic computer skills and career guidance for local residents. Many of the services it provides are available in Spanish, Amharic, French, and Swahili—in addition to English—ensuring that immigrant populations in the area are able to enjoy the benefits.

Community colleges also train students in technical skills that they can then use to find a footing in the local economy. This is especially important in rural and suburban areas, where technological change and globalization have reduced the number of unskilled jobs available. The American Association of Community Colleges estimates that former community college students contributed $806.4 billion in added income to the U.S. economy in 2012. Harry Holzer, an economist at Georgetown's McCourt School of Public Policy, has been among those calling on community colleges to build even stronger ties with local businesses. Holzer argues that community colleges need to direct more of their resources to offering programs aimed at training students—especially those who will not go on to four-year colleges—for better-paying jobs in the new economy. Rebuilding civil society thus becomes part of a strategy to rebuild local economies. Community-centered education systems can simultaneously act as local conveners and as partners in apprenticeship and other programs aimed at enhancing individual skills.[14]

Not-for-profit organizations themselves will also have to change. Theda Skocpol, a Harvard University sociologist and political scientist, has spent decades studying civic participation. She has shown that the decline in civic participation is in part driven by the increasing professionalization of civil society. Member-led community groups have lost ground to staff-run advocacy organizations, which tend to be based in Washington, state capitals, and other sites of political power. As a result, public engagement for many Americans devolves into mailing a check. Existing national membership organizations need to examine their operating practices and find innovative ways to connect their grassroots constituents with work in their own communities. The ACLU, for example, has launched People Power, an online platform for grassroots mobilization of its members. More work needs to be done to build the capacity of people to act locally.

Some of the gap created by the centralization of mass membership organizations is being filled by community organizing—again, often in partnership with faith communities. For example, the PICO National Network is a federation of state and local groups that organize religious congregations to drive change in their neighborhoods on issues of economic, racial, and immigrant justice. PICO staffers train and develop volunteers, who then take on leadership roles in shaping PICO's campaigns. Congregations work in coalitions across lines of racial, socioeconomic, and religious difference to build power collectively and influence local decision makers. The result is bottom-up, broad-based community action.

The Industrial Areas Foundation (IAF), the community-organizing group founded in 1940 by the legendary organizer Saul Alinsky, is engaged in work similar to PICO's. Its Do Not Stand Idly By campaign is a national effort to reduce gun violence by mobilizing people of faith to pressure local and state officials as well as members of the firearms industry into adopting safer standards for gun manufacturing and sale.

One of the most successful organizing efforts of the last decade has been around undocumented immigrants who were brought to the United States as children. United We Dream has mobilized over 100,000 Dreamers and allies in their communities and is now comprised of 55 affiliate organizations across dozens of states. Activists lobby local, state, and federal officials to adopt more humane immigration laws and to provide protections and social services for undocumented immigrants. United We Dream and the Dreamers movement were influential in pressing for President Obama's Deferred Action for Childhood Arrivals (DACA) program, announced in June 2012. DACA granted relief from deportation to hundreds of thousands of Dreamers. The influence of the Dreamers and the moral story they tell are such that, in June 2017, Trump reversed a major campaign promise and announced that his administration would continue the DACA program, at least for the near future.[15]

The focus of this book is on the need to turn back Trumpism, so we have necessarily devoted considerable attention to progressive civil society initiatives. But the urgency of rebuilding civil society, of reengaging and reempowering citizens, transcends particular policy or political goals. Community work, in fact, can make its largest contribution by building bridges across partisan divides as citizens come together to solve shared problems and rebuild the neighborhoods, towns, cities, and regions to which they are devoted. By reviving a sense of shared identity based in mutual interest, communities can begin to counteract the mistrust and sense of hopelessness that helped fuel Trump's rise.

TEN

What "Draining the Swamp" Really Looks Like

Bringing a New Democracy to Life

At a moment when liberal democracy is under challenge as it has not been since the 1930s, two classic observations on the subject are worth remembering.

"If we desire a society that is democratic," said the civil rights legend Bayard Rustin, "then democracy must become a means as well as an end."

And Molly Ivins, the brilliant, cheeky, and hard-nosed Texas scribe who loved democracy as much as anyone, offered this advice to her regular readers: "The thing about democracy, beloveds, is that it is *not* neat, orderly, or quiet. It requires a certain relish for confusion."

If Trump and Trumpism continue to weaken our democracy and threaten our freedoms, those who would reinvigorate democratic life must combine Rustin's aspirations with Ivins's realism. This applies not only to our attitudes—toward each other and toward the ultimate wisdom of the citizenry—but also to how we approach reform. Rustin is right that undemocratic means should not be expected to produce democratic results. Nothing is more critical to the long-term legitimacy of a political system built on democratic values than guaranteeing that all eligible citizens are able to exercise their fundamental right to vote and have that vote matter. Getting more citizens into the democratic fray is essential to defending and repairing our republic.

But as Ivins would insist, democracy is not for wimps or for those who seek purity in all things. Ours is a complex, pluralistic, representative democracy, one in which political parties play an essential role in elections and policymaking. People pursue their right "to petition the Government for a redress of grievances" in many ways, some of them boisterous and inconvenient. Powerful group identities shape the relations between representatives and the represented. Getting into the fight will mean devoting ourselves to the often-hard work of politics, even when it makes us uncomfortable. It will require recognizing that we will not always be successful but that each experience will sharpen our skills. It will demand creative approaches to effecting change. It will mean becoming involved with some of the oldest forms of political action, inside parties and at the precinct level, while at the same time being willing to embrace new political alliances.[1]

There are many structural reforms that could make our system work better and confront the challenges of Trump and Trumpism. These include changes to voting practices and new rules for regulating the financing of campaigns. But the most important obstacles we face are cultural and normative. If one group of Americans sees another as evil, or as "not like us," or as promoting policies designed to undermine the American way of life, our democracy is in jeopardy. If Americans in large numbers start with premises built on faulty information, or facts that are not facts, the finest and most carefully constructed institutions will not function properly. If our top elected representatives cynically distort or misuse the laws and rules to fit their short-term political objectives or ideological agendas, simply changing the laws and rules is unlikely to deter them from further misbehavior.

Nonetheless, our constitutional democracy is a system with strong antibodies. When large numbers of Americans turn up, turn out, and speak forcefully, their voices are eventually heard. The widespread backlash against Republicans' efforts to repeal and replace Obamacare is an encouraging example of how active citizens can alter the trajectory of a debate. When politicians repeatedly lie and mislead, the free exchange of ideas and information can ensure that they are, eventually, called out for their deceit. When regular elections are the rule, elected officials are required, over time, to respond to movements in public opinion— and all the more so if one side's arguments are not drowned out by the financial power of the other, and if legislative districts are drawn in ways that maximize the opportunity that voters have to effect change.

> Ours is a complex, pluralistic, representative democracy, one in which political parties play an essential role.

Responding to the challenge before us will be all the more difficult because many reforms that might once have enjoyed bipartisan support have fallen victim to hyperpolarization. We will thus need to think broadly and innovatively about how to improve our system of self-government. Our democracy already offers citizens many tools. But we need to make the ones they have work better, and put more in their hands.

Start with the most basic: the right to vote itself. Over the last decade, voting rights have come under siege. Empowered by the Supreme Court under Chief Justice John Roberts, many Republican-controlled state legislatures have passed new measures to restrict access to the ballot. The Trump administration has shown it will bolster these efforts whenever possible, all in the name of combating widespread "voter fraud" that simply does not exist.

The most urgent task for advocates and activists is to roll back these pernicious efforts to suppress voting rights, which are aimed largely at African Americans, Latinos, and younger voters. According to the Brennan Center for Justice, 14 states had new voting restrictions in place for the first time in a presidential election in 2016. Among the most common are voter identification laws, which require those who would cast ballots to provide one of a limited number of state-issued forms of photo ID to be able to vote. These laws seem neutral but are not. Americans of color, the poor, the young, and the elderly are far less likely to have these documents. In a parody of how political priorities trumped voting rights, Texas's voter ID law, passed in 2011, prohibited young people from using their public-university student IDs to vote, but declared that a handgun license was a sufficient form of identification.

Other voter suppression measures, pushed by Republican governors and state legislators in states such as North Carolina, Florida, and Arizona, have included reductions in early voting, the closing of polling locations (often targeted at minority neighborhoods), and the elimination of same-day registration. And some states have even made it harder for low-income voters to secure required IDs by closing or relocating offices where those legal forms of identification might be obtained. In 2015, Alabama announced that it would close or drastically reduce the hours for 35 motor vehicle offices, purportedly because of budget cuts. These closures were overwhelmingly concentrated in the part of the state with the highest proportion of black residents.

The discriminatory nature of the action was so egregious that the Obama administration's Department of Transportation opened an investigation into whether the state had violated Title VI of the Civil Rights Act of 1964.

Encouragingly, a wide array of public interest, civil rights, and civil liberties organizations have successfully challenged voter suppression laws in the courts. They include the NAACP Legal Defense Fund, the Campaign Legal Center, the Lawyers' Committee for Civil Rights Under Law, the Advancement Project, the ACLU, and the Brennan Center. In July 2016, the full U.S. Circuit Court of Appeals for the Fifth Circuit upheld a lower court's ruling that the Texas voter ID bill had a discriminatory effect on African American and Latino voters. Then, in April 2017, a federal judge ruled that the law had been written with the specific intent to discriminate. Additionally, a three-judge panel of the Fourth Circuit Court of Appeals struck down North Carolina's voter ID law in 2016, finding that the "new provisions target African Americans with almost surgical precision."[2]

During the Obama presidency, the Department of Justice played a key role in supporting challenges to state voting restrictions. But under Attorney General Jeff Sessions, a longtime opponent of government-protected voting rights, Justice has begun switching sides. In February, for example, the department filed a motion asking that the judge in the Texas case dismiss Justice's earlier claim that the state legislature had passed its voter ID bill with discriminatory intent, arguing that Texas had demonstrated its willingness to amend the law and correct its flaws. When the judge ruled, in effect, in favor of the original department position, Ari Berman, one the country's premier journalists writing on voting rights, called the decision "a big loss for Jeff Sessions." It was, and for Donald Trump, too.

Support for ongoing efforts to combat voter suppression is key to protecting the right to vote. So is challenging the ongoing false claims by Trump, Sessions, and others that there is widespread illegal voting, which serve as the rationale for laws whose real purpose is to block access to the ballot. A report by the Brennan Center found incident rates of illegal voting at between 0.0003 and 0.0025 percent of total votes cast. The report noted that it is more likely an American "will be struck by lightning than that he will impersonate another voter at the polls." In May, Trump sought to give the unsubstantiated allegations of fraud a veneer of legitimacy by issuing an executive order, against the advice of Democrats and also many Republicans, to create the Advisory Commission on Election Integrity. The commission is chaired by Vice President Mike Pence and vice-chaired by Kansas Secretary of State Kris Kobach, a key architect of restrictive voting legislation in Kansas and around the country. Sherrilyn Ifill, president of the NAACP Legal Defense and Educational Fund, said it was "a thinly veiled voter suppression task force . . . designed to impugn the integrity of African-American and Latino participation in the political process." And it got off to a very bumpy start. In late June, when the commission asked states to provide sweeping, detailed information on all voters, 45 refused to comply with at least part of the request.

The path to increased voter suppression was first reopened in 2013 when the Supreme Court, in a 5–4 ruling in *Shelby County v. Holder,* gutted the Voting Rights Act. The narrow majority nullified the law's "preclearance" provision, which had required certain states and counties with a long history of voting restrictions to seek approval from the Justice Department or the federal courts before making any changes to election procedures. But the Court's finding was only that the formula used to determine who would qualify for preclearance was outdated, not that the measure itself was unconstitutional. Even if a Republican Congress under Trump is unlikely to act, supporters of equal rights must press their elected officials to speak out against voter suppression and in support of equal access to the ballot. The long-term goal should be new legislation to restore the Voting Rights Act to its full power by updating the preclearance formula and adding additional protections against new forms of voter suppression. A new Voting Rights Act should be the centerpiece of a new democracy.[3]

An updated version of the act could also encourage other reforms that would make the system work better. Universal voter registration, under which citizens are registered automatically unless they explicitly request not to be—something that is routine in most democracies—could be joined with automatic preregistration of 16- and 17-year-olds when they get driver's licenses.

It was not until 1845 that Congress established Election Day as the first Tuesday after the first Monday in November to accommodate the needs of what was then still largely a nation of farmers. (Holding elections on Tuesdays did not interfere with Wednesday "Market Days.") More than a century and a half on, a very different kind of society should be willing to revisit this decision. Moving Election Day from Tuesday to the weekend, ideally over a 24-hour period from noon Saturday to noon Sunday, would eliminate the "rush hours" that occur early in the morning and at the end of the day. It would ease participation by voters with irregular or inflexible working hours who are generally less well-off economically. Election Day itself should be a national holiday. And all states should have an extended period of early voting.

At a time of sharp partisan division, a bipartisan commission headed by two prominent partisan election lawyers, Democrat Robert Bauer and Republican Ben Ginsberg, recommended a series of changes in how we run elections and enunciated what should be a basic right: the ability to vote within a half hour of showing up at the polls. Their reforms included:

- Online voter registration in every state, allowing eligible citizens to register to vote and to update their registrations via the Internet.
- Exchanging voter registration lists across states, so that voters are correctly registered at one location, that registration lists are more accurate and not a source of polling-place congestion, and that these more accurate lists can assist in identifying individuals who are eligible to vote but are not registered.
- Expanding voting before Election Day to limit congestion on Election Day and to give more opportunities for people who can't show up on Election Day, via alternatives like mail balloting and in-person early voting.
- Using more schools as polling places, with Election Day scheduled as an in-service day for students and teachers.
- Managing polling places through a resource allocation calculator, to optimize the number of voting machines and staff at polling places, thereby reducing the potential for long lines.
- Replacing voting machines—most of which are nearing the end of their useful lives—with equipment incorporating new technology that can help voters with disabilities or limited English, and those in the military and overseas,

while also making sure ballots are not too complicated and polling places are accessible.

"Let's put it this way," said Stuart Stevens, one of the Republican Party's most experienced strategists, in a July tweet responding to the controversies surrounding Trump's vote fraud commission, "far more votes are lost due to long lines at polls than any voting fraud. Making it easier to vote is first remedy."

America should also harness the powerful technology of the Digital Age to facilitate faster and easier democratic participation. The technology that enables people to rent a car and receive a personalized receipt within 30 seconds of returning it could also enable voters to go to any convenient polling place and get a personalized ballot that matches the one they would receive at their regular precinct. These reforms have already been introduced in some places for early voting. But in much of the country, current practices limit voting to a predetermined location near one's home. Poll stations are often understaffed and can have extremely long lines, particularly before and after normal business hours. Wide adoption of new voter technology would also broaden the opportunities to create vote centers in shopping malls, supermarkets, and any other places with ample parking and easy access. In Larimer County, Colorado, vote centers have been both popular and effective at increasing voter turnout.

The tens of thousands of Americans who volunteer to work the polls on Election Day are national assets, and the management of elections is uncontroversial in most of our jurisdictions. Nonetheless, America is unusual in that the election officials who preside over the election process are themselves typically partisan and thereby prone to efforts to advantage one party's voters over another—or, perhaps just as important, likely to be suspected of such behavior by those who don't share their partisan leanings. Imagine Super Bowl referees on the payroll of one of the competing teams. Having our elections run instead by nonpartisan professionals would increase the credibility of the electoral process and the trust of voters. It would, for example, reduce the controversies we now have over locating polling places in ways that benefit one party over the other, and make recounts in close races somewhat less contentious. (And we would still value those volunteers, who should receive the best training available.)[4]

Finally, we urge an idea that is controversial but has worked well elsewhere: universal voting. Australia, a country of democratic innovation that gave the world the secret ballot (it was known as "the Australian ballot"), has provided a model for how it works.

Alarmed by a decline in voter turnout to less than 60 percent in the early 1920s, Australia adopted a law in 1924 requiring all citizens to present themselves at the polling place on Election Day. This is often referred to as "mandatory voting," although Australian voters are not required to cast marked ballots—they can draw a cartoon character on them if they wish, and some voters do. It is thus more appropriately labeled "compulsory attendance at the polls." Enforcing the law is a small fine (now set at $20). The law also establishes permissible reasons for not voting, such as illness and foreign travel.

The results have been remarkable. In the 1925 election, the first held under the new law, turnout soared to 91 percent, and it has stood at over 90 percent ever since.[5]

The small fine is, in effect, a "nudge." It is also a declaration of responsibility. Democracy cannot be strong if citizenship is weak. With the abolition of the universal draft, citizens are asked to pay their taxes and obey the law, show up for jury duty when summoned, and not a lot more. Universal voting sends a message: we all have the duty to participate in the great act of self-government.

Universal voting would have a powerful effect on voting rights as well. If citizens had a duty to vote (and if they faced a small penalty if they didn't), then the obligations of those who run our elections would be to make it as easy as possible for citizens to do their duty, not create barriers to voting. Universal registration, keeping voter lists current, providing for easy access to the polls and to early voting—all would become the rule. And voter suppression efforts would become obsolete.

High turnout is not an automatic sign of a flourishing democracy. But Australia shows the values of universal voting for improving political discourse. Both parties know that their bases will already be voting, so Australian candidates aim to persuade the voters in the middle, using less inflammatory language, fewer scare tactics, and a greater emphasis on large issues rather than "wedge" issues (even if wedge issues are not unknown Down Under). Bringing less-partisan voters into the electorate presents parties and candidates with new challenges and opportunities. The balance of electoral activities would shift from mobilizing the highly committed to persuading the less committed. Political rhetoric might cool, and the intensity of polarization could diminish. Universal voting might, if we can use the term, leave politics less "Trumpified."

We don't pretend that compulsory attendance at the polls would cure all our ills and are under no illusion that it will catch on anytime soon in the United States. Americans resist mandates and penalties, especially for something like voting. But it would be enormously valuable for at least some states to initiate universal voting. We suspect Americans could use this innovation as effectively as we have used the Australian ballot.

We also know that changing the Electoral College system will be extremely difficult. But as we argued in chapter 1, there is reason to worry that going forward, we will have many more outcomes in which the winner of the Electoral College will be the loser of the popular vote. The Electoral College is increasingly out of line with popular sentiment in the country.

We noted, for example, that the Electoral College disadvantages metropolitan areas, particularly large ones. Since metropolitan areas tend to be younger and more diverse than rural areas, the current system also discriminates against the new generation, and against African Americans, Latinos, and Asians. Aggravating this discrimination, white voters are more likely to live in swing states, while nonwhites are concentrated in "safe" states. One study of voting power on the Electoral College outcome found that, while every registered white non-Hispanic voter in 2012 had the potential influence of 1.05 registered voters, the influence of registered Asian voters stood at 0.58 and of Hispanic voters at 0.87. If the growth of metropolitan areas will make the Electoral College increasingly unrepresentative, so too will the rise of the nation's nonwhite population concentrated in the non-swing states.

In a democracy that invests such great power in the presidency, choosing the chief executive through a system that empowers the old over the young, whites over non-whites, and voters from declining regions over those in growing areas is a recipe for division, reaction, and long-term instability. It runs the risk of electing a string of leaders who do not represent even a plurality of the voting population and are out of touch with the concerns of the rising sectors of the American electorate.

Defenders of the Electoral College offer a series of arguments that either are self-contradictory or overlook the arbitrary way in which the Electoral College can work. They regularly speak of the "wisdom of the founders," as if the way we elect the president now has anything to do with the way the founders envisioned the process. In fact, the founders always saw the Electoral College as a deliberative body. They never imagined that electors would be chosen by popular vote. There is nothing deliberative about the current Electoral College. Indeed, many states have passed laws binding electors to state electoral results, and those electors who depart from their party's candidates are criticized as "faithless electors."[6]

The Electoral College is supposed to encourage the election of candidates who can assemble a coalition with geographical breadth. But this is a relative term. The existing rules and the nature of politics, state by state, encourage candidates to campaign in 10 or 12 swing states and skip the rest. Where's the breadth? The winner is picked not by the laws of elections but by the serendipity of the casino. If you're lucky enough to hit the right numbers, narrowly, in a few states, you can override your opponent's big margins in other states.

After the 2016 election, many of the Electoral College's defenders, particularly among conservatives, argued that Clinton's popular vote lead could be ascribed entirely to her 4.27-million-vote victory over Trump in California. Some asked why California should have such influence. It was not a question that occurred to conservatives when Ronald Reagan carried the state. And the questions can be reversed: Why should Americans who choose to live in California be punished by having their electoral power reduced? Should it not be more troubling that 4.27 million voters in California mattered far less than 10,704 voters in Michigan, 22,748 voters in Wisconsin, and 44,292 voters in Pennsylvania? Either we are a democratic republic, or we're not. We either believe in one person, one vote, or we don't.

There is a remaining rationale for the Electoral College—that if there is an exceedingly close presidential election, like 1960, in which the popular vote division is about one-tenth of 1 percent of the national vote, or one vote per precinct, a challenge to the outcome could require a nationwide recount. It would certainly be a spectacle. But it is a risk far smaller than that of having a series of elections in which a plurality or a majority of Americans find themselves governed by the choice of a far smaller group of their fellow citizens.

The cleanest way to reform the system would be to amend the Constitution to eliminate the Electoral College and mandate an outcome based on a national popular vote. This should be the ultimate goal, but it is unlikely to be achieved anytime soon, given the number of smaller states advantaged by the current system that could block a constitutional amendment.

In the meantime, the National Popular Vote Interstate Compact is a promising path. It envisions the legislatures of states representing a majority of the Electoral College forging a formal agreement through state law to cast their electoral votes for the winner of the popular vote, thereby creating a de facto popular vote system. Its supporters have won enactment of the compact in states with 165 votes, still short of the 270 needed for a majority. This is an area where citizens in states that have not yet joined the compact can mobilize to effect change on behalf of popular rule.[7]

Less of a reach is the enactment of "instant runoff" systems under which voters rank candidates in the order of their preferences, marking a "1" for their first choice, a "2" for their second choice and on through the list if they wish. If no candidate wins a majority on the first round, the ballots for candidates with the fewest first preferences are redistributed to their second preferences. This process continues until one candidate reaches a majority.

The instant runoff would, on the one hand, empower third-party voters because they would know expressing their first choice would not automatically lead to the election of their least-favored candidate; their second or third preferences would count. At the same time, it would prevent third-party votes from distorting what are likely to remain two-party contests—something we saw in full measure with both Jill Stein's Green Party and Gary Johnson's Libertarian Party in 2016. An instant runoff system could be included in a constitutional amendment to replace the Electoral College with a direct national vote system. Or it could be adopted individually by states to determine which candidate wins their electoral votes under the current system. Other proposals for changing the way in which states allocate their electoral vote, such as by the winner of congressional districts, would introduce more, not less, bias into the system and should be avoided.

How politicians draw the boundaries of congressional and legislative districts is another serious problem for American democracy. It can lead to two undesirable outcomes: both parties can conspire to protect all their incumbents by creating "safe" districts for them; or one party can distort lines to award itself more seats than its votes, fairly apportioned, would give it. The latter is known as partisan "gerrymandering," named after an early-nineteenth-century Massachusetts governor who was a pioneer of the practice. Some gerrymanders have been particularly outrageous, producing vast distortions of the popular will as measured in votes.

Gerrymandering is not the sole reason for the difficulty in matching votes and seats. How voters sort themselves before any lines are drawn has an important effect. With Democrats concentrated in urban and suburban areas and Republicans spread out over more geographically spacious exurbs and rural areas, many districts are naturally homogeneous and thus safe for one party. Elected officials from such districts have few incentives for listening to or representing those with different views or backgrounds. These districts can pull lawmakers and candidates toward the extremes to accommodate the ideological activist bases that dominate party primaries. Further, because so many Democrats live in densely populated areas, they represent more districts decided by overwhelming margins. The votes of Democrats are thus more likely to be "wasted" in producing big victory margins in cities, while Republicans win more seats with somewhat smaller margins.

Still, gerrymandering matters enormously, as the Brennan Center report cited in chapter 1 suggests. And redistricting reform would produce important benefits. Research by political scientists Ryan D. Williamson, Michael Crespin, Maxwell Palmer, and Barry C. Edwards shows that independent redistricting commissions, where districts are drawn by nonpartisan actors or agencies, can make districts fairer. Independent commissions already exist in some states, such as Arizona and California. In states that do not have any independent redistricting authority, strong and continuing efforts, among them the Democratic Party's initiative led by former attorney general Eric Holder and former president Obama, are essential.[8]

Also important is the multipronged effort to create a workable standard for the courts to use when a redistricting plan is unfairly rigged for partisan advantage. This is still a relatively new area of jurisprudence (most redistricting cases heretofore have focused on racial gerrymandering). In June 2017, the Supreme Court announced that it would hear the Wisconsin case *Gill v. Whitford,* in which the plaintiffs have proposed to evaluate partisan gerry-mandering based on the "efficiency gap." This model encompasses not only a measure of the size of the difference between the votes a party receives and the number of seats it wins but also various for-mulas, including how many votes cast for candidates of each party were "wasted." Having an unbiased empirical measure of what constitutes a gerrymander could revolutionize Supreme Court ju-risprudence on the subject, in light of previous opinions in this area by Justice Anthony Kennedy.

It may also be time to consider bolder redistricting reform, recognizing that such change will not come easily or quickly. Un-til 1980, state legislative districts in Illinois had three members, and voters could cast three ballots—all for one candidate, or split among three. Those in the legislature at the time said the cumu-lative system created broader representation, a better stream of candidates, and more incentives for lawmakers to cooperate with one another, all of which eroded sharply after its repeal. Ten other states, including Arizona, New Jersey, Maryland, Vermont, and West Virginia, currently allow for some form of multimember dis-tricts in their state legislatures. Applying this principle, Congress might ameliorate some of its problems, and do so without a con-stitutional amendment. Congress would simply need to amend the 1967 federal law requiring single-member districts.[9]

The advantages and disadvantages of multimember districts can be debated, but it is an example of how building a new de-mocracy requires thinking outside of accepted frameworks and rediscovering our institutional inventiveness. Ideas such as the di-rect election of U.S. senators were products of the Progressive Era's reforming imagination. We need a similar spirit of civic innovation in our time.

A spirit of innovation would certainly be useful in the House of Representatives. When the parties are ideologically polarized and compete closely for control, it is inevitable that the majority party in the House will use the rules to advance its strategic interests. That means fewer opportunities for participation by the minority, less transparency, little genuine deliberation in committees and on the floor, and diminished incentives for aggressive oversight of the executive. Standing rules of the House can be and are routinely suspended by the majority when it is in their interest to do so.

There is little prospect of altering these incentives in a fundamental way. But the House could improve the quality of its deliberation and policy making. Currently, the House typically meets from the late afternoon on Tuesday to mid-afternoon on Thursday. Moving to a 9–5, Monday-through-Friday schedule three weeks a month, with the fourth week off for constituent meetings, would have multiple benefits. It would provide incentives for House members to bring their families to Washington, creating more opportunities for social interaction within and across party lines. It would provide more time for debate and deliberation, and for real congressional oversight. If the schedule change were combined with a change to the rules banning fundraising during the fifteen days a month in Washington, it would reduce the spectacle of lawmakers racing off the Capitol grounds at every spare moment to do "call time"—i.e., pleading with contributors for campaign money. A similar adjustment in work habits would benefit the Senate as well.

Both houses could also improve their performance by hiring additional professional staff with specific areas of expertise.

Such reforms would help, but only public pressure has any real chance of changing the political calculus. "Do your job" chants at raucous, well-attended town halls, and persistent calls and letters to congressional offices are a good place to start. As we discussed in chapter 3, the intense public outcry when House Republicans tried to weaken their own ethics watchdog shows that public pressure can work.

There are also deep structural problems in the Senate, and they are not easy to resolve. As we have seen, the Senate is becoming less and less representative of the population, as it tilts more toward the smaller, rural, and ethnically homogeneous (read, white) states. Legislation can pass with support from senators who represent significantly less than 50 percent of the country. At the same time, obstructionism has often thwarted majority will and brought the chamber to a halt. Short of abolishing the representational system in the Senate (made almost impossible by the Constitution), what is to be done?

Start with the filibuster, which has been controversial for more than a century, but was rarely used during most of the modern era. When it became a flash point over judicial nominations in 2006 as Democratic senators tried to block a number of conservative Bush nominees to the appeals courts, a bipartisan group known as the Gang of Fourteen defused the conflict by agreeing to allow votes on some of the picks but not others. This détente crumbled in the Obama era when Senate Republicans effectively distorted the rule to use the filibuster routinely on issues and nominations.

The threat of abolishing the filibuster for executive and judicial appointments came to be known as the "nuclear option," a name suggesting that doing so would wreak unimaginable havoc. Yet the nuclear option itself was, as law professor Josh Chafetz has pointed out, simply part of a trend toward weakening the filibuster that goes back to 1975. That is when the threshold for closing down debate was lowered from two-thirds of senators voting to three-fifths of the Senate, the current 60 votes. This reform may have inadvertently made it much easier for the minority to misuse the rule. The frustration of the majority that followed is part of a natural evolution in response to changing political circumstances and tactics. "When the use of a parliamentary procedure becomes so obstructionist that it brings its chamber to a halt," Chafetz writes, "that procedure is changed."

The filibuster on legislation remains intact, and there has been growing support for abolishing it entirely. The partisan identities of advocates of this course often change, depending on who is in the majority. It was disconcerting that Trump, in an effort to explain his lack of legislative accomplishment, sought to shift the blame to what he called the "archaic" rules of the House and Senate. He told Fox News that "the filibuster concept is not a good concept to start off with." It was an odd point for Trump to make, since his problems at the time were in the House, which gives the majority nearly unlimited power. *The Washington Post*'s Aaron Blake described the interview as Trump "talking about consolidating his own power," a disturbing portent from a president who, as Blake wrote, had expressed "admiration for strongman leaders."[10]

If there was ever a debate that the president should stay out of and that should be disentangled from partisanship—however difficult that is—it is the argument over the filibuster. And there are steps short of abolition that could keep the minority relevant without giving it the capacity to foster mass obstruction.

When Senate Republican Leader Mitch McConnell misused the filibuster during the Obama years by routinely forcing Democrats to undertake time-consuming cloture votes on even seemingly noncontroversial issues, he had an easy time of it so long as he could keep some unity among Republican senators. They did not have to exert themselves at all—by, for example, speaking for hours on the Senate floor. Currently 60 votes are required to close down debate and move toward a vote. Even when Democrats had 60 senators for a brief time in 2009 and 2010, they could not force action if even one in their ranks was ill or absent. One rule change to speed action would shift the burden to those trying to block legislation. Instead of requiring the majority to muster 60 votes to act, the minority could be required to muster 41 votes to continue debate and maintain a filibuster. This approach would begin to answer concerns over excessive minority power without instituting a radical change at an especially contentious moment in our politics.

Compromise on this issue is especially vital now. In the past, Senate Democrats and Republicans alike have been restrained when it came to rules changes governing the passage of legislation. Restraint is a wise principle in the Age of Trump.

When it comes to the Supreme Court, it is time to lower the stakes, and to take away the ability of accidents and actuarial tables to enable a president to stack the court for decades. The best way to do so would be to move from lifetime appointments to single 18-year terms for justices, staggered so that each president in a term could nominate two justices to fill posts. There would be less incentive to pick younger justices in the interests of influencing the Court over multiple generations, and less opportunity to stack its membership.

The executive branch is also facing deep challenges from Trump and Trumpism. Civil servants in particular face immense pressures. Trump has called for reforms ranging from removing civil service protections and allowing civil servants to be fired without cause to budget cuts aimed at diminishing agency employment and continuing education. This is partly a partisan effort to reshape the civil service, but also an attack on professional expertise. Thus has the arcane term "kakistocracy," meaning government by the least competent among us, taken on a surprising resonance with the advent of the Trump administration.

Protecting the independence and integrity of the civil service and of government managers, including but not limited to whistle-blowers, is an important goal. But so is attracting talent to government service, rewarding and recognizing those who do the work, and finding ways to make government work better. Groups such as the Partnership for Public Service, which distributes the Sammie Awards to honor outstanding federal employees, and the Volcker Alliance, with its efforts to improve implementation of government budgeting and legislation, have pushed for reforms to create a better government. Every American has an interest in an efficient and responsive government, but progressives especially need to be more invested in improving the civil service. Progressives, after all, insist that government can do much good; voters who doubt government's capacity and efficiency will be less likely to put faith in their promises.[11]

In June 2016, a poll jointly conducted by Ipsos and Issue One found that 80 percent of Americans believed money had a greater influence on politics than at any other point in their lives, and 70 percent believed that this posed grave risks to democracy. They are not mistaken. Billions of dollars are now spent each election cycle on political campaigns, much of it in the form of dark money donated by independent groups that do not need to disclose their donors.

Our money system also has an invidious impact on policy-making and problem solving. The intense focus on fundraising—all that "call time"—means that politicians are required to spend a great deal of their time and attention with the nation's most affluent citizens, and less with voters who do not have large bank accounts. It also draws away from politics many who could make large contributions to our public life but simply do not want to spend so much of their energy seeking money from others.

It was not only the Supreme Court's *Citizens United* ruling that shattered any balance in or constraint on the role of money in politics. Another decision, written by Chief Justice John Roberts in *McCutcheon v. Federal Election Commission,* diluted the definition of corruption in politics, essentially limiting it to the Abscam/*American Hustle* variety—a direct bribe, which in the case of Abscam was captured on videotape.

At the same time, the partisan distortion of the Federal Election Commission (FEC), tasked with overseeing federal campaign and election procedures, has eviscerated its capacity to police violations of campaign finance laws. The Internal Revenue Service, through a combination of badly drafted regulations for nonprofits, clumsy implementation of the regulations on 501(c)(4) social welfare organizations, and intimidation by Republicans in Congress, has opened the door to in-your-face abuse of the law. And the failure of Congress to enact new disclosure rules that might enable at least some transparency about the role of big money has dealt yet another blow to our democracy.[12]

Disclosure, a necessary but not sufficient remedy, should remain a legislative priority. Pushing Congress to pass a disclosure law—with the help of Tea Party reformer John Pudner and his organization, Take Back Our Republic—might create a new coalition of campaign reformers from right to left. While the FEC, the IRS, the Federal Communications Commission, and the Securities and Exchange Commission will be controlled through this presidential term by commissioners unwilling to push for greater transparency for contributions, laying the groundwork for such actions by a future administration is important.

More broadly, we need a new regimen of campaign finance reform focused on empowering small donors and encouraging candidates to raise funds through small contributions. The goal is to balance the overwhelming force of billionaires and corporations. Several proposals would push in the right direction. Senator Tom Udall has regularly called for a constitutional amendment to overturn *Citizens United*. While this has brought attention to the increasing role of big and dark money in our politics, the daunting threshold for passing constitutional amendments means it is unlikely to pass in the near future.

The Empowering Citizens Act, introduced in 2012 by Representatives David Price and Chris Van Hollen (who is now a senator), would allow candidates to focus on small-dollar donors by creating a six-to-one matching system for small donations. Additionally, it would blunt the impact of super PACs unleashed by *Citizens United* by strengthening anti-coordination rules to ensure that super PACs are truly independent and not acting as an arm of a candidate's campaign to skirt election contribution laws.

Representative John Sarbanes's innovative Government by the People Act would provide every voter with $25 a year to give to political campaigns, in the form of a 50 percent refundable tax credit for donations up to $50. Donations up to $150 would be matched six-to-one with public money (and nine-to-one for those candidates who renounce big money and *only* accept donations up to $150). A variant on this idea proposed by Bruce Ackerman of Yale Law School would create "Patriot Dollars," $25 or $50 vouchers that every citizen could use to contribute to political candidates. Seattle became the first place to adopt this system for local elections in 2015.

Under the Sarbanes proposal, candidates relying on small contributions could receive additional help in the last 60 days of a campaign if they were confronted with a huge influx of dark money, a provision that would require a change in the Supreme Court's approach to campaign finance. This, in turn, means that lawyers focused on reform need to prepare for a future Court willing to reexamine the basics, including the landmark *Buckley v. Valeo* ruling that contributions, but not campaign spending, can be regulated to prevent corruption or the appearance of corruption. It is time to focus on a different basis for reform, one not as constraining as simply the desire to limit corruption. In our view, the best approach is to emphasize the Constitution's guarantees of a republican form of democracy. Big money and dark money tilt the playing field sharply toward would-be oligarchs and wealthy ideologues, distorting democratic politics in such fundamental ways that they threaten the very nature of our government.[13]

> It is time to focus on a different basis for campaign finance reform than the one used in *Buckley v. Valeo.*

In chapter 2, we cited the important critique of our current way of talking about politics offered by Cass Sunstein in *#republic*. We return to this issue because finding new ways of talking to each other and informing ourselves will be an important part of building a new democracy. "In a well-functioning democracy," Sunstein writes, "people do not live in echo chambers or information cocoons." Increasingly, though, that is exactly where so many of us do live. "Members of a democratic public will not do well," Sunstein continues, "if they are unable to appreciate the views of their fellow citizens, if they believe 'fake news,' or if they see one another as enemies or adversaries in some kind of war. Learned Hand, a renowned federal circuit court judge from many decades ago, put his finger on the point when he said that the 'spirit of liberty' is 'that spirit which is not too sure that it is right.'"

Among Sunstein's intriguing suggestions is the creation of "deliberative domains," places on the web designed to foster discussions and debates involving divergent views. Some efforts already exist, including Stanford professor James Fishkin's deliberative opinion polls, as well as the Deliberative Democracy Consortium. Sunstein suggests creating a website called deliberativedemocracy .com or deliberativedemocracy.org.

Perhaps Sunstein's most important recommendation is to provide more generous subsidies to public media in order to create a vibrant, civil public square focusing on important issues and including a broad array of views. That means not only fighting the effort to cut federal funds from public broadcasting on television and radio but also finding a robust way of financing this work. The best approach would be to eliminate the public interest obligations of broadcasters—a requirement given to them in return for free use of public airwaves and often observed only symbolically—and instead charge a kind of rent for their access, with the revenues put into a trust for various forms of public media.

The major social media outlets also need to examine their role in our democracy and ask if they have contributed to the spread of false information and the decline of dialogue across our various dividing lines. In one view, they are similar to telephone companies, "common carriers" simply providing a utility to all who subscribe. How others use the service is essentially not a common carrier's business. But social media companies are also, in effect, publishers. Do they thus have responsibilities similar to those of newspaper editors and visual-media producers? Should those who run social media platforms prevent their use in the spread of false information?

We are very alive to the problem of censorship, and our inclination is to err on the side of free speech. But traditional media have always operated under an obligation to the truth, even if they have sometimes failed to fulfill it, and there is a strong case that social media companies have a comparable responsibility. At a meeting in June, Facebook's shareholders rejected a proposal that would have required the company to publish a report on the impact of fake news disseminated through its website. Partly in response to the shareholder initiative, Mark Zuckerberg, Facebook's founder and CEO, said the company would have a "special focus on trying to reduce the prevalence of false news in the system," but added that it did not want to "block content from being shared." This issue will not go away, and the nation needs a searching national discussion over how social media fit into our information ecosystem.

Many of these media innovations we've suggested rest on a faith in "if you build it, they will come." The current incentives and our media habits push us away from engagement with each other and bring to mind the late historian Christopher Lasch's meditation more than two decades ago on "the lost art of argument." In real argument, Lasch wrote, "we have to enter imaginatively into our opponents' arguments, if only for the purpose of refuting them, and we may end up being persuaded by those we sought to persuade. Argument is risky and unpredictable—and therefore educational." His view of argument as a form of education shaped his view of democracy. "We will defend democracy," he wrote, "not as the most efficient but as the most educational form of government—one that extends the circle of debate as widely as possible."

This is not what democracy looks like in the Trump era, but it is the democracy we should seek.

We are aware that many of our democratizing proposals will be seen, especially by conservatives, as broadly "progressive" or "liberal." Yet we would insist that Republicans and conservatives have, throughout our history, played important roles in movements for political reform. The Civil Rights and Voting Rights Acts would never have passed without strong Republican support, and Republicans played a leading role in shaping both at a time when most southern Democrats opposed them. Repairing our system of campaign finance was once a bipartisan cause. The most important reforming law of the last two decades bears the name of Republican John McCain as well as that of Democrat Russ Feingold. On a longer view, Daniel Ziblatt, a Harvard government professor, showed in his recent book *Conservative Parties and the Birth of Democracy* that responsible and pragmatic conservatives were essential to the development of democratic systems from the moment of their birth. Conservatives who are opposed to a politics rooted in the far right are now called upon to renew their democratic commitments.[14]

Our democratic system has undergone a profound evolution since its founding over two hundred years ago: from the end of slavery and enfranchisement for African Americans to women's suffrage; from the civil service reforms of the Progressive Era to the social welfare programs of the New Deal and the Great Society. In each case, reformers from both parties enacted fundamental changes to strengthen our republican democracy and ensure fuller and more inclusive participation in social and political life. The rise of Trump underscores the need for a new era of democratic reform rivaling the most transformational periods in our nation's history. And we will create that era only through persistent, patient, creative, and determined political engagement.

ELEVEN

"Show Up, Dive In, Stay at It"

Building One Nation After Trump

On January 10, 2017, President Obama traveled to Chicago to offer a farewell address under circumstances that he never expected to face—and had certainly hoped to avoid. He spoke 10 days before the inauguration of the man who had questioned his very right to be president, and who had spent eight years charging darkly that the incumbent had presided over American decline.

Obama, as is his way, declined to be gloomy and insisted that his confidence in the American Experiment was undiminished. He mentioned Donald Trump only once, to express his commitment to a smooth transition. But Obama did not ignore the dangers Trump represented—even if he couched them by speaking of "autocrats in foreign capitals." His audience seemed to know he was talking about dangers at home, too.

The perils democracy faced, Obama declared, were "more far-reaching than a car bomb or a missile," and included "the fear of change, the fear of people who look or speak or pray differently, a contempt for the rule of law that holds leaders accountable, an intolerance of dissent and free thought." He defended "science" and "reason" and warned against scapegoating newcomers to

America's shores, noting that the "stereotypes about immigrants today were said, almost word for word, about the Irish, Italians, and Poles."

Above all, he called on Americans to take responsibility for their own democracy. "Not just when there's an election, not just when your own narrow interest is at stake, but over the full span of a lifetime. If you're tired of arguing with strangers on the Internet, try talking with one of them in real life. If something needs fixing, then lace up your shoes and do some organizing. If you're disappointed by your elected officials, grab a clip board, get some signatures, and run for office yourself.

"Show up, dive in, stay at it."[1]

This is just what Americans began to do from the day after Trump took office. The Women's March of January 21 was about women, their rights, and the demand that they not be denied. But it embodied a broader message to Trump and the country as well. Less than 24 hours after the new president took the oath of office, millions of Americans came together to say that they would not stand by in silence if the new administration threatened the advances of the previous 8 years—or the previous 50. Trump's election jarred many out of quiescence. The passion, energy, and commitment in politics had shifted decisively.

The Washington march drew upward of 700,000 people, and the sentiments in the capital were echoed by large crowds in cities and towns across the country, and around the world. The marches grew organically from the bottom up. They drew 3 million to 4.5 million people determined to show that they would not be cowed into silence or sullen indifference. The demonstrators were more jubilant than angry, buoyed by the knowledge that in the face of political troubles to come, those who chose to stand up against Trump would have allies and friends.

Just as striking was the nonsectarian nature of the protests. Different parts of the anti-Trump coalition reinforced one another's messages. The signs the marchers carried showed how varied these were: about his attitude and behavior toward women especially, given the theme of the day, but also about Russia's role in the election and Trump's bromance with Vladimir Putin. There were signs in support of voting rights and against voter suppression, and in favor of the Affordable Care Act ("I Obamacare About You," read one), the Black Lives Matter movement, and gay rights. There were loud calls for the defense of free speech. If Trump didn't talk about freedom in his inaugural address, the protesters picked up the slack the next day.[2]

The January 21 marches proved to be more than a spasm of good feeling. They were followed by continued, focused activity that combined spontaneity with coordination. The enormous crowds that gathered at airports to oppose Trump's travel ban were a dramatic example of citizens setting boundaries around behavior they saw as both illegal and un-American.

The pressure was brought not only on Trump but also on his corporate supporters, and it was felt almost instantaneously by Uber. At Kennedy Airport, the New York City Taxi Workers Alliance called on its drivers to cease all pickups in a show of solidarity for those affected by the travel ban. But Uber, taking advantage of the chaos, announced it would lower its prices to increase its business. In response, activists used social media to urge customers to #DeleteUber. Only days later, some 200,000 people had deleted their accounts. This prompted Uber's CEO, Travis Kalanick, to apologize publicly, to leave Trump's business council, and to pledge $3 million to set up a legal defense fund for people affected by what he called the "wrong and unjust" ban. The social media campaign, along with other problems that eventually forced Kalanick to resign, also had a long-term effect. Citing the impact of the #DeleteUber effort, the *Financial Times* reported that Uber's market share had fallen from 84 percent at the beginning of the year to 77 percent in June, to the benefit of its chief competitor, Lyft.

The success of the Women's March encouraged Trump's opponents to take to the streets to highlight other challenges. On April 15, traditionally Tax Day, protesters in hundreds of coordinated events called on Trump to release his tax returns. The following week, thousands participated in the March for Science, a series of formally nonpartisan rallies around the United States supporting the use of scientific evidence in crafting public policy. A week after that, thousands of demonstrators descended on Washington for the People's Climate March, timed to coincide with Trump's hundredth day in office, to demand that the president reverse course in his efforts to roll back all of Obama's environmental rules and regulations.[3]

Perhaps even more remarkable was the sustained pressure in congressional districts around the country. The anti-Trump forces learned from the Tea Party mobilizations in the early Obama years, and as was true then, the television coverage amplified the power of the protests. Even Republican members of Congress representing deeply red districts discovered that a large number of their constituents were unhappy over any show of complicity with Trump. Charles M. Blow, a persistent and consistent anti-Trump voice on *The New York Times* op-ed page, wrote of the "Resilience of the Resistance" in noting the power of the protests.

The issues Trump's opponents raised were varied, but there was enormous attention to preserving the Affordable Care Act. In a tribute to the folk singer Joni Mitchell's long-ago insight that "you don't know what you've got 'till it's gone," many Americans who benefited from the act rallied to resist the very personal threat repeal posed to them. Obamacare, which had never been adequately defended by Democrats while Obama was in office, finally found its champions at the grassroots.

The demonstrations clearly had an effect. As we have seen, Trump and House Speaker Paul Ryan were embarrassed when their bill to repeal the Affordable Care Act initially was kept off the House floor because of a shortage of votes. Much of the attention at the time went to the right-wing Freedom Caucus's refusal to embrace the repeal bill because many of its members felt it did not go far enough. A *New York Times* vote count found, however, that many opponents of the bill were pragmatic conservatives who represented Clinton districts. Reflecting the views of the protesters, they opposed the bill from the left, seeing it as insufficiently generous to those who needed help to buy insurance.

When the House passed its modestly amended version of the repeal plan in May, constituents packed town halls to oppose it. Representative Tom MacArthur of New Jersey, one of the chief architects of the revised bill, faced five hours of hostile questioning and chants of "shame" at his public event with voters. And after Senate Republicans unveiled the first version of their health care bill in late June, supporters of the ACA renewed their activism and made clear that the political costs of any repeal would be high.[4]

Anti-Trump constituents also focused on the failure of Republicans in Congress to press Trump on his conflicts of interest and his refusal to release his tax returns. And they protested the reluctance of the GOP, particularly in the House, to investigate possible ties between Trump's campaign and Russian intervention in the election. Representative Jason Chaffetz, chair of the House Oversight Committee, confronted angry rebukes from his constituents over his relaxed approach to the conflict and disclosure issues. He eventually found himself with a well-financed opponent for 2018 who took advantage of the activist mood and the capacity of new technologies to channel it. Kathryn Allen, a physician angered by Chaffetz's remarkably obtuse comment that low-income Americans had to decide whether they wanted a new cell phone or health insurance, announced that she would oppose him if she could raise enough seed money. In one day, she raised $40,000 on a Crowdpac fundraising page, breaking the platform's records. She decided to run. It's not clear what role Allen's challenge played in Chaffetz's late-April announcement that he would not seek reelection, but the emergence of opposition to Trump in surprising places gave many Republicans pause about a full embrace of Trump's agenda.

"What is striking is how many people Trump has mobilized who previously didn't pay very much attention to what happens in Washington," the *New Yorker*'s John Cassidy wrote in April 2017. "He has politicized many formerly apolitical people; ultimately, this may be among his biggest achievements as President."[5]

Trump's opponents can also take heart from how professional and grassroots strategists moved quickly to give the anti-Trump movement a sense of strategic coherence. Citizens were hungry for ways to identify their own unique skills and strengths ("What do I bring to this fight?"), and then to figure out how to work strategically with others to direct their collective power where it could have the most impact ("What can we do together?"). These efforts helped build the protests and reinforced a commitment to long-term engagement.

One of the most successful of these was the movement spearheaded by four former congressional staffers, Ezra Levin, Jeremy Haile, Leah Greenberg, and Angel Padilla, who studied the Tea Party for lessons in how to organize a parallel response to Trump.

They published a document called "Indivisible: A Practical Guide for Resisting the Trump Agenda" online after the election, and regularly updated and supplemented it. "Indivisible" quickly became the equivalent of an online bestseller. Drawing on many years of combined experience on Capitol Hill, the authors detailed easy-to-follow instructions to effect political change by turning up at town halls, contacting lawmakers by telephone and in writing, attending public events in large numbers, and creating local associations of like-minded activists. "Indivisible" was widely embraced because it retaught the basics of democratic politics: individual citizens can have far more impact than they realize, especially when they act in concert with others.

A similarly successful initiative was Daily Action, which sends texts each morning with marching orders for those who sign up to take action to combat Trump's policies. Created by Laura Moser, a writer and mother of two young children, the messages offered by Daily Action are simple and direct. In late January, for example, her subscribers—they quickly numbered in the hundreds of thousands—got this on their phones at 10:15 a.m.: "Today's daily action is to urge your Senator to place a 'hold' on Sessions' AG nomination until Trump shows some respect for the rule of law." Its alerts were part of the upsurge that forced House Republicans to back off their plan to gut the Office of Congressional Ethics. The group was also part of the phone campaign against Trump's initial nominee for labor secretary, Andrew Puzder, who later withdrew. "If we can sustain this energy and this anger," Moser told *The Washington Post*, "maybe we can reclaim our country." Other groups followed similar models, linking advanced technology with the most old-fashioned forms of engagement.

Nonprofit organizations, so vital, as we have seen, in opposing Trump's specific actions, have also mobilized broadly to engage more Americans in politics. Citizen University, a Seattle group founded by Eric Liu, launched an innovative program called "Civic Saturday." Liu described it as "a civic analogue to church: a gathering of friends and strangers in a common place to nurture a spirit of shared purpose." The faith being celebrated, Liu noted, was the creed of America's civic religion. He was regularly forced to find larger venues for the events, and other communities have followed his lead in creating civic liturgies of their own.

Liu's effort is consciously nonpartisan, even if, in a Democratic stronghold, many of those he is bringing into politics are Democrats. Greater civic engagement across the political and ideological spectrum is something to be welcomed. But the larger issue of partisanship must be confronted squarely at this moment.[6]

While there was a substantial anti-Trump movement among conservative writers and intellectuals, the Republican Party's leadership stayed closely allied with Trump during his first months in office. Most Republicans in Congress, as we have noted, still hoped Trump might help them achieve many long-standing policy goals and strengthen their hold on lifelong judicial appointments. GOP politicians are unlikely to break with Trump as long as their principal fears involve angering conservative media, alienating their base voters, and being ousted in primaries. Only the risk of losing their seats in general elections—or control of one or both houses of Congress, or power in state governments—will push them toward second thoughts in their approach to Trump.

This in turn means that, within our two-party system, the Democratic Party must be the agent to contain and ultimately defeat Trump and Trumpism. Democratic victories will demonstrate that the time has arrived for Republicans to abandon Trump. Democrats must thus become a "fusion" party, to use a term once popular among urban reformers, most famously New York City's longtime mayor Fiorello La Guardia. The idea of fusion involved ignoring old party fights and differences to build broad coalitions, typically aimed at bringing down corrupt political machines. Fusionism was a way of saying that narrow partisanship needed to give way to a larger and more urgent cause. Democrats must not only bring together their own factions (a difficult enough task) and win back white working-class voters who once stood with them. They must also gain the support of Independents and Republicans (in the electorate if not among the elected politicians) willing to suspend old loyalties to deal with the emergency Trump represents.

The heightened political engagement among Democrats that Trump brought about has already had an impact in a series of special elections in longtime Republican congressional districts—in Kansas, Montana, Georgia, and South Carolina—where Democratic nominees ran far ahead of the normal party vote. Their showings augured well for the 2018 elections. So did Democratic victories in a variety of local and state legislative contests in Pennsylvania, Delaware, Virginia, Illinois, and elsewhere. Democratic successes will be correctly interpreted as a blow to Trumpism, which is why anti-Trump Republicans will welcome them. So will at least some Republican officeholders who would never publicly say so. They understand that defeating the Trumpian version of Republicanism is essential to rebuilding the more responsible, forward-looking center-right party that the country needs.[7]

The imperative of turning back Trump and Trumpism will require unusual forms of discipline and commitment. It will mean not allowing the ideological and tactical battles within the

> To defeat Trumpism, Democrats must gain the support of Independents and Republicans willing to suspend old loyalties.

Democratic Party between factions loosely defined as Clinton and Sanders Democrats to tear it asunder and allow pro-Trump Republicans to prevail in general elections. While there are real and important differences of opinion among Democrats (and within the larger anti-Trump coalition) on issues such as trade and health care, these differences are far smaller than those between the entire movement and Trump.

For example, there may be disagreements about moving toward single-payer health care, but not on the need to preserve and expand the gains of Obamacare. There are certainly differences on trade, but not on the imperative of lifting up those left out of our prosperity, whether because of globalization or technological change. Outside Democratic ranks, Trump's critics may have their differences with both Clinton and Sanders Democrats, but they share with both groups a belief that Trump's divisiveness, his indifference to political norms, and his lack of respect for basic American institutions are a threat to the kind of politics all three groups value.

This certainly does not mean suspending intellectual and policy debate. On the contrary, we have offered our ideas for a new economy, a new patriotism, a new civil society, and a new democracy in order to promote debate in four areas where we see creative action as central to healing the rifts in our country that Trump exploited and is now deepening. But serious debate need not descend into bitter sectarianism. The movement against Trump needs to model a politics in which honest differences do not mean enmity, and disagreements over one or two issues do not lead to the disruption of coalition building on so many others. As the political commentator Mark Shields has often observed, political movements, like religious traditions, have to decide whether their emphasis will be on courting converts or hunting heretics. This is not a moment for heretic hunting.

Independent mass movements have often found that alliances with political parties are the most effective way—in many cases, the only way—to achieve their ends. As Daniel Schlozman showed in his innovative book *When Movements Anchor Parties,* such alliances were important to both the labor movement (in the case of the Democrats) and the Christian Conservative movement (in its alliance with the Republicans). As Schlozman writes, "only political parties form the government," and leaders of major causes always face tough political choices over how "to take movement fervor and translate it into durable change."[8]

The abolitionists and the progressives, the civil rights, environmental, and women's movements—all found ways of relating to partisan and political power. Those seeking to get our nation past Trumpism must understand the inevitability of party politics even as they seek to broaden their reach across party lines.

There is reason to hope that the anti-Trump writers and intellectuals within the conservative movement are a harbinger of a larger realignment in our politics and of a more moderate conservatism, or even moderation itself. We have cited many of these conservatives in our account, and as the Trump presidency has moved from one crisis and outrage to another, they have become increasingly alienated from a timid GOP leadership. They have also criticized the willingness of their onetime comrades in the conservative movement to apologize for or brush off actions taken by Trump that would have drawn furious condemnation had they come from a Democratic administration. Will these restive conservatives abandon their traditional loyalties altogether?

It would not be the first time that a group of thinkers opened the way for political realignment. History, it's said, sometimes rhymes. The anti-Trump distemper on the right has some of the rhythms and sounds of an earlier intellectual rebellion in the mid-1960s involving an uneasy group of liberals. They remained staunch supporters of Franklin Roosevelt's New Deal but worried about what they saw as liberal excesses and the overreach of some Great Society policies.

Over time, this collection of magazine- and university-based rebels—among them Irving Kristol, Nathan Glazer, Daniel Patrick Moynihan, Daniel Bell, and Norman Podhoretz—came to be known as "neoconservatives." They were not party bosses, but they certainly knew how to write essays.

The history of this movement, well told in books by Peter Steinfels, Justin Vaïsse, and Gary Dorrien, is winding and complicated. Some of the neocons never abandoned liberalism or the Democrats. This category includes Bell and Moynihan, who eventually served with distinction as a Democratic senator from New York. Glazer's views have always been hard to pigeonhole. Others (notably Kristol and Podhoretz) moved steadily toward old-fashioned conservatism. By the beginning of this century, neoconservatism came to be associated more with a muscular foreign policy than with its initial focus on domestic issues.

What cannot be doubted is that the neocons helped prepare the ground for Ronald Reagan's political revolution. Will the anti-Trumpers—a fair number of them philosophical descendants of neoconservatism, and some of them the sons and daughters of the original neoconservatives—have a comparable impact?

Much depends on whether their critique of Trump carries into a broader critique of contemporary conservatism and the Republican Party. This is already starting to happen, as we have seen in the case of writers and commentators such as Michael Gerson, Jennifer Rubin, Peter Wehner, David Frum, Ana Navarro, Tom Nichols, Charlie Sykes, and Max Boot.

Evan McMullin, who ran as an independent conservative against Trump in 2016, explicitly raised the prospect of realignment (and nodded toward the fusion idea) in a tweet: "In our Trumpian era, is there any longer a traditional right and left? Or are there only those who fight for liberty and those against it."

Another factor could push the anti-Trump conservatives out of their ideological home: attacks on them from onetime comrades. Writing on *National Review*'s website, author and radio host Dennis Prager described the anti-Trump right as "a very refined group of people" who live in a "cultural milieu" in which "to support Trump is to render oneself contemptible at all elite dinner parties." Those were fighting words.[9]

Like the intellectuals of a half-century ago who developed qualms about liberalism but insisted they were still in the liberal camp, conservatives standing against Trump today still see themselves as being true to their old loyalties. Still, between the mid-1960s and 1980, a large cadre of those liberal dissenters accepted that they were, in fact, conservatives. Something similar may be happening in the other direction as members of the anti-Trump right, battling against immoderation, irrationality, and irresponsibility, become ever more distant from their old allies and come to recognize the damage inflicted on contemporary conservatism by long-standing habits and impulses. Let's call them "neomoderates." They, too, could emerge as a major force in our politics and make a difference in our history by moving the country away from the far right. The progressive wing of the anti-Trump movement should not only welcome their witness but also engage them in seeking to create a politics that is less harsh, more intellectually honest, and more focused on solving the problems the Trump era has brought into such relief.

The anti-Trump movement may seem unusual because it is primarily directed against one man and his impulses. In fact, it is about much more than opposition and resistance. It is, and should be, driven by affirmation.

Consider the aspects of Trump's persona and approach that incite such disquiet and rage: the ease with which he demonizes whole groups of Americans; his indifference to fact; his willingness to lie with impunity; his lack of even elementary knowledge or intellectual curiosity about policy; his proclivity toward shifting positions again and again; his quest to tote up "wins" without any concern about the content of the proposals he is pushing; his lack of any historical sense; his belief that everything is about a "deal"; and his refusal to acknowledge any need to separate his personal financial interests from his public duties.

Those riled by each of these traits and habits are, in their revulsion, affirming a series of moral and practical commitments and a vision of how a democratic republic is supposed to work. Lies and untruths are the enemy of honest democratic deliberation. Policymaking needs to be taken seriously because government matters. Being a politician of any sort—and especially being president—is a deadly serious responsibility and requires attention to detail and history, as well as a willingness to study and learn. While deals are certainly part of politics, the notion that the deal is the only thing that counts denigrates the idea that what the deal sets into motion can have a powerful impact on our citizens and our country's future. There is a point to political arguments, and they are supposed to lead somewhere better. And it is always a problem when public office is turned into an opportunity for private enrichment.

To insist on these things is to demand that we restore our sense of the dignity and, yes, majesty of self-government. We need a new appreciation of what an extraordinary achievement it is. Trump's rise was made possible by a long-term war on public life that cast public endeavor, the public sector, and public concerns as inferior to private striving and private interests.

This certainly resulted from elite failures and even elite self-enrichment. It also arose from a feeling within a large part of the public that its interests were not being properly represented. The exit polls showed that 61 percent of voters believed Trump to be unqualified for the presidency—and about a sixth of these voters supported him anyway. This shows how deep the revulsion toward Washington, politics, and government runs. It also reflects the impact of approaches to politics that have demeaned public service and of a culture that no longer celebrates it. Politicians (and, it must be said, especially Republican politicians) have delegitimized government for political gain. And campaigns run by both parties have become a long-running advertisement against government. No one selling a commercial product treats competitors with a contempt even remotely like the insolence politicians demonstrate toward each other in their television advertisements and social media messages.

We are under no illusions that campaigns were once graceful affairs. "Politics ain't beanbag" is a very old warning, and it has always been apt. Competition can bring out hostility. Still, while athletes may occasionally trash-talk each other, they treat their rivals far more respectfully than candidates treat their adversaries. Technologies—from television ads to the creation of fake news—have been used far more to denigrate, demean, and divide than to inform, ennoble, and unite.

And setting up a freely elected government as the enemy casts democracy as being little different from despotism. "Let us never forget that government is ourselves and not an alien power over us," Franklin Roosevelt declared. "The ultimate rulers of our democracy are not a President and senators and congressmen and government officials, but the voters of this country."

But we *have* forgotten, and this helped pave the way for a politician who sees little difference between a despot and a democratically elected president—who was willing to declare Vladimir Putin a better leader than Barack Obama. The fight against Trump is thus ultimately a fight to reclaim the dignity of public life and the honor of democratic politics.[10]

The battle against Trump is also an affirmation of a very different vision of what the United States is and can be. The most disturbing aspect of Trumpism—beyond whatever we come to discover about his and his campaign's relationship with Putin and Russia—is its dark pessimism about liberal democracy, an open society, and the achievements of the American Experiment. If the fruits of the American economy are not shared as fairly as they should be, the fact remains that the recovery of our economy after the Great Recession was a remarkable and insufficiently heralded achievement. As soon as he took office, Trump himself began taking credit for a recovery he had nothing to do with—and which, until January 20, 2017, he insisted had never occurred. We remain the strongest country on earth, endowed with an ambitious and inventive people, exceptional natural resources including great supplies of energy, a powerful military, and, perhaps most importantly, a culture of freedom

> The fight against Trump is ultimately a fight to reclaim the dignity of public life and the honor of democratic politics.

and fairness that still makes us a magnet for the world's people and defines our aspirations. Being hopeful about our nation's capacities is not only truer to who we are, it is also the disposition that will serve us best in facing up to the problems confronted by Americans who are demanding a fair shot, a degree of security, and a better life for their children and grandchildren.

In our debates over how to reform and improve our immigration system, we should retain our pride in the desire of immigrants to flock to our shores. As we have stressed, our approaches to economics must uplift the native-born and the immigrant alike. The idea that immigrants come to the United States to affirm American values rather than to undermine them has always regained the upper hand in our history—despite outbreaks of nativism—because it reflects the reality of our experiences.

Similarly, Trumpism ignores the ways in which liberal democracy has strengthened the power of the United States by establishing us, at our best moments, as an example of what freedom and self-rule can achieve.

Of course, there have been times of national exhaustion after inconclusive or mistaken wars. There is a widespread impatience with the role of the United States as "the world's policeman," and a realistic acknowledgment that our country cannot and will not intervene in all of the world's trouble spots. But the alternative to promiscuous intervention is not wholesale withdrawal from our responsibilities. And, as we have argued, the paradox is that an "America First" foreign policy does not, in fact, put the interests of the United States first (as the country came to understand during and after World War II). American power and influence grew as a result of the extraordinary period of international institution building in the postwar period. And the United States' leadership in providing foreign and development aid through the Marshall

Plan helped create a more prosperous and stable world—to our own benefit.

We are stronger with allies among like-minded democratic nations than we are on our own. We are also stronger when we do not pretend that autocratic regimes and nationalist movements will advance our interests in the long run. That Trump chose to offer his indirect endorsement of Marine Le Pen's National Front during the French presidential campaign would at any other time have been a national scandal. The United States will necessarily deal with many sorts of powers in the world to keep the peace, and we have not always been true to our democratic commitments. But our deep sympathies for democratic systems, the rule of law, and minority rights should never be in doubt. Under Trump, they are.

Rejecting Trumpism means rejecting a wholesale rollback of our nation's extraordinary progress toward equal rights—for African Americans, for women, for Latinos, for the LGBTQ community, for religious minorities, and for so many of our other fellow citizens. It means acknowledging that this progress is still incomplete and repudiating the idea that any airing of complaints about ongoing injustices is "political correctness." Throughout this book, we have insisted that an embrace of equal rights for racial minorities and women should not in any way foreclose the rights of working Americans who are white and male to the redress of their own legitimate grievances. Casting the white working class and racial or ethnic minority groups as enemies is the unspoken but very clear strategy of Trumpian politics. Down this path lies a repudiation of the American promise of a just and prosperous society that will allow all of our citizens, as Dr. King insisted, "to sit down together at the table of brotherhood."[11]

A broad and powerful movement has arisen to defeat Trump and Trumpism. Its success will be a triumph worthy of celebration.

But this is not just an end in itself; it is also an essential first step toward a new politics. It will be a politics that takes seriously the need to solve the problems that Trump has exposed. It will reclaim our country's faith in the future and its natural inclination toward hope. And it will nurture our dedication to the raucous but ultimately unifying project of democratic self-government. For it is our shared commitment to republican institutions and democratic values that makes us one nation.

ACKNOWLEDGMENTS

We begin by thanking two people who truly did make this book possible.

It is customary to thank your publisher toward the end of brief essays of this sort, but we think it appropriate to break with this unwritten rule by thanking Tim Bartlett, our editor at St. Martin's Press, right at the start. It was Tim who encouraged us to write this book, and he was there with us from beginning to end with enormously helpful counsel on large ideas and small details, on the state of American politics and the nature of the arguments that need to be made at this moment in our history. He provoked, encouraged, advised, and inspired us, and we are deeply grateful. Mann and Ornstein gratefully acknowledge this is the third book they have written at Tim's initiative and with his unbending support.

Adam Waters is, in principle, the research assistant who kept track of this manuscript from beginning to end. He made certain all three of us got things done, offered running critiques, cuts, and trims, caught last-minute errors, and got everything into the proper form. In practice, he was much more. We so often adopted Adam's words, sentences, and paragraphs as our own that we are tempted not to offer the usual disclaimer that he has no responsibility for what is here. We'll just say he's accountable only for the parts that readers like and agree with. Adam is brilliant, and he was indispensable, an overused word that in this case does not fully do him justice.

We thank all of the institutions that have offered us support over many years: in Dionne's case, *The Washington Post*, the Brookings Institution, and Georgetown University, particularly the McCourt School of Public Policy; in Ornstein's case, the American Enterprise Institute; and in Mann's case, Brookings and the Institute of Governmental Studies at the University of California at Berkeley.

All of us wish to thank outlets where we incubated some of the ideas reflected here in earlier writing. Dionne thanks the great editors on the *Post* editorial staff and at the Washington Post Writers Group. Parts of chapter 8 are drawn from the Navin Narayan Memorial Lecture at Harvard University and a lecture at the Walter H. Capps Center at University of California at Santa Barbara. The Harvard lecture was the basis of an article for the *Post*'s Outlook section. He's grateful for those opportunities. Ornstein is deeply appreciative of *The Atlantic*, especially his editor Yoni Applebaum. Mann would like to thank the editors of the *FixGov* blog at Brookings.

At Berkeley, Jake Grumbach was a generous and resourceful colleague who offered us many valuable ideas. At AEI, thanks to Eleanor O'Neill and Heather Sims. Adam worked at Brookings, with support from Georgetown, and thanks also to Donald Stephens, Carter Goodwin, and Stephen Imburgia.

We appreciated the very useful comments on our manuscript from Al Franken and Daniel Ornstein.

Thank you to our agent Gail Ross for working on very short notice with her usual efficiency and commitment in organizing our agreement with St. Martin's. At St. Martin's, we are grateful not only to Tim but also to Laura Clark, associate publisher, who championed this book from the start, and to George Witte, editor-in-chief, and Sally Richardson, publisher. Alan Bradshaw, managing editor for *One Nation After Trump*, performed a variety of miracles to move the manuscript quickly. Thanks also to Martin Quinn, senior marketing manager, Tracey Guest, vice president and director of publicity, and the incomparable publicist Gabrielle Gantz for all her work on our behalf. Alice Pfeifer kept all of the pieces moving seamlessly and India Cooper did an excellent job as copy editor.

We express our deepest appreciation to our families, three loving, opinionated, supportive, and thoughtful tribes: Mary Boyle and James, Julia and Margot Dionne; Judy Harris and Danny Ornstein; and Sheilah, Steph, Ted, Suzanne Miazga, and Leo and Luca Mann.

Last, we thank each other. If this seems odd, consider that a three-way partnership could have been difficult. This one wasn't. We started as dear friends and ended as even dearer friends. We're deeply grateful for that.

NOTES

INTRODUCTION

1. Philip Rucker, "Trump reacts to London terror by stoking fear and renewing feud with mayor," *The Washington Post,* June 4, 2017, https://www.washingtonpost.com/politics/trump-reacts-to-london-terror-by-stoking-fear-and-renewing-feud-with-mayor/2017/06/04/2811bcce-4931-11e7-a186-60c031eab644_story.html?utm_term=.8a061fa98171; Glenn Thrush and Maggie Haberman, "Trump mocks Mika Brzezinski; says she was 'bleeding badly from a face-lift'," *The New York Times,* June 29, 2017, https://www.nytimes.com/2017/06/29/business/media/trump-mika-brzezinski-facelift.html; Michael M. Grynbaum, "Trump tweets a video of him wrestling 'CNN' to the ground," *The New York Times,* July 2, 2017, https://www.nytimes.com/2017/07/02/business/media/trump-wrestling-video-cnn-twitter.html?mcubz=1.
2. Edmund Burke, *Reflections on the Revolution in France* (London: Everyman's Library, 1971), p. 153.
3. John F. Kennedy's inaugural address, January 20, 1961; Donald Trump's Republican nomination acceptance speech, July 21, 2016.
4. William Julius Wilson, *When Work Disappears: The World of the New Urban Poor* (New York: Alfred A. Knopf, 1996).
5. Martin Luther King, Jr., "I have a dream" speech, August 28, 1963, retrieved from the Martin Luther King, Jr., Research and Education Institute at Stanford University, https://kinginstitute.stanford.edu/king-papers/documents/i-have-dream-address-delivered-march-washington-jobs-and-freedom; Donald J. Trump, "Dishonest media is trying their absolute best to depict a star in a tweet as the Star of David rather than a Sheriff's Star, or a plain star!" July 4, 2016 [Tweet]; for Mexican Americans as "rapists," see Trump's campaign announcement speech, June 16, 2015.
6. Robert D. Putnam, *Bowling Alone: The Collapse and Revival of American Community* (New York: Simon & Schuster, 2000); Charles Murray, *Coming Apart: The State of White America, 1960–2010* (New York: Crown Forum, 2012); J. D. Vance, *Hillbilly Elegy: A Memoir of a Family and Culture in Crisis* (New York: HarperCollins, 2016); Anne Case and Angus Deaton, "Mortality and morbidity in the 21st century," Brookings Institution, May 1, 2017, https://www.brookings.edu/wp-content/uploads/2017/03/casedeaton_sp17_finaldraft.pdf.

CHAPTER ONE

1. Trump on *Good Morning America,* March 17, 2011, video available at http://abcnews.go.com/GMA/video/gma-exclusive-trump-birther-13155432; Trump on *The View,* March 23, 2011, video available at http://www.realclearpolitics.com/video/2011/03/23/donald_trump_to_obama_show_the_birth_certificate.html; Brat quoted in John B. Judis, "Dave Brat and the triumph of

rightwing populism," *The New Republic,* June 11, 2014, https://newrepublic.com /article/118097/dave-brat-and-triumph-rightwing-populism.

2. Gallup, Presidential Job Approval Center, June 26, 2017, http://www.gallup .com/interactives/185273/presidential-job-approval-center.aspx?g_source =WWWV7HP&g_medium=topic&g_campaign=tiles; Nate Silver, "The Comey letter probably cost Clinton the election," *FiveThirtyEight,* May 3, 2017, https://fivethirtyeight.com/features/the-comey-letter-probably-cost-clinton -the-election/; Karoun Demirjian and Devlin Barrett, "How a dubious Russian document influenced the FBI's mishandling of the Clinton probe," *The Washington Post,* May 24, 2017, https://www.washingtonpost.com/world/national -security/how-a-dubious-russian-document-influenced-the-fbis-handling-of -the-clinton-probe/2017/05/24/f375c07c-3a95-11e7-9e48-c4f199710b69 _story.html?utm_term=.097107fabca6.

3. David Wasserman, "2016 National Popular Vote Tracker," *Cook Political Report,* http://cookpolitical.com/file/2016_vote.pdf; David Wasserman, "2012 National Popular Vote Tracker," *Cook Political Report,* https://docs.google.com /spreadsheets/d/1PV-jK0kov7-w-xuj6DhyL7gP9VGKIv0-c_hY0UN1Un0/edit; for 2016 exit poll data, see CNN exit polls, updated November 23, 2016, http:// edition.cnn.com/election/results/exit-polls.

4. Nate Silver, "Donald Trump's base is shrinking," *FiveThirtyEight,* May 24, 2017, https://fivethirtyeight.com/features/donald-trumps-base-is-shrinking/; Michael A. Cohen, "French election is a backlash to the backlash," *The Boston Globe,* April 23, 2017, https://www.bostonglobe.com/opinion/2017/04/23/fre nch-election-backlash-backlash/b6x1kooHnKlJy9stI18khJ/story.html.

5. For Erie County 2012 and 2016 results, see Pennsylvania Board of Elections, http://www.electionreturns.pa.gov/Home/SummaryResults; for Obama's share of the white voters without college degrees in Wisconsin in 2012, see Peyton M. Craighill and Scott Clement, "Can unions save the white working-class vote for Democrats?" *The Washington Post,* November 20, 2012, https:// www.washingtonpost.com/news/the-fix/wp/2012/11/20/can-unions-save -the-white-working-class-vote-for-democrats/?utm_term=.4b791a2a79a8; for Clinton, and Trump's share of white voters without college degrees in Wisconsin and nationally, see CNN exit polls; for Obama's, and Romney's shares of the white working-class vote nationally, see Ruy Teixeira and John Halpin, *The Obama Coalition in the 2012 Election and Beyond,* Center for American Progress, December 2012, https://www.americanprogress.org/wp-content/uploads /2012/12/ObamaCoalition-5.pdf; for Trump support in working-class counties, see Perry County results in 2012 and 2016, Kentucky State Board of Elections, http://elect.ky.gov/results/2010-2019/Pages/2012primaryandgeneralelection results.aspx; Nicholas Carnes and Noam Lupu, "It's time to bust the myth: Most Trump voters were not working class," *The Washington Post,* June 5, 2017, https://www.washingtonpost.com/news/monkey-cage/wp/2017/06/05 /its-time-to-bust-the-myth-most-trump-voters-were-not-working-class/?utm _term=.f71b0c302bee.

6. Sophie Tatum, "Trump: Clinton 'doesn't have the stamina' to be president," *CNN,* September 27, 2016, http://www.cnn.com/2016/09/27/politics/donald -trump-hillary-clinton-stamina/; Justin Gest, *The New Minority: White Working Class Politics in an Age of Immigration and Inequality* (New York: Oxford University Press, 2016), p. 200; Guy Molyneux, "Mapping the white working class," *The American Prospect,* December 20, 2016, http://prospect.org/article /mapping-white-working-class; Martin Wolf, "Conservatism buries Ronald Reagan and Margaret Thatcher," *Financial Times,* May 23, 2017, https://www .ft.com/content/970bbdcc-3f1e-11e7-82b6-896b95f30f58.

7. D'Angelo Gore, "A short history lesson on presidents winning without the popular vote," *USA Today,* November 8, 2016, https://www.usatoday

.com/story/news/politics/onpolitics/2016/11/07/presidents-winning-without
-popular-vote/93441516/; The American Presidency Project, "Election of
1888," http://www.presidency.ucsb.edu/showelection.php?year=1888; Gregory Krieg, "It's official: Clinton swamps Trump in popular vote," December 22,
2016, http://www.cnn.com/2016/12/21/politics/donald-trump-hillary-clinton
-popular-vote-final-count/.

8. Jordan Fischer and Fazley Siddiq, "Trends in metropolitan and non-metropolitan
populations in Canada and the United States over fifty years," Woodrow
Wilson International Center for Scholars, May 2013, https://www.wilson
center.org/sites/default/files/fazley_final_paper.pdf; for California and Wyoming population estimates, see U.S. Census Bureau, Annual Estimates of the Res-
ident Population for the United States, Regions, States, and Puerto Rico, 2016,
https://www.census.gov/data/tables/2016/demo/popest/state-total.html; 1790
Census, https://www2.census.gov/prod2/decennial/documents/1790a.pdf;
Lisa L. Miller, "Gun control reforms failed the Senate. But it wasn't a fair vote," The
Guardian, June 21, 2016, https://www.theguardian.com/commentisfree/2016
/jun/21/gun-control-reforms-senate-vote-not-fair-republican-congress.

9. Philip Bump, "The Senate may be developing an electoral college issue," The
Washington Post, April 10, 2017, https://www.washingtonpost.com/news/poli
tics/wp/2017/04/10/the-senate-may-be-developing-an-electoral-college-issue
/?utm_term=.5da842545ce2; Adam Wisnieski, "Next 100 days: In the era of
Trump, NYS is out of step and in the crosshairs," City Limits, June 30, 2017,
http://citylimits.org/2017/06/30/next-100-days-in-the-era-of-trump-nys-is
-out-of-step-and-in-the-crosshairs/; David Wasserman quoted in Chris Cillizza,
"It could be a very long time before Democrats are in the House majority again,"
The Washington Post, January 29, 2015, https://www.washingtonpost.com
/news/the-fix/wp/2015/01/29/it-could-be-a-while-before-democrats-are-in-the
-house-majority-again/?utm_term=.a4564f5a92bd; Laura Royden and Michael Li, Extreme Maps, Brennan Center for Justice, May 9, 2017, https://www
.brennancenter.org/publication/extreme-maps.

10. For "one person, one vote," see Supreme Court of the United States, Reynolds
v. Sims (1964); Michael D. Shear and Peter Baker, "After his claim of voter
fraud, Trump vows 'major investigation,'" The New York Times, January 25,
2017, https://www.nytimes.com/2017/01/25/us/politics/trump-voting-fraud
-false-claim-investigation.html.

11. Michael Gerson, "The conservative mind has become diseased," The Washington Post, May 25, 2017, https://www.washingtonpost.com/opinions/the-conser
vative-mind-has-become-diseased/2017/05/25/523f0964-4159-11e7-9869-ba
c8b446820a_story.html?utm_term=.38aa7aa0c3bd; Jennifer Rubin, "A week
that reveals how rotten today's Republican Party is," The Washington Post,
May 26, 2017, https://www.washingtonpost.com/blogs/right-turn/wp/2017
/05/26/a-week-that-reveals-how-rotten-todays-republican-party-is/?utm
_term=.56a07c2366b0.

12. NBC News, Meet the Press transcript for February 13, 2011, http://www.nbc
news.com/id/41536793/ns/meet_the_press-transcripts/t/meet-press-transcript
-feb/#.WQnqnLIrJpg.

CHAPTER TWO

1. Donald J. Trump, "The FAKE NEWS media (failing @nytimes, @NBCNews,
@ABC, @CBS, @CNN) is not my enemy, it is the enemy of the American
people!" February 17, 2017 [Tweet]; Michael M. Grybaum, "Trump strategist
Stephen Bannon says media should 'keep its mouth shut,'" The New York Times,
January 26, 2017, https://www.nytimes.com/2017/01/26/business/media/ste
phen-bannon-trump-news-media.html.

2. For Trump on inauguration crowd size, see Jenna Johnson, "In his first major TV interview as president, Trump is obsessed with his popularity," *The Washington Post*, January 26, 2017, https://www.washingtonpost.com/news /post-politics/wp/2017/01/26/in-his-first-major-tv-interview-as-president -trump-is-endlessly-obsessed-about-his-popularity/?utm_term=.dad8c010 cfaa; Glenn Kessler, "Spicer earns four Pinocchios for false claim on inauguration crowd size," *The Washington Post*, January 22, 2017, https://www .washingtonpost.com/news/fact-checker/wp/2017/01/22/spicer-earns-four -pinocchios-for-a-series-of-false-claims-on-inauguration-crowd-size/?utm _term=.20806eb4e606; Kimiko de Freytas-Tamura, "George Orwell's '1984' is suddenly a best-seller," *The New York Times*, January 25, 2017, https://www.ny times.com/2017/01/25/books/1984-george-orwell-donald-trump.html; *NBC News' Meet the Press*, "Conway: Press secretary gave 'alternative facts,'" January 22, 2017, http://www.nbcnews.com/meet-the-press/video/conway-press-secre- tary-gave-alternative-facts-860142147643 [Video].

3. Timothy Snyder, *On Tyranny: Twenty Lessons from the Twentieth Century* (New York: Tim Duggan Books, 2017), pp. 65–66.

4. Nicholas Confessore and Karen Yourish, "$2 Billion worth of free media for Donald Trump," *The New York Times*, March 15, 2016, https://www .nytimes.com/2016/03/16/upshot/measuring-donald-trumps-mam moth-advantage-in-free-media.html?smid=tw-share&_r=0; Alex Weprin, "CBS CEO Les Moonves clarifies Donald Trump 'good for CBS' comment," *Politico*, October 19, 2016, http://www.politico.com/blogs/on-media/2016 /10/cbs-ceo-les-moonves-clarifies-donald-trump-good-for-cbs-comment-22 9996.

5. Thomas E. Patterson, "News coverage of the 2016 General Election: How the press failed the voters," Shorenstein Center on Media, Politics, and Public Policy, December 7, 2016, https://shorensteincenter.org/news-coverage -2016-general-election/; Jeffrey Gottfried, "More say press is too easy on Trump than said so of Romney, McCain," *Pew Research Center*, September 22, 2016, http://www.pewresearch.org/fact-tank/2016/09/22/more-say-press -is-too-easy-on-trump-than-said-so-of-romney-mccain/.

6. Michael M. Grynbaum, "Matt Lauer fields storm of criticism over Clinton– Trump forum," *The New York Times*, September 8, 2016, https://www.ny times.com/2016/09/08/us/politics/matt-lauer-forum.html; "Pelosi: Media was Russian 'accomplice' in 2016," *CNN*, March 5, 2017, https://www.you tube.com/watch?v=e2C6Z6tjY0w [Video]; David Leonhardt, "A French lesson for the American media," *The New York Times*, May 9, 2017, https:// www.nytimes.com/2017/05/09/opinion/a-french-lesson-for-the-american -media.html; Paul Farhi, "Washington Post's David Fahrenthold wins Pulitzer Prize for dogged reporting of Trump's philanthropy," *The Washington Post*, April 10, 2017, https://www.washingtonpost.com/lifestyle/style/washington -posts-david-fahrenthold-wins-pulitzer-prize-for-dogged-reporting-of-trumps -philanthropy/2017/04/10/dd535d2e-1dfb-11e7-be2a-3a1fb24d4671_story .html?utm_term=.8f423423caf6.

7. David A. Graham, "The many scandals of Donald Trump: A cheat sheet," *The Atlantic*, January 23, 2017, https://www.theatlantic.com/politics/ar chive/2017/01/donald-trump-scandals/474726/; User MrCallvin, "Trump University intro," YouTube, December 5, 2009, https://www.youtube.com/watch ?v=BvaaeHP9xtQ [Video]; Steve Eder and Jennifer Medina, "Trump University suit settlement approved by judge," *The New York Times*, March 31, 2017, https://www.nytimes.com/2017/03/31/us/trump-university-settlement.html.

8. Richard A. Oppel, Jr., "In tribute to son, Khizr Khan offered citizenship lesson at convention," *The New York Times*, July 29, 2016, https://www .nytimes.com/2016/07/29/us/elections/khizr-humayun-khan-speech

.html; Steve Turnham, "Donald Trump to father of fallen soldier: 'I've made a lot of sacrifices,'" *ABC News,* July 30, 2016, http://abcnews.go.com /Politics/donald-trump-father-fallen-soldier-ive-made-lot/story?id=41015051; Scott Wong, "Trump memo calls for 'urgent pivot' from Khan controversy," *The Hill,* August 2, 2016, http://thehill.com/homenews/campaign/290179 -trump-memo-calls-for-urgent-pivot-from-khan-controversy.

9. Patterson, "News coverage of the 2016 General Election"; The White House, "The inaugural address," January 20, 2017, https://www.whitehouse.gov/in augural-address.

10. Nate Silver, "The Comey letter probably cost Clinton the election," *FiveThirty Eight,* May 3, 2017, https://fivethirtyeight.com/features/the-comey-letter -probably-cost-clinton-the-election/; Brian Beutler, "Shame on us, the American media," *The New Republic,* November 8, 2016, https://newrepublic.com /article/138502/shame-us-american-media.

11. David Remnick, "Nattering Nabobs," *The New Yorker,* July 10, 2006, http:// www.newyorker.com/magazine/2006/07/10/nattering-nabobs; Sarah Kaplan, "George Will exits the Republican Party over Trump," *The Washington Post,* June 25, 2016; for "congenital liar," see William Safire, "Blizzard of lies," *The New York Times,* January 8, 1996, http://www.nytimes.com/1996/01/08 /opinion/essay-blizzard-of-lies.html; Eric Alterman, *What Liberal Media? The Truth about Bias and the News* (New York: Basic Books, 2003); Michael M. Grynbaum, "Corey Lewandowski, Donald Trump's former campaign manager, leaves CNN," *The New York Times,* November 11, 2016, https://www .nytimes.com/2016/11/12/business/corey-lewandowski-donald-trumps-former -campaign-manager-leaves-cnn.html?mcubz=1.

12. For Limbaugh's audience, see Lewis Grossberger, "The Rush hours," *The New York Times,* December 16, 1990, http://www.nytimes.com/1990/12/16/maga zine/the-rush-hours.html?pagewanted=all; Center for American Progress and Free Press, "Talk radio by the numbers," June 20, 2007, https://www.ameri canprogress.org/issues/general/reports/2007/06/20/3087/the-structural-im balance-of-political-talk-radio/; Yashar Ali, "Montana NBC affiliate refused to cover Gianforte's 'body slam,'" *New York Magazine,* May 25, 2017, http://ny mag.com/daily/intelligencer/2017/05/montana-nbc-affiliate-refused-to-cover -gianforte-body-slam.html; for Fox News' 1996 numbers, see Steven Barnett, *The Rise and Fall of Television Journalism: Just Wires and Lights in a Box?* (New York: Bloomsbury Academic, 2011), p. 215; for the 2000 numbers, see Allan Johnson, "Is there life after Florida? The count battle gave cable news a wild rating ride, but now it needs an encore," *The Chicago Tribune,* December 18, 2000, http://articles.chicagotribune.com/2000-12-18/features/0012180033_1_cable -news-channels-identity-crisis-channel-and-msnbc; for the 2002 numbers, see Fox News, "Fox News Channel marks decade as the number one cable news network," January 2012, http://press.foxnews.com/2012/01/fox-news-channel -marks-decade-as-the-number-one-cable-news-network/.

13. Joe Otterson, "MSNBC reaches No. 1 for first time in Weekly Primetime Ratings, Fox News drops to third," *Variety,* May 22, 2017, http://variety .com/2017/tv/news/msnbc-fox-news-ratings-cable-news-cnn-1202440320/; Amy Mitchell, Jeffrey Gottfried, Jocelyn Kiley, and Katerina Eva Matsa, "Political polarization and media habits," *Pew Research Center,* October 21, 2014, http://www.journalism.org/2014/10/21/political-polarization-media-habits/; Charlie Sykes, "Charlie Sykes on where the Right went wrong," *The New York Times,* December 15, 2016, https://www.nytimes.com/2016/12/15/opinion /sunday/charlie-sykes-on-where-the-right-went-wrong.html.

14. For 1980 share, see Pew Project for Excellence in Journalism, "Network TV audience," *The State of the News Media 2004,* http://www.stateofthemedia

.org/2004/network-tv-intro-2/audience/; for 1980 viewership, see Pew Project for Excellence in Journalism, "Audience," *The State of the News Media 2009,* http://www.stateofthemedia.org/2009/network-tv-intro/audience/; for 2017 ratings, see Chris Ariens, "Evening News ratings: Q1 2017 and Week of March 20," *TV Newser,* March 28, 2017, http://www.adweek.com/tvnewser /evening-news-ratings-q1-2017-week-of-march-20/324571/.

15. Paul Starr, "Goodbye to the age of newspapers (hello to a new era of corruption)," *The New Republic,* March 4, 2009, https://newrepublic.com/article /64252/goodbye-the-age-newspapers-hello-new-era-corruption; American Society of News Editors, *2015 Newsroom Diversity Census,* http://asne.org/content .asp?contentid=415; Bureau of Labor Statistics, "Unemployment trends in newspaper publishing and other media, 1990–2016," June 2, 2016, https:// www.bls.gov/opub/ted/2016/employment-trends-in-newspaper-publishing -and-other-media-1990-2016.htm; WashPostPR, "The Washington Post surges to 76 million monthly users," *The Washington Post,* January 14, 2016, https:// www.washingtonpost.com/pr/wp/2016/01/14/the-washington-post-surges-to -76-million-monthly-users-2/?utm_term=.3b744904329b.

16. Michiko Kakutani, "Critic's notebook; opinion vs. reality in an age of pundits," *The New York Times,* January 28, 1994, http://www.nytimes.com/1994 /01/28/books/critic-s-notebook-opinion-vs-reality-in-an-age-of-pundits.html ?pagewanted=all&mcubz=1; George Will, "The wisdom of Pat Moynihan," *The Washington Post,* October 3, 2010, http://www.washingtonpost.com/wp -dyn/content/article/2010/10/01/AR2010100105262.html; Cass Sunstein, *#republic: Divided Democracy in the Age of Social Media* (Princeton, NJ: Princeton University Press, 2017), pp. 6, x.

17. Yochai Benkler, Robert Faris, Hal Roberts, and Ethan Zuckerman, "Study: Breitbart-led right-wing media ecosystem altered broader media agenda," *Columbia Journalism Review,* March 3, 2017, https://www.cjr.org/analysis/breit bart-media-trump-harvard-study.php; Greg Sargent, "Trump's lies are working brilliantly. This new poll proves it," *The Washington Post,* April 27, 2017, https:// www.washingtonpost.com/blogs/plum-line/wp/2017/04/27/trumps-lies-are -working-brilliantly-this-new-poll-proves-it/?utm_term=.1b929665925f.

18. For Lippmann's quote, see Craufurd D. Goodwin, *Walter Lippmann: Public Economist* (Cambridge, MA: Harvard University Press, 2014), p. 30; Alexander Hamilton, "Enclosure: Objections and answers respecting the administration of the government," National Archives: Founders Online, August 18, 1792, https://founders.archives.gov/documents/Hamilton/01-12-02-0184-0002; Maquita Peters and Domenico Montanaro, "Trump will be first president in 36 years to skip White House Correspondents' Dinner," *NPR,* February 25, 2017, http://www.npr.org/2017/02/25/517257273/trump-will-be-first-president-in -36-years-to-skip-white-house-correspondents-din; Kathryn Watson, "Trump happy to be with 'much better people' than Washington press corps," *CBS News,* April 29, 2017, http://www.cbsnews.com/news/watch-live-president -trump-rally-speech-in-pennsylvania/; Abby Ohlheiser and Emily Yahr, "A different sort of White House correspondents' dinner," *The Washington Post,* April 29, 2017, https://www.washingtonpost.com/news/reliable-source/wp /2017/04/29/a-different-sort-of-white-house-correspondents-dinner/?utm _term=.307e37b18765; for Havel's quote, see Thomas B. Farrell, *Norms of Rhetorical Culture* (New Haven, CT: Yale University Press, 1993), p. 291.

CHAPTER THREE

1. Abigail Abrams, "George H.W. Bush's 1993 letter to Bill Clinton shows how to lose gracefully," *Time,* October 20, 2016, http://time.com/4538329/george-hw

-bush-letter-bill-clinton-donald-trump/; Nancy Perry Graham, "What's next for George W. Bush?" *AARP: The Magazine,* January/February 2011, http:// www.aarp.org/politics-society/government-elections/info-11-2010/george -bush-interview.html.

2. Donald J. Trump, March 4, 2017 [Tweets]; Emmarie Huetteman, "Devin Nunes to step aside from House investigation on Russia," *The New York Times,* April 6, 2017, https://www.nytimes.com/2017/04/06/us/politics/devin -nunes-house-intelligence-committee-russia.html; Kathryn Watson, "Schiff be- lieves Nunes violated his recusal with 'unmasking' subpoenas," *CBS News,* June 2, 2017, http://www.cbsnews.com/news/schiff-believes-nunes-in-violation-of -ethics-rules-by-issuing-subpoenas; Austin Wright, "McCain on Trump's wire- tap claim: 'I haven't seen anything like this,'" *Politico,* March 6, 2017, http:// www.politico.com/story/2017/03/mccain-trump-wiretapping-235749.

3. Bret Stephens, "The Vertigo Presidency," *The Wall Street Journal,* March 6, 2017, https://www.wsj.com/articles/the-vertigo-presidency-1488847239?tesla=y; for Trump's claims about illegal voting and his inauguration crowd, see Lau- ren Carroll and Linda Qiu, "Fact-checking what Donald Trump got wrong in his ABC News interview," *PolitiFact,* January 26, 2017, http://www.politifact .com/truth-o-meter/article/2017/jan/26/fact-checking-what-donald-trump -got-wrong-his-abc-/; for Trump's claims about Muslims in New Jersey on 9/11, see Lauren Carroll, "Fact-checking Trump's claim that thousands in New Jersey cheered when World Trade Center tumbled," *PolitiFact,* November 22, 2015, http://www.politifact.com/truth-o-meter/statements/2015/nov/22/donald -trump/fact-checking-trumps-claim-thousands-new-jersey-ch/; for definition of "norm," see *Oxford Living Dictionaries,* https://en.oxforddictionaries.com /definition/norm; Rod Dreher, "Conservatism does not equal anti-liberalism," *The American Conservative,* February 17, 2017, http://www.theamericanconser vative.com/dreher/conservatism-anti-liberalism/.

4. Donald R. Matthews, *U.S. Senators and Their World* (Chapel Hill: University of North Carolina Press, 1960), pp. 92–102.

5. David R. Mayhew, *Divided We Govern: Party Control, Lawmaking, and Inves- tigations, 1946–1990* (New Haven, CT: Yale University Press, 1991); see also Sarah A. Binder, *Stalemate: Causes and Consequences of Legislative Gridlock* (Washington, DC: Brookings Institution Press, 2003).

6. For S-CHIP enrollment, see https://www.medicaid.gov/chip/chip-program -information.html; for McCormack's quote, see Norman Ornstein, "Foul mouths in Congress? Big [expletive] deal," *The Washington Post,* March 28, 2010, http://www.washingtonpost.com/wp-dyn/content/article/2010/03/25 /AR2010032500943.html.

7. For Gingrich's quote, see John M. Barry, *The Ambition and the Power* (New York: Viking, 1989), p. 162; for competition and hyperpartisanship, see Fran- ces E. Lee, *Insecure Majorities: Congress and the Perpetual Campaign* (Chicago, IL: University of Chicago Press, 2016); for Office of Technology Assessment, see Jathan Sadowski, "The much-needed and sane Congressional Office that Gingrich killed off and we need back," *The Atlantic,* October 26, 2012, https:// www.theatlantic.com/technology/archive/2012/10/the-much-needed-and -sane-congressional-office-that-gingrich-killed-off-and-we-need-back/264160/.

8. Charles Babington, "Ethics panel rebukes DeLay," *The Washington Post,* Octo- ber 1, 2004, http://www.washingtonpost.com/wp-dyn/articles/A63387-2004 Sep30.html; for McConnell's quote, see Glenn Kessler, "When did Mitch Mc- Connell say he wanted to make Obama a one-term president?" *The Washington Post,* January 11, 2017, https://www.washingtonpost.com/news/fact-checker /wp/2017/01/11/when-did-mitch-mcconnell-say-he-wanted-to-make-obama-a -one-term-president/?utm_term=.1395db87a51f; for Voinovich's quote, see

Michael Grunwald, "The Party of No: New details on the GOP plot to obstruct Obama," *Time*, August 23, 2012, http://swampland.time.com/2012/08/23/the -party-of-no-new-details-on-the-gop-plot-to-obstruct-obama/; Sarah Binder, "How we count Senate filibusters and why it matters," *The Washington Post*, May 15, 2014, https://www.washingtonpost.com/news/monkey-cage/wp/2014 /05/15/how-we-count-senate-filibusters-and-why-it-matters/?utm_term =.8ab94b44a234; Richard S. Beth and Elizabeth Rybicki, Congressional Distribution Memorandum, "Nominations with cloture motions, 2009 to the present," November 21, 2013, https://assets.documentcloud.org/documents/83 8702/crs-filibuster-report.pdf.

9. Burgess Everett and Glenn Thrush, "McConnell throws down the gauntlet: No Scalia replacement under Obama," *Politico*, February 13, 2016, http://www.politico.com/story/2016/02/mitch-mcconnell-antonin-scalia -supreme-court-nomination-219248; for Hatch's quote, see Garrett Epps, "Merrick Garland is a great pick; that may not matter," *The Atlantic*, March 16, 2016, https://www.theatlantic.com/politics/archive/2016/03/merrick-gar land-is-a-great-choice-that-may-not-matter/474093/.

10. Sarah Binder, "Yes, Mitch McConnell's secretive lawmaking is really unusual—in these 4 ways," *The Washington Post*, June 19, 2017, https://www .washingtonpost.com/news/monkey-cage/wp/2017/06/19/yes-mitch-mccon nells-secretive-lawmaking-is-really-unusual-in-these-4-ways/?utm_term=.a33 741f3fbb6; Sean Sullivan, Kelsey Snell, and Juliet Eilperin, "Trump, Senate leaders attempt to regroup after postponing vote to overhaul Obamacare," *The Washington Post*, June 27, 2017, https://www.washingtonpost.com/powerpost/senate -republicans-scramble-to-keep-alive-plans-to-overhaul-obamacare/2017/06 /27/c8ea4c02–5b37–11e7–9fc6-c7ef4bc58d13_story.html?utm_term=.3559 1fe432b0 for "disservice to the American people," see Thomas Ferraro and Donna Smith, "Democrats near deal to 'fast-track' health bill," *Reuters*, April 24, 2009, http://www.reuters.com/article/us-usa-healthcare-congress-idUSTR E53N6LC20090424; Robert Pear, "Obamacare took months to craft; repeal may be much swifter," *The New York Times*, March 7, 2017, https://www .nytimes.com/2017/03/07/us/politics/obamacare-repeal-of-health-law-repub licans.html?_r=0.

11. Eric Cantor, Paul Ryan, and Kevin McCarthy, *Young Guns: A New Generation of Conservative Leaders* (New York: Threshold Editions, 2010); for "big government Republican," see Richard A. Viguerie, "The GOP must reject big government," *Los Angeles Times*, December 29, 2008, http://www.latimes.com /la-oe-viguerie29-2008dec29-story.html; "Election 2010," *The New York Times*, https://www.nytimes.com/elections/2010/results/house.html; Michael McAuliff, "House Republicans spent millions of dollars on Benghazi Committee to exonerate Clinton," *The Huffington Post*, June 29, 2016, http://www.huffington post.com/entry/benghazi-report-clinton_us_57727ed2e4b017b379f74880; Jeffrey M. Jones, "Americans' trust in political leaders, public at new lows," Gallup, September 21, 2016, http://www.gallup.com/poll/195716/americans -trust-political-leaders-public-new-lows.aspx/; Jenna Johnson, "Donald Trump to African American and Hispanic voters: 'What do you have to lose?'" *The Washington Post*, August 22, 2016, https://www.washingtonpost.com/news/po st-politics/wp/2016/08/22/donald-trump-to-african-american-and-hispanic -voters-what-do-you-have-to-lose/?utm_term=.f65874cde851.

12. For "hell" and "law and order," see Matthew Nussbaum, "Trump at debate: Minorities in cities 'are living in hell,'" *Politico*, September 26, 2016, http://www .politico.com/story/2016/09/trump-minorities-living-in-hell-228726; Robert Kagan, "Republicans are becoming Russia's accomplices," *The Washington Post*, March 6, 2017, https://www.washingtonpost.com/opinions/republicans

-are-becoming-russias-accomplices/2017/03/06/8616c2f4-027a-11e7-ad5b
-d22680e18d10_story.html?utm_term=.019890891143; Jonathan Martin and
Matt Flegenheimer, "G.O.P. lawmakers like what they see in Trump. They just
have to squint," *The New York Times,* February 12, 2017, https://www.nytimes
.com/2017/02/12/us/politics/trump-gop-lawmakers.html.

13. The Editorial Board, "House fires at ethics and shoots self," *The New York
    Times,* January 3, 2017, https://www.nytimes.com/2017/01/03/opinion/house
    -fires-at-ethics-and-shoots-self.html; Susan Davis and Brian Naylor, "Af-
    ter backlash, including from Trump, House GOP drops weakening of Eth-
    ics Office," *NPR All Things Considered,* January 3, 2017, http://www.npr
    .org/2017/01/03/508043376/after-trump-tweets-criticism-house-gop-drops
    -weakening-of-house-ethics-office; Louis Nelson, "Conway: GOP has 'man-
    date' to gut Congressional Ethics Office," *Politico,* January 3, 2017, http://
    www.politico.com/story/2017/01/office-of-congressional-ethics-oce-kelly
    anne-conway-233121.

14. For history of release of tax returns, see Tom Kertscher, "Is Donald Trump the
    only major-party nominee in 40 years not to release his tax returns?" *PolitiFact,*
    September 28, 2016, http://www.politifact.com/wisconsin/statements/2016
    /sep/28/tammy-baldwin/donald-trump-only-major-party-nominee-40-years
    -not/; for Trump's quote on tax release, see David Wright, "Trump says pub-
    lic doesn't care 'at all' about his taxes," *CNN,* January 11, 2017, http://www
    .cnn.com/2017/01/11/politics/trump-tax-returns-answer-news-conference/;
    Washington Post–ABC News Poll, January 12–15, 2017, https://www.wash
    ingtonpost.com/politics/polling/washington-postabc-news-poll-january-1215
    /2017/01/19/5c82bb38-dc27-11e6-8902-610fe486791c_page.html; Donald J.
    Trump, April 16, 2017 [Tweet].

15. For a description of Trump's conflicts plan and criticism, see Karen Yourish and
    Larry Buchanan, "It 'falls short in every respect': Ethics experts pan Trump's
    conflicts plan," *The New York Times,* January 12, 2017, https://www.nytimes
    .com/interactive/2017/01/12/us/politics/ethics-experts-trumps-conflicts-of
    -interest.html; Donald J. Trump, "My daughter Ivanka has been treated so un-
    fairly by @Nordstrom. She is a great person—always pushing me to do the right
    thing! Terrible!" February 8, 2017 [Tweet].

16. Craig Holman, "The curious case of President Trump's ethics executive or-
    der," *The Hill,* March 15, 2017, http://thehill.com/blogs/pundits-blog/the-ad
    ministration/323619-the-curious-case-of-trumps-ethics-order; for a summary
    of executive order on lobbying, see Sarah Posner, "Under Trump, the Washing-
    ton 'swamp' is as bogged down as ever," *The Washington Post,* April 26, 2017,
    https://www.washingtonpost.com/blogs/plum-line/wp/2017/04/26/under
    -trump-the-washington-swamp-is-as-bogged-down-as-ever/?utm_term=.39
    57c10904fb; Matea Gold, "White House grants ethics waivers to 17 appointees,
    including four former lobbyists," *The Washington Post,* May 31, 2017, https://
    www.washingtonpost.com/news/post-politics/wp/2017/05/31/white-house
    -grants-ethics-waivers-to-17-appointees-including-four-former-lobbyists/?utm
    _term=.cf05f142203f.

17. Benjamin Haas, "Ivanka Trump brand secures China trademarks on day US
    president met Xi Jinping," *The Guardian,* April 19, 2017, https://www.theguard
    ian.com/us-news/2017/apr/19/ivanka-trump-brand-china-trademarks-day
    -us-president-met-xi-jinping; Javier C. Hernández, Cao Li, and Jesse Drucker,
    "Jared Kushner's sister highlights family ties in pitch to Chinese investors,"
    The New York Times, May 6, 2017, https://www.nytimes.com/2017/05/06
    /world/asia/jared-kushner-sister-nicole-meyer-china-investors.html; Norman
    Eisen and Noah Bookbinder, "Jared Kushner and Ivanka Trump should re-
    cuse themselves from China policy," *The Washington Post,* May 8, 2017, https://

www.washingtonpost.com/opinions/jared-kushner-and-ivanka-trump-should
-recuse-themselves-from-china-policy/2017/05/08/2cca5498-342c-11e7-b4ee
-434b6d506b37_story.html?utm_term=.e277d35e00a0.

18. For Trump cabinet conflicts of interest, see Jeremy Venook, "The Trump administration's conflicts of interest: A crib sheet," *The Atlantic*, January 18,
2017, https://www.theatlantic.com/business/archive/2017/01/trumps-appoin
tees-conflicts-of-interest-a-crib-sheet/512711/; for Pruitt controversy, see Steven Mufson, "New EPA head told Congress he never used personal email for
government business. But it turns out he did," *The Washington Post*, March 2,
2017, https://www.washingtonpost.com/news/energy-environment/wp/2017
/03/02/new-epa-head-told-congress-he-never-used-personal-email-for-govern
ment-business-but-it-turns-out-he-did/?utm_term=.557453ebc9f1; Steve Benen,
"Orrin Hatch lashes out at the 'idiots' he works with," *MSNBC*, February 1,
2017, http://www.msnbc.com/rachel-maddow-show/orrin-hatch-lashes-out
-the-idiots-he-works; Mitch McConnell, Remarks on the Senate floor, "Mc-
Connell: The American people are ready for solutions," January 23, 2017,
https://www.republicanleader.senate.gov/newsroom/remarks/mcconnell-the
-american-people-are-ready-for-solutions.

19. For "Muslim ban," see Amy B. Wang, "Trump asked for a 'Muslim ban,' Giuliani
says—and ordered a commission to do it 'legally,'" *The Washington Post*, January 29, 2017, https://www.washingtonpost.com/news/the-fix/wp/2017/01/29
/trump-asked-for-a-muslim-ban-giuliani-says-and-ordered-a-commission-to
-do-it-legally/?utm_term=.ad0f159bfec3; Justin Jouvenal, Rachel Weiner, and
Ann E. Marimow, "Justice Dept. lawyer says 100,000 visas revoked under travel
ban; State Dept. says about 60,000," *The Washington Post*, February 3, 2017,
https://www.washingtonpost.com/local/public-safety/government-reveals
-over-100000-visas-revoked-due-to-travel-ban/2017/02/03/7d529eec-ea2c-11
e6-b82f-687d6e6a3e7c_story.html?utm_term=.5289e6a3e2b6; for Ryan's June
2016 comments, see Jake Sherman, "Ryan breaks with Trump on Muslim immigrant ban," *Politico*, June 14, 2016, http://www.politico.com/story/2016/06
/ryan-trump-muslim-ban-224312; for Ryan's January 2017 comments, see Paul
Ryan, "Statement on President Trump's executive actions on national security,"
January 27, 2017, http://www.speaker.gov/press-release/statement-president
-trump-s-executive-action-national-security; Rachael Bade, Jake Sherman, and
Josh Dawsey, "Hill staffers secretly worked on Trump's immigration order,"
January 30, 2017, http://www.politico.com/story/2017/01/trump-immigration
-congress-order-234392; Donald J. Trump, "The opinion of this so-called
judge, which essentially takes law-enforcement away from our country, is ridiculous and will be overturned," February 4, 2017 [Tweet]; Donald J. Trump,
"Because the ban was lifted by a judge, many very bad and dangerous people
may be pouring into our country. A terrible decision," February 4, 2017 [Tweet].

20. The White House, "Statement by President Trump on the shooting in Virginia,"
June 14, 2017, https://www.whitehouse.gov/the-press-office/2017/06/14/state
ment-president-trump-shooting-virginia; Hadas Gold, "Some on right blame
anti-Trump rhetoric for shooting," *Politico*, June 14, 2017, http://www.politico
.com/story/2017/06/14/congress-baseball-shooting-blame-anti-trump
-239549; Donald J. Trump, "You are witnessing the single greatest WITCH HUNT
in American political history—led by some very bad and conflicted people!
#MAGA," June 15, 2017 [Tweet].

21. Michael S. Schmidt, Mark Mazzetti, and Matt Apuzzo, "Trump campaign
aides had repeated contacts with Russian intelligence," *The New York Times*,
February 14, 2017, https://www.nytimes.com/2017/02/14/us/politics/russia
-intelligence-communications-trump.html; Greg Miller and Adam Entous,
"Trump administration sought to enlist intelligence officials, key lawmakers

to counter Russia stories," *The Washington Post,* February 24, 2017, https://www.washingtonpost.com/world/national-security/trump-adminis tration-sought-to-enlist-intelligence-officials-key-lawmakers-to-counter-russia -stories/2017/02/24/c8487552-fa99-11e6-be05-1a3817ac21a5_story.html?utm _term=.217abc21d117; Uri Friedman, "America isn't having a constitutional crisis," *The Atlantic,* May 11, 2017, https://www.theatlantic.com/politics/ar chive/2017/05/constitutional-crisis-trump-comey/526089/; Matthew Rosen berg and Matt Apuzzo, "Days before firing, Comey asked for more resources for Russia inquiry," *The New York Times,* May 10, 2017, https://www.nytimes .com/2017/05/10/us/politics/comey-russia-investigation-fbi.html?hp&action =click&pgtype=Homepage&clickSource=story-heading&module=span-ab -top-region&region=top-news&WT.nav=top-news; Noah Bierman and Da vid Lauter, "Trump fires FBI chief, citing handling of Clinton email inves tigation," *Los Angeles Times,* May 9, 2017, http://www.latimes.com/politics /washington/la-na-essential-washington-updates-trump-fires-fbi-director -comey-1494366975-htmlstory.html; James Griffiths, "Trump says he consid ered 'this Russia thing' before firing FBI Director Comey," *CNN,* May 12, 2017, http://www.cnn.com/2017/05/12/politics/trump-comey-russia-thing/index .html; Matt Apuzzo, Maggie Haberman, and Matthew Rosenberg, "Trump told Russians that firing 'nut job' Comey eased pressure from investigation," *The New York Times,* May 19, 2017, https://www.nytimes.com/2017/05/19/us /politics/trump-russia-comey.html?mcubz=1.

22. Derek Hawkins, "'Monday night massacre'? After firing of Yates, Nixon's sordid moment has been repurposed for Trump," *The Washington Post,* January 31, 2017, https://www.washingtonpost.com/news/morning-mix/wp/2017/01/31 /monday-night-massacre-after-firing-of-yates-nixons-sordid-moment-has-been -repurposed-for-trump/?utm_term=.c2b923535dc1; Glenn Kessler, "The fall of Michael Flynn: A timeline," *The Washington Post,* February 15, 2017, https:// www.washingtonpost.com/news/fact-checker/wp/2017/02/15/the-firing-of -michael-flynn-a-timeline/?utm_term=.edfc757d06f0.

23. Jeff Stein, "Comey explains why he kept notes on Trump: 'I was honestly concerned he might lie,'" *Vox,* June 8, 2017, https://www.vox.com/2017/6/8 /15762134/comey-fbi-trump-character; Zachary Cohen, "The tweet that got James Comey to go to the press," *CNN,* June 8, 2017, http://www.cnn.com /2017/06/08/politics/james-comey-leaking-memo/index.html; Amber Phillips, "Trump thinks he got 'total vindication' from Comey. Except he didn't," *The Washington Post,* June 9, 2017, https://www.washingtonpost.com/news/the-fix /wp/2017/06/09/trump-thinks-he-got-total-vindication-from-comey-except -he-didnt/?utm_term=.1425cf813c50.

24. Michael D. Shear and Maggie Haberman, "Friend says Trump is consider ing firing Mueller as special counsel," *The New York Times,* June 12, 2017, https://www.nytimes.com/2017/06/12/us/politics/robert-mueller-trump .html?mcubz=1; Kellyanne Conway, "FEC report: Mueller's team includes some big Democrat donors. Some maxed out, none wanted Trump to be POTUS. @CNNPolitics," June 13, 2017 [Tweet]; Devlin Barrett, Adam Entous, Ellen Nakashima, and Sari Horwitz, "Special counsel is investigating Trump for pos sible obstruction of justice, officials say," *The Washington Post,* June 14, 2017, https://www.washingtonpost.com/world/national-security/special-counsel-is -investigating-trump-for-possible-obstruction-of-justice/2017/06/14/9ce02 506-5131-11e7-b064-828ba60fbb98_story.html?utm_term=.b200e14d18e4; Michael D. Shear, Charlie Savage, and Maggie Haberman, "Trump attacks Rosenstein in latest rebuke of Justice Department," *The New York Times,* June 16, 2017, https://www.nytimes.com/2017/06/16/us/politics/trump-investigation -comey-russia.html?mcubz=1; for Trump campaign statements, see Eli Stokols,

"Clinton and Trump beg base to get excited," *Politico,* November 2, 2016, http://www.politico.com/story/2016/11/donald-trump-hillary-clinton-230652.

25. Jamelle Bouie, "Is there anything Trump could do to lose GOP support?" *Slate,* May 10, 2017, http://amp.slate.com/articles/news_and_politics/politics/2017/05/comey_s_gone_and_the_gop_doesn_t_care_is_there_anything_trump_could_do_to.html.

CHAPTER FOUR

1. Amy B. Wang, "Trump lashes out at 'so-called judge' who temporarily blocked travel ban," *The Washington Post,* February 4, 2017, https://www.washingtonpost.com/news/the-fix/wp/2017/02/04/trump-lashes-out-at-federal-judge-who-temporarily-blocked-travel-ban/?utm_term=.0bf390182eab; Glenn Kessler, "Recidivism Watch: Trump's claim that millions of people voted illegally," *The Washington Post,* January 24, 2017, https://www.washingtonpost.com/news/fact-checker/wp/2017/01/24/recidivism-watch-trumps-claim-that-3-5-million-people-voted-illegally-in-the-election/?utm_term=.f0d1927b9655; Karen DeYoung and David Filipov, "Trump and Putin: A relationship where mutual admiration is headed toward reality," *The Washington Post,* December 30, 2016, https://www.washingtonpost.com/world/national-security/trump-and-putin-a-relationship-where-mutual-admiration-is-headed-toward-reality/2016/12/30/f900b3e2-cebd-11e6-b8a2-8c2a61b0436f_story.html?utm_term=.12c6ddbb8b30; Philip Rucker, "Trump keeps praising international strongmen, alarming human rights advocates," *The Washington Post,* May 2, 2017, https://www.washingtonpost.com/politics/trump-keeps-praising-international-strongmen-alarming-human-rights-advocates/2017/05/01/6848d018-2e81-11e7-9dec-764dc781686f_story.html?utm_term=.2398bb543fa7; David Weigel, "With election in rear view, Trump keeps talking about Clinton's campaign," *The Washington Post,* February 16, 2017, https://www.washingtonpost.com/news/post-politics/wp/2017/02/16/with-election-in-rear-view-trump-keeps-talking-about-clintons-campaign/?utm_term=.e2d0f758e322; Andrew Higgins, "Trump embraces 'Enemy of the People,' a phrase with a fraught history," *The New York Times,* February 26, 2017, https://www.nytimes.com/2017/02/26/world/europe/trump-enemy-of-the-people-stalin.html?_r=0.

2. Fareed Zakaria, "The rise of illiberal democracy," *Foreign Affairs,* November/December 1997, https://www.foreignaffairs.com/articles/1997-11-01/rise-illiberal-democracy; Basharat Peer, *A Question of Order: India, Turkey, and the Return of Strongmen* (New York: Columbia Global Reports, 2017), p. 15; see Masha Gessen, "Autocracy: Rules for survival," *The New York Review of Books,* November 10, 2016, http://www2.nybooks.com/daily/s3/nov/10/trump-election-autocracy-rules-for-survival.html; David Frum, "How to build an autocracy," *The Atlantic,* March 2017, https://www.theatlantic.com/magazine/archive/2017/03/how-to-build-an-autocracy/513872/; Timothy Snyder, "The Reichstag warning," *The New York Review of Books,* March 26, 2017, http://www.nybooks.com/daily/2017/02/26/reichstag-fire-manipulating-terror-to-end-democracy/.

3. Jeff Colgan, "Risk of democratic erosion—reading list," November 2016, https://docs.google.com/viewer?a=v&pid=sites&srcid=ZGVmYXVsdGRvbWFpbnxqZWZmZGNvbGdhbnxneDozN2RmZGMzMmEyOWRmNjM5.

4. Peter Pomerantsev, *Nothing Is True and Everything Is Possible: The Surreal Heart of the New Russia* (New York: PublicAffairs, 2014), p. 231; John Podesta, "Trump's dangerous strategy to undermine reality," *The Washington Post,* February 16, 2017, https://www.washingtonpost.com/opinions/trumps

-dangerous-attempts-to-undermine-reality/2017/02/16/f5d9b826-f3ca-11e6
-b9c9-e83fce42fb61_story.html?utm_term=.735442790806.

5. "Donald Trump's New York Times interview: Full transcript," *The New York Times,* November 23, 2016, https://www.nytimes.com/2016/11/23/us/politics /trump-new-york-times-interview-transcript.html?hp&action=click&pgtype =Homepage&clickSource=story-heading&module=b-lede-package-region &region=top-news&WT.nav=top-news&_r=0; The Constitution of the United States of America, https://www.archives.gov/founding-docs/constitu tion-transcript.

6. Norman L. Eisen, Richard Painter, and Laurence H. Tribe, "The Emoluments clause: Its text, meaning, and application to Donald J. Trump," Brookings Institution, December 16, 2016, https://www.brookings.edu/wp-content/up loads/2016/12/gs_121616_emoluments-clause1.pdf; Steve Reilly, "Trump hasn't donated hotel profits from foreign governments yet," *USA Today,* March 17, 2017, https://www.usatoday.com/story/news/politics/2017/03/17/trump -wait-until-after-end-year-donate-profits-foreign-governments/99313784/; Eric Lipton and Jesse Drucker, "Trump couple, now White House employees, can't escape conflict laws," *The New York Times,* April 1, 2017, https://www .nytimes.com/2017/04/01/us/politics/ivanka-trump-jared-kushner-conflicts -business-empire.html?mcubz=1.

7. The Constitution of the United States of America; Jason Dearan, "Teed off: Critics say Trump water rule helps his golf links," *Associated Press,* March 5, 2017, https://apnews.com/a8d9fefa9e9848e1be2f74b38f0b6ca7/teed-critics -say-trump-water-rule-helps-his-golf-links; Robert Frank, "Mar-a-Lago membership fee doubles to $200,000," *CNBC,* January 25, 2017, http://www .cnbc.com/2017/01/25/mar-a-lago-membership-fee-doubles-to-200000 .html; on presidential tax returns, see Marlena Baldacci, "Presidential candidates have long history of releasing tax returns," *CNN,* July 16, 2012, http:// politicalticker.blogs.cnn.com/2012/07/16/presidential-candidates-have-long -history-of-releasing-tax-returns/.

8. For Donald Trump, Jr.'s comments on Russia, see Tom Hamburger, Rosalind S. Helderman, and Michael Birnbaum, "Inside Trump's financial ties to Russia and his unusual flattery of Vladimir Putin," *The Washington Post,* June 17, 2016, https://www.washingtonpost.com/politics/inside-trumps-financial-ties -to-russia-and-his-unusual-flattery-of-vladimir-putin/2016/06/17/dbdcaac8 -31a6-11e6-8ff7-7b6c1998b7a0_story.html?utm_term=.d2ef4d111085; for congressional suit, see Tom Hamburger and Karen Tumulty, "Congressional Democrats to file emoluments suit against Trump," *The Washington Post,* June 14, 2017, https://www.washingtonpost.com/politics/congressional-democrats -to-file-emoluments-lawsuit-against-trump/2017/06/13/270e60e6-506d-11e7 -be25-3a519335381c_story.html?utm_term=.3e4ec66e6b23; for details on the CREW suit, see Andrew Rice, "Is Trump Inc. the president's greatest vulnerability," *New York Magazine,* June 12, 2017, http://nymag.com/daily/intellig encer/2017/06/donald-trump-emoluments-clause-crew.html; Aaron C. Davis, "D.C. and Maryland sue President Trump, alleging breach of constitutional oath," *The Washington Post,* June 12, 2017, https://www.washingtonpost.com /local/dc-politics/dc-and-maryland-to-sue-president-trump-alleging-breach -of-constitutional-oath/2017/06/11/0059e1f0-4f19-11e7-91eb-9611861a988f _story.html?utm_term=.2ec119216959&wpisrc=nl_headlines&wpmm=1.

9. Jonathan O'Connell, "Foreign payments to Trump's businesses are legally permitted, argues Justice Department," *The Washington Post,* June 10, 2017, https://www.washingtonpost.com/politics/foreign-payments-to-trumps-busi nesses-are-legally-permitted-argues-justice-department/2017/06/10/e66c7 312-4d8c-11e7-a186-60c031eab644_story.html?utm_term=.d73b88d6681e;

for Trump tweets on judge, see Reena Flores, "Trump tweets on 'so-called judge' after travel ban stay," *CBS News,* February 4, 2017, http://www.cbsnews.com/news/trump-tweets-on-so-called-judge-after-travel-ban-stay/.

10. For the second travel ban, see Matt Zapotosky, "Second federal judge blocks revised Trump travel ban," *The Washington Post,* March 16, 2017, https://www.washingtonpost.com/local/social-issues/second-federal-judge-blocks-revised-trump-travel-ban/2017/03/16/dc47cd1e-0a2a-11e7-93dc-00f9bdd74ed1_story.html; for Trump's response in Nashville, see Katie Reilly, "Read President Trump's response to the travel ban ruling: It 'makes us look weak,'" *Time,* March 16, 2017, http://time.com/4703622/president-trump-speech-transcript-travel-ban-ruling/; Donald J. Trump, June 5, 2017 [Tweet]; Laura Jarrett and Ariane de Vogue, "9th Circuit deals Trump travel ban another defeat," *CNN,* June 13, 2017, http://www.cnn.com/2017/06/12/politics/9th-circuit-travel-ban/index.html; Derek Hawkins, "Trump takes up GOP tradition of bashing 9th Circuit, a.k.a. '9th Circus,'" *The Washington Post,* April 27, 2017, https://www.washingtonpost.com/news/morning-mix/wp/2017/04/27/trump-takes-up-hoary-gop-tradition-of-bashing-9th-circuit-aka-9th-circus/?utm_term=.b7e2dfa6df10; Charlie Savage, "Jeff Sessions dismisses Hawaii as 'an island in the Pacific,'" *The New York Times,* April 20, 2017, https://www.nytimes.com/2017/04/20/us/politics/jeff-sessions-judge-hawaii-pacific-island.html.

11. For the Holt interview, see Ali Vitali and Corky Siemaszko, "Trump interview with Lester Holt: President asked Comey if he was under investigation," *NBC News,* May 11, 2017, http://www.nbcnews.com/news/us-news/trump-reveals-he-asked-comey-whether-he-was-under-investigation-n757821; for CNN dossier story, see Evan Perez, Jim Sciutto, Jake Tapper, and Carl Bernstein, "Intel chiefs presented Trump with claims of Russian efforts to compromise him," *CNN,* January 12, 2017, http://www.cnn.com/2017/01/10/politics/donald-trump-intelligence-report-russia/index.html; for *BuzzFeed* dossier reporting, see Ken Bensinger, Miriam Elder, and Mark Schoofs, "These reports allege Trump has deep ties to Russia," *BuzzFeed,* January 10, 2017, https://www.buzzfeed.com/kenbensinger/these-reports-allege-trump-has-deep-ties-to-russia?utm_term=.kl6eN2JRYd#.vgXYRN3Gbx; Donald J. Trump, January 11, 2017 [Tweet].

12. Paul Farhi, "Taunted by Trump, 'Little Katy' stood her ground. And she became a star because of it," *The Washington Post,* January 31, 2017, https://www.washingtonpost.com/lifestyle/style/taunted-by-trump-little-katy-stood-her-ground-and-became-a-star-because-of-it/2017/01/31/288fc01a-de8d-11e6-ad42-f3375f271c9c_story.html?utm_term=.0fa2146996a2; for full Trump tweets on Brzezinski, see Emily Heil, "Trump labels MSNBC hosts 'Crazy Mika' and 'Psycho Joe' and mocks her 'face-lift'," *The Washington Post,* June 29, 2017, https://www.washingtonpost.com/news/reliable-source/wp/2017/06/29/trump-labels-msnbc-hosts-crazy-mika-and-psycho-joe-and-mocks-her-face-lift/?utm_term=.c5585d5b0a15; J. Freedom du Lac and Jenna Johnson, "Mika Brzezinski explains what President Trump's tweets reveal about him," *The Washington Post,* June 30, 2017, https://www.washingtonpost.com/news/arts-and-entertainment/wp/2017/06/30/mika-brzezinski-on-trumps-twitter-attack-it-does-worry-me-about-the-country/?utm_term=.dbae8f2caaf2; Mark Kornblau, June 29, 2017 [Tweet].

13. For "save American jobs," see Donald J. Trump, "TOGETHER we can save American JOBS, American LIVES, and American FUTURES. #AmericaFirst," January 23, 2017 [Tweet]; Donald J. Trump, June 4, 2017 [Tweet]; Scott Horsley, "Trump's latest tweets on travel ban could raise new legal hurdles," *NPR,* June 5, 2017, http://www.npr.org/2017/06/05/531558813/trumps-latest-tweets-on-travel-ban-could-raise-new-legal-hurdles; Julie Hirschfeld, Robert Pear, and Thomas Kaplan,

"Trump tells G.O.P. it's now or never, demanding House vote on health bill," *The New York Times,* March 23, 2017, https://www.nytimes.com/2017/03/23 /us/politics/health-republicans-vote.html?mcubz=1&_r=0; Ezra Klein, "Has anyone told Donald Trump that he runs the government?" *Vox,* June 6, 2017, https://www.vox.com/policy-and-politics/2017/6/6/15740376/trump-govern ment-alienation.

14. For Bybee, see Garrett Epps, "Why Trump's revised travel ban could still succeed," *The Atlantic,* March 16, 2017, https://www.theatlantic.com/poli tics/archive/2017/03/trumps-revised-travel-ban-could-still-succeed/519807/; *Donald J. Trump, President of the United States, et al. v. International Refu- gee Assistance Project, et al.,* 582 U.S., 2017, https://www.supremecourt.gov /opinions/16pdf/16-1436_l6hc.pdf; Kate Brumback, "Immigration courts: Record number of cases, many problems," *Associated Press,* March 4, 2017, https://apnews.com/1cf71a90b61745d697b3800e08efb52e; Ingrid V. Eagly and Steven Shafer, "A national study of access to counsel in immigration court," *University of Pennsylvania Law Review,* Vol. 164, No. 1, December 2015, http://scholarship.law.upenn.edu/cgi/viewcontent.cgi?article=9502&con text=penn_law_review; Oliver Laughland, "Inside Trump's secretive immi- gration court: Far from scrutiny and legal aid," *The Guardian,* June 7, 2017, https://www.theguardian.com/us-news/2017/jun/07/donald-trump-immigra tion-court-deportation-lasalle?CMP=share_btn_link.

15. Philip Rucker and Robert Costa, "Bannon vows a daily fight for 'deconstruction of the administrative state,'" *The Washington Post,* February 23, 2017, https:// www.washingtonpost.com/politics/top-wh-strategist-vows-a-daily-fight-for -deconstruction-of-the-administrative-state/2017/02/23/03f6b8da-f9ea -11e6-bf01-d47f8cf9b643_story.html?utm_term=.b8154bee4232; Scott W. Johnson, "A new old regime," *National Review,* July 31, 2014, http://www.nati onalreview.com/article/384183/new-old-regime-scott-w-johnson.

16. Max Fisher, "What happens when you fight a 'deep state' that doesn't exist," *The New York Times,* March 10, 2017, https://www.nytimes.com/2017/03/10 /world/americas/what-happens-when-you-fight-a-deep-state-that-doesnt-exist .html; David Remnick, "There is no deep state," *The New Yorker,* March 20, 2017, http://www.newyorker.com/magazine/2017/03/20/there-is-no-deep -state; Rebecca Savransky, "Gingrich: Mueller tip of 'deep state spear,'" *The Hill,* June 15, 2017, http://thehill.com/homenews/house/337912-gingrich-mu eller-tip-of-the-deep-state-spear; Michael Gerson, "Republicans are defining lunacy down," *The Washington Post,* March 13, 2017, https://www.washington post.com/opinions/republicans-are-defining-lunacy-down/2017/03/13/7f50 5ba4-0821-11e7-b77c-0047d15a24e0_story.html?utm_term=.1017df707656.

17. Matthew Cole, Richard Esposito, Sam Biddle, and Ryan Grim, "Top-secret NSA report details Russian hacking effort days before 2016 Election," *The In- tercept,* June 5, 2017, https://theintercept.com/2017/06/05/top-secret-nsa-re port-details-russian-hacking-effort-days-before-2016-election/.

CHAPTER FIVE

1. The White House, "Remarks by the president on 250th anniversary of the birth of President Andrew Jackson," March 15, 2017, https://www.whitehouse.gov /the-press-office/2017/03/15/remarks-president-250th-anniversary-birth-presi dent-andrew-jackson; The White House, "The inaugural address," January 20, 2017, https://www.whitehouse.gov/inaugural-address.

2. Peter Baker, "Jackson and Trump: How two populist presidents compare," *The New York Times,* March 15, 2017, https://www.nytimes.com/2017/03/15/us /politics/donald-trump-andrew-jackson.html; Susan Page, "Analysis: Trump's

cabinet dubbed 'Goldman, generals and gazillionaires,'" *USA Today,* December 11, 2016, https://www.usatoday.com/story/news/2016/12/11/trumps-cabinet -goldman-generals-and-gazillionaires/95299216/; Congressional Budget Office, "H.R. 1628, American Health Care Act of 2017," May 24, 2017, https:// www.cbo.gov/publication/52752; Robert Costa and Amy Goldstein, "Trump vows 'insurance for everybody' in Obamacare replacement plan," *The Washington Post,* January 15, 2017, https://www.washingtonpost.com/politics/trump -vows-insurance-for-everybody-in-obamacare-replacement-plan/2017/01/15 /5f2b1e18-db5d-11e6-ad42-f3375f271c9c_story.html?utm_term=.82ed10 cca6a4; Max Ehrenfreund, "Trump's tax proposal: What it means for the rich, for the world and for you," *The Washington Post,* April 26, 2017, https://www .washingtonpost.com/news/wonk/wp/2017/04/26/trumps-tax-proposal-what -it-means-for-the-rich-for-the-world-and-for-you/?utm_term=.005b073f8c92.

3. Donald J. Trump, May 7, 2015 [Tweet]; Cristiano Lima, "Trump: It's 'big league,' not 'bigly,'" *Politico,* October 27, 2016, http://www.politico.com/story /2016/10/donald-trump-big-league-bigly-230431; James B. Stewart, "Trump lands a blow against carried interest tax loophole," *The New York Times,* September 17, 2015, https://www.nytimes.com/2015/09/18/business/with-trump -as-foe-carried-interest-tax-loophole-is-vulnerable.html.

4. Tracy Jan, "Trump's 'big, beautiful wall' will require him to take big swaths of other people's land," *The Washington Post,* March 21, 2017, https://www .washingtonpost.com/news/wonk/wp/2017/03/21/trumps-big-beautiful-wall -will-require-him-to-take-big-swaths-of-other-peoples-land/?utm_term=.a270 d8fdb18e; "Here's what we know about Trump's Mexico wall," *Bloomberg,* March 29, 2017, https://www.bloomberg.com/graphics/2017-trump-mexico -wall/how-much-would-the-wall-cost/; Nicholas Fandos, "Trump weighs cuts to Coast Guard, T.S.A. and FEMA to bolster border plan," *The New York Times,* March 9, 2017, https://www.nytimes.com/2017/03/09/us/politics/trump-bud get-coast-guard.html.

5. Vivian Salama and Alicia A. Caldwell, "AP exclusive: DHS report disputes threat from banned nations," *Associated Press,* February 24, 2017, https://www .apnews.com/39f1f8e4ceed4a30a4570f693291c866; Damian Paletta, "White House split on import tax puts Congress in limbo," *The Washington Post,* March 3, 2017, https://www.washingtonpost.com/business/economy/white -house-fight-on-import-tax-puts-congress-in-limbo/2017/03/03/89ca2298-00 44-11e7-8ebe-6e0dbe4f2bca_story.html?utm_term=.b7453f4b1481; Bob Davis and William Mauldin, "Trump administration signals it would seek mostly modest changes to NAFTA," *The Wall Street Journal,* March 30, 2017, https:// www.wsj.com/articles/trump-administration-signals-it-would-seek-mostly -modest-changes-to-nafta-1490842268?mod=e2tw; for "compromise" between "trade hawks" and "moderates," see Alayna Treene, "Trump might keep controversial NAFTA provisions," *Axios,* March 30, 2017, https://www.axios.com /trump-might-keep-some-of-naftas-most-controversial-provisions-23363882 27.html.

6. Ashley Parker, Philip Rucker, Damian Paletta, and Karen DeYoung, "'I was all set to terminate': Inside Trump's sudden shift on NAFTA," *The Washington Post,* April 27, 2017, https://www.washingtonpost.com/politics/i-was-all-set-to -terminate-inside-trumps-sudden-shift-on-nafta/2017/04/27/0452a3fa-2b65 -11e7-b605-33413c691853_story.html?utm_term=.44c15ee1372e; Peter Nicholas and Paul Vieira, "Why Donald Trump decided to back off NAFTA threat," *The Wall Street Journal,* April 27, 2017, https://www.wsj.com/articles/trump -says-nafta-partners-persuaded-him-to-keep-u-s-in-trade-pact-1493320127; Jenna Johnson, "Trump on NATO: 'I said it was obsolete. It's no longer obsolete,'" *The Washington Post,* April 12, 2017, https://www.washingtonpost.com

/news/post-politics/wp/2017/04/12/trump-on-nato-i-said-it-was-obsolete-its
-no-longer-obsolete/?utm_term=.ab417fceaf6a.

7. Susan B. Glasser, "Trump national security team blindsided by NATO speech,"
   Politico, June 5, 2017, http://www.politico.com/magazine/story/2017/06/05
   /trump-nato-speech-national-security-team-215227; Henry Farrell, "Thanks
   to Trump, Germany says it can't rely on the United States. What does that
   mean?" *The Washington Post,* May 28, 2017, https://www.washingtonpost
   .com/news/monkey-cage/wp/2017/05/28/thanks-to-trump-germany-says-it
   -cant-rely-on-america-what-does-that-mean/?utm_term=.7e2cf13b45a1; Peter Baker, "Trump commits United States to defending NATO nations," *The
   New York Times,* June 9, 2017, https://www.nytimes.com/2017/06/09/world
   /europe/trump-nato-defense-article-5.html?mcubz=1; for Trump's quote on
   the Paris Agreement, see The White House, "Statement by President Trump
   on the Paris Climate Accord," June 1, 2017, https://www.whitehouse.gov
   /the-press-office/2017/06/01/statement-president-trump-paris-climate
   -accord.

8. Zack Beauchamp, "Trump wants to cut the State Department's budget by
   37 percent. Congress isn't buying it," *Vox,* March 1, 2017, https://www.vox
   .com/world/2017/3/1/14777248/trump-state-department-budget-congress
   -opposition; Paul Krugman, "Populism, real and phony," *The New York
   Times,* December 23, 2016, https://www.nytimes.com/2016/12/23/opinion
   /populism-real-and-phony.html; Jeremy Diamond, "Donald Trump: Banks
   have 'total control' over Ted Cruz," *CNN,* February 19, 2016, http://www
   .cnn.com/2016/02/19/politics/donald-trump-ted-cruz-goldman-sachs/; Peter
   Schroeder, "Goldman Sachs accounts for a quarter of Dow Jones gains since
   election," *The Hill,* December 20, 2016, http://thehill.com/policy/finance/311
   169-goldman-sachs-good-for-a-quarter-of-dows-trump-rally; Zachary Mider
   and Jennifer A. Dlouhy, "Trump adviser Carl Icahn lobbies for rule change
   that benefits Icahn," *Bloomberg Businessweek,* March 16, 2017, https://
   www.bloomberg.com/news/articles/2017-03-16/trump-adviser-carl-icahn-lob
   bies-for-rule-change-that-benefits-icahn.

9. Andrew Restuccia and Nancy Cook, "Inside Trump's war on regulations,"
   Politico, May 28, 2017, http://www.politico.com/interactives/2017/trump
   -war-on-regulations/; Brian Fung, "The House just voted to wipe away the
   FCC's landmark Internet privacy protections," *The Washington Post,* March
   28, 2017, https://www.washingtonpost.com/news/the-switch/wp/2017/03/28
   /the-house-just-voted-to-wipe-out-the-fccs-landmark-internet-privacy-pro
   tections/?utm_term=.64514fb10da6; Gerard Baker, Carol E. Lee, and Michael
   C. Bender, "Trump says dollar 'getting too strong,' won't label China a currency manipulator," *The Wall Street Journal,* April 12, 2017, https://www.wsj
   .com/articles/trump-says-dollar-getting-too-strong-wont-label-china-currency
   -manipulator-1492024312; Donald J. Trump, April 16, 2017 [Tweet].

10. Amy Goldstein, "Trump says Congress must 'save Americans from this implod-
    ing Obamacare disaster,'" *The Washington Post,* February 28, 2017, https://
    www.washingtonpost.com/politics/2017/live-updates/trump-white-house
    /real-time-fact-checking-and-analysis-of-trumps-address-to-congress/trump
    -says-congress-must-save-americans-from-this-imploding-obamacare-disaster
    /?utm_term=.4fb6b936f5e0; Aaron Blake, "Trump's forbidden love: Single-
    payer health care," *The Washington Post,* May 5, 2017, https://www.washington
    post.com/news/the-fix/wp/2017/05/05/trumps-forbidden-love-singe-payer
    -health-care/?utm_term=.66c995fdbe2b; Robert Costa and Amy Goldstein,
    "Trump vows 'insurance for everybody' in Obamacare replacement plan," *The
    Washington Post,* January 15, 2017; Congressional Budget Office, "American
    Health Care Act cost estimate," March 13, 2017, https://www.cbo.gov/publi

cation/52486; Nate Cohn, "Trump supporters have the most to lose in the G.O.P. Repeal Bill," *The New York Times*, March 10, 2017, https://www.nytimes.com/2017/03/10/upshot/why-trump-supporters-have-the-most-to-lose-with-the-gop-repeal-bill.html; Matthew Buettgens, Linda J. Blumberg, John Holahan, and Siyabonga Ndwandwe, "The cost of ACA repeal," Urban Institute, June 2016, http://www.urban.org/sites/default/files/publication/81296/2000806-The-Cost-of-the-ACA-Repeal.pdf.

11. Paul Krugman, "Republicans party like it's 1984," *The New York Times*, May 8, 2017, https://www.nytimes.com/2017/05/08/opinion/republicans-party-like-its-1984.html; Quinnipiac University, "21% of U.S. voters approve of revised GOP Health Plan, Quinnipiac University National Poll finds; voters reject Trump Tax Plan almost 2–1," May 11, 2017, https://poll.qu.edu/images/polling/us/us05112017_Uqjw42xw.pdf/; Christopher Warshaw and David Broockman, "G.O.P. senators might not realize it, but not one state supports the Republican Health Bill," *The New York Times*, June 14, 2017, https://www.nytimes.com/2017/06/14/upshot/gop-senators-might-not-realize-it-but-not-one-state-supports-the-ahca.html?mcubz=1.

12. Kelsey Snell and Sean Sullivan, "Trump calls House health bill that he celebrated in the Rose Garden 'mean,'" *The Washington Post*, June 13, 2017, https://www.washingtonpost.com/powerpost/trump-calls-house-health-bill-that-he-celebrated-in-the-rose-garden-mean/2017/06/13/ede11784-5060-11e7-b064-828ba60fbb98_story.html?utm_term=.79162374b5e0; Dylan Scott, "What we know so far about what's in the secret Senate health bill," *Vox*, June 15, 2017, https://www.vox.com/policy-and-politics/2017/6/15/15808238/senate-republicans-health-care-obamacare-repeal-deals; Madeline Conway, "Trump: 'Nobody knew that health care could be so complicated,'" *Politico*, February 27, 2017, http://www.politico.com/story/2017/02/trump-nobody-knew-that-health-care-could-be-so-complicated-235436; Madeline Berg, "Steve Bannon worth as much as $48 million, blockbuster filings reveal," *Forbes*, April 1, 2017, https://www.forbes.com/sites/maddieberg/2017/04/01/steve-bannon-worth-as-much-as-48-million-blockbuster-filings-reveal/#4d3a99401f59.

13. Nicholas Clairmont, "The many ways 'Buy American' can harm the economy," *The Atlantic*, April 19, 2017, https://www.theatlantic.com/business/archive/2017/04/buy-american-trump/523584/; Glenn Thrush, Nick Wingfield, and Vindu Goel, "Trump signs order that could lead to curbs on foreign workers," *The New York Times*, April 18, 2017, https://www.nytimes.com/2017/04/18/us/politics/executive-order-hire-buy-american-h1b-visa-trump.html; Dana Varinsky, "Trump just signed a 'Buy American' order, but his businesses don't," *Business Insider*, April 20, 2017, http://www.businessinsider.com/trump-buy-american-order-hotel-imports-2017-4.

14. Julie Hirschfeld Davis and Alan Rappeport, "White House proposes slashing tax rates, significantly aiding wealthy," *The New York Times*, April 26, 2017, https://www.nytimes.com/2017/04/26/us/politics/trump-tax-cut-plan.html; Senator Ron Wyden, "Wyden statement on unprincipled Trump tax plan," April 26, 2017, https://www.finance.senate.gov/ranking-members-news/wyden-statement-on-unprincipled-trump-tax-plan-; Ross Douthat, "Donald Trump, establishment sellout," *The New York Times*, May 20, 2017, https://www.nytimes.com/2017/05/20/opinion/donald-trump-establishment-sellout.html; Tim Devaney, "AFL-CIO chief: Trump pulled 'bait-and-switch' on working-class voters," *The Hill*, April 4, 2017, http://thehill.com/regulation/labor/327239-labor-boss-trump-pulled-a-bait-and-switch-on-working-class-voters.

15. Michael Kazin, *The Populist Persuasion: An American History* (Ithaca, NY: Cornell University Press, 1998), pp. 271, 290; Richard Hofstadter, *The Age*

of Reform (New York: Vintage Books, 1955); Lawrence Goodwyn, *Democratic Promise: The Populist Movement in America* (New York: Oxford University Press, 1976); Charles Postel, *The Populist Vision* (New York: Oxford University Press, 2007), p. 6; Thomas Frank, *Listen, Liberal: Or, What Ever Happened to the Party of the People?* (New York: Metropolitan Books, 2016).

16. John Judis, *The Populist Explosion: How the Great Recession Transformed American and European Politics* (New York: Columbia Global Reports, 2016), pp. 14–15, 17; Benjamin Moffitt, *The Global Rise of Populism: Performance, Political Style, and Representation* (Stanford, CA: Stanford University Press, 2016), pp. 43–45; Larry Bartels, "The 'wave' of right-wing populist sentiment is a myth," Monkey Cage blog, *The Washington Post*, June 21, 2017, https://www.washingtonpost.com/news/monkey-cage/wp/2017/06/21/the-wave-of-right-wing-populist-sentiment-is-a-myth/?utm_term=.a377d2e969d8.

17. Jan-Werner Müller, *What Is Populism?* (Philadelphia: University of Pennsylvania Press, 2016), p. 3; Mudde quoted in Uri Friedman, "What is a populist?" *The Atlantic,* February 27, 2017, https://www.theatlantic.com/international/archive/2017/02/what-is-populist-trump/516525/.

18. Daniel Kreiss, "Trump, Breitbart, and the rejection of multicultural democracy," *Medium,* January 29, 2017, https://medium.com/@dkreiss/trump-breitbart-and-the-rejection-of-multicultural-democracy-90f3f776bebd.

19. Bannon's remarks published in J. Lester Feder, "This is how Steve Bannon sees the entire world," *BuzzFeed,* November 16, 2016, https://www.buzzfeed.com/lesterfeder/this-is-how-steve-bannon-sees-the-entire-world?utm_term=.pm66oRNBXK#.bo14DpaG5v.

20. Ryan Lizza, "How Steve Bannon conquered CPAC—and the Republican Party," *The New Yorker,* February 24, 2017, http://www.newyorker.com/news/ryan-lizza/how-steve-bannon-conquered-cpac-and-the-republican-party; Ryan Teague Beckwith, "Read Steve Bannon and Reince Preibus' joint interview at CPAC," *Time,* February 23, 2017, http://time.com/4681094/reince-priebus-steve-bannon-cpac-interview-transcript/; Ashley Parker, Robert Costa, and Abby Phillip, "Bannon wants a war on Washington. Now he's part of one inside the White House," *The Washington Post,* April 6, 2017, https://www.washingtonpost.com/politics/bannon-wants-a-war-on-washington-now-hes-part-of-one-inside-the-white-house/2017/04/06/ec4a135a-1ada-11e7-9887-1a5314b56a08_story.html?utm_term=.c79dc62f70d3.

21. For "rapists," see "Full text: Donald Trump announces a presidential bid," *The Washington Post,* June 16, 2015, https://www.washingtonpost.com/news/post-politics/wp/2015/06/16/full-text-donald-trump-announces-a-presidential-bid/?utm_term=.1c4943296481; Matthew Rozsa, "WATCH: Donald Trump's last campaign ad is a fitting end to an anti-Semitic campaign," *Salon,* November 7, 2016, http://www.salon.com/2016/11/07/watch-donald-trumps-last-campaign-ad-is-a-fitting-end-to-an-anti-semitic-campaign/.

22. The White House, "Remarks by President Trump at United States Holocaust Memorial Museum National Days of Remembrance," April 25, 2017, https://www.whitehouse.gov/the-press-office/2017/04/25/remarks-president-trump-united-states-holocaust-memorial-museum-national; Adam Serwer, "Jeff Sessions's agenda for the Civil-Rights Division," *The Atlantic,* May 25, 2017, https://www.theatlantic.com/article/528126/; Juliet Eilperin, Emma Brown, and Darryl Fears, "Trump administration plans to minimize civil rights efforts in agencies," *The Washington Post,* May 29, 2017, https://www.washingtonpost.com/politics/trump-administration-plans-to-minimize-civil-rights-efforts-in-agencies/2017/05/29/922fc1b2-39a7-11e7-a058-ddbb23c75d82_story.html?tid=sm_tw&utm_term=.af472beeaa72; Müller, *What Is Populism?* pp. 3–4.

CHAPTER SIX

1. John Judis, "Opposing everything is the wrong way to stop Trump," *The New Republic,* April 10, 2017, https://newrepublic.com/article/141705/opposing -everything-wrong-way-stop-trump; CNN 2016 Exit Polls, http://www.cnn .com/election/results/exit-polls.

2. For Wallace and class-consciousness, see Richard M. Scammon and Ben J. Wattenberg, *The Real Majority: An Extraordinary Examination of the American Electorate* (New York: Coward-McCann, 1970), pp. 195–196; Benjamin M. Friedman, "The moral consequences of economic growth," *Society,* January/ February 2006, https://web.stanford.edu/group/scspi/_media/pdf/key_issues /philosophy_journalism.pdf; for discussion of economics and anti-immigrant sentiment, see Nicholas A. Valentino, Ted Brader, and Ashley E. Jardina, "Immigration opposition among U.S. whites: General ethnocentrism or media priming of attitudes about Latinos?" *Political Psychology,* Vol. 34, No. 2, 2013, https://deepblue.lib.umich.edu/bitstream/handle/2027.42/97221/pops928 .pdf?sequence=1; Migration Policy Institute, "U.S. immigrant population and share over time, 1850–present," http://www.migrationpolicy.org/programs /data-hub/charts/immigrant-population-over-time?width=1000&height=850 &iframe=true.

3. Robert P. Jones, *The End of White Christian America* (New York: Simon & Schuster, 2016); for Weber and Barbour's quotes, see E. J. Dionne, Jr., *Why the Right Went Wrong: Conservatism—From Goldwater to Trump and Beyond* (New York: Simon & Schuster, 2016), p. 237.

4. Ronald F. Inglehart and Pippa Norris, "Trump, Brexit, and the rise of populism: Economic have-nots and cultural backlash," Harvard Kennedy School Faculty Research Working Paper Series, August 2016; Brian F. Schaffner, Matthew MacWilliams, and Tatishe Nteta, "Explaining white polarization in the 2016 vote for president: The sobering role of racism and sexism," Paper prepared for the Conference on the U.S. Elections of 2016 at IDC Herzliya Campus, 2017, http://people.umass.edu/schaffne/schaffner_et_al_IDC_conference.pdf; Michael Tesler, "Trump is the first modern Republican to win the nomination based on racial prejudice," *The Washington Post,* August 1, 2016, https://www .washingtonpost.com/news/monkey-cage/wp/2016/08/01/trump-is-the-first -republican-in-modern-times-to-win-the-partys-nomination-on-anti-minority -sentiments/?utm_term=.dcfdcaa0de3f.

5. Philip Klinkner, "The easiest way to guess if someone supports Trump? Ask if Obama is a Muslim," *Vox,* June 2, 2016, https://www.vox.com/2016 /6/2/11833548/donald-trump-support-race-religion-economy; Bruce Stokes, "As Republicans' views improve, Americans give the economy its highest marks since financial crisis," *Pew Research Center,* April 3, 2017, http://www .pewresearch.org/fact-tank/2017/04/03/americans-give-economy-highest -marks-since-financial-crisis/; Sean McElwee and Jason McDaniel, "Fear of diversity made people more likely to vote Trump," *The Nation,* March 14, 2017, https://www.thenation.com/article/fear-of-diversity-made-people-more-likely -to-vote-trump/; Perry Bacon Jr., "The identity politics of the Trump administration," *FiveThirtyEight,* May 4, 2017, https://fivethirtyeight.com/features /the-identity-politics-of-the-trump-administration/.

6. Theda Skocpol and Vanessa Williamson, *The Tea Party and the Remaking of Republican Conservatism* (New York: Oxford University Press, 2012), pp. 56, 68–69; Alec MacGillis, "Who turned my blue state red?" *The New York Times,* November 20, 2015, https://www.nytimes.com/2015/11/22/opinion/sunday /who-turned-my-blue-state-red.html; for Limbaugh, see Rebecca Sinderbrand, "RNC chairman candidate defends 'Barack the Magic Negro' song," *CNN,*

December 26, 2008, http://www.cnn.com/2008/POLITICS/12/26/rnc.obama .satire/.

7. Emma Green, "It was cultural anxiety that drove white, working-class voters to Trump," *The Atlantic*, May 9, 2017, https://www.theatlantic.com/politics /archive/2017/05/white-working-class-trump-cultural-anxiety/525771/; Daniel Cox, Rachel Lienesch, and Robert P. Jones, "Beyond economics: Fears of cultural displacement pushed the white working class to Trump," PRRI, May 9, 2017, https://www.prri.org/research/white-working-class-attitudes-economy -trade-immigration-election-donald-trump/; CNN 2016 Exit Polls, http:// www.cnn.com/election/results/exit-polls; *Pew Research Center*, "Partisan identification is 'sticky,' but about 10% switched parties over the past year," May 17, 2017, http://www.people-press.org/2017/05/17/partisan-identification-is -sticky-but-about-10-switched-parties-over-the-past-year/.

8. For "radical Islam," see Jose A. DelReal, "Trump blames Clinton's 'weakness' for attacks," *The Washington Post*, September 19, 2016, https://www.wash ingtonpost.com/news/post-politics/wp/2016/09/19/trump-blames-clintons -weakness-for-attacks/?tid=a_inl&utm_term=.8182698f7330; Russell Moore, "Have evangelicals who support Trump lost their values?" *The New York Times*, September 17, 2015, https://www.nytimes.com/2015/09/17/opinion/have-eva ngelicals-who-support-trump-lost-their-values.html?_r=0; for Moore's comments to Baptist pastors, see Rod Dreher, "Why Russell Moore matters," *The American Conservative*, December 21, 2016, http://www.theamericanconserva tive.com/dreher/why-russell-moore-matters/comment-page-1/.

9. Data on evangelicals and Trump received from PRRI; Julie Lyons, "Robert Jeffress wants a mean 'son of a gun' for president, says Trump isn't a racist," *Dallas Observer*, April 5, 2016, http://www.dallasobserver.com/news /robert-jeffress-wants-a-mean-son-of-a-gun-for-president-says-trump-isnt-a -racist-8184721; for Trump's comments on abortion in the third presidential debate, see Aaron Blake, "The final Trump–Clinton debate transcript, annotated," *The Washington Post*, October 19, 2016, https://www.washington post.com/news/the-fix/wp/2016/10/19/the-final-trump-clinton-debate-tran script-annotated/?utm_term=.04956c01d608; Gregory A. Smith and Jessica Martínez, "How the faithful voted: A preliminary 2016 analysis," *Pew Research Center*, November 9, 2016, http://www.pewresearch.org/fact-tank/2016/11/09 /how-the-faithful-voted-a-preliminary-2016-analysis/.

10. PRRI/Brookings Survey, October 19, 2016, https://www.prri.org/research/prri -brookings-oct-19-poll-politics-election-clinton-double-digit-lead-trump/; Sarah Posner, "Amazing disgrace," *The New Republic*, March 20, 2017, https://newrepublic.com/article/140961/amazing-disgrace-donald-trump-hi jacked-religious-right.

11. Richard Florida, "How U.S. metro area votes changed between 2012 and 2016," *CityLab*, December 7, 2016, http://www.citylab.com/politics/2016/12 /where-metro-areas-swung-for-trump-and-clinton/509633/; Ben Casselman, "Stop saying Trump's win had nothing to do with economics," *FiveThirtyEight*, January 9, 2017, https://fivethirtyeight.com/features/stop-saying-trumps-win -had-nothing-to-do-with-economics/.

12. Jed Kolko, "Trump was stronger where the economy is weaker," *FiveThirty Eight*, November 10, 2016, https://fivethirtyeight.com/features/trump-was -stronger-where-the-economy-is-weaker/; Mark Muro and Sifan Liu, "Another Clinton–Trump divide: High-output America vs low-output America," Brookings Institution, November 29, 2016, https://www.brookings.edu/blog /the-avenue/2016/11/29/another-clinton-trump-divide-high-output-america -vs-low-output-america/; Jim Tankersley, "Donald Trump lost most of the American economy in this election," *The Washington Post*, November 22, 2016,

https://www.washingtonpost.com/news/wonk/wp/2016/11/22/donald-trump
-lost-most-of-the-american-economy-in-this-election/?utm_term=.1aede1e
8d7ac; Greg Sargent, "Why did Trump win? New research by Democrats offers a worrisome answer," *The Washington Post,* May 1, 2017, https://www.wash
ingtonpost.com/blogs/plum-line/wp/2017/05/01/why-did-trump-win-new
-research-by-democrats-offers-a-worrisome-answer/?utm_term=.bd442f3
912fa.

13. "Election 2016: Trump voters on why they backed him," *BBC News,* November 9, 2016, http://www.bbc.com/news/election-us-2016-36253275; Sam Altman, "I'm a Silicon Valley liberal, and I traveled across the country to interview
100 Trump supporters—here's what I learned," *Business Insider,* February
23, 2017, http://www.businessinsider.com/sam-altman-interview-trump-sup
porters-2017-2.

CHAPTER SEVEN

1. Alana Semuels, "Poor at 20, poor for life," *The Atlantic,* July 14, 2016, https://
www.theatlantic.com/business/archive/2016/07/social-mobility-america/491
240/; Elise Gould, "U.S. lags behind peer countries in mobility," Economic Policy Institute, October 10, 2012, http://www.epi.org/publication/usa-lags-peer
-countries-mobility/; Alan B. Krueger, "The great utility of the Great Gatsby
Curve," Brookings Institution, May 19, 2015, https://www.brookings.edu
/blog/social-mobility-memos/2015/05/19/the-great-utility-of-the-great-gatsby
-curve/.

2. Todd Arrington, "Homesteading by the numbers," U.S. National Park Service,
April 24, 2007, https://www.nps.gov/home/learn/historyculture/bynumbers
.htm.

3. Jacob S. Hacker and Paul Pierson, *American Amnesia: How the War in Government Led Us to Forget What Made America Prosper* (New York: Simon &
Schuster, 2016), pp. 8, 338; Steven Pearlstein, "Social capital, corporate purpose and the revival of American capitalism," Brookings Institution, January
2014, https://www.brookings.edu/wp-content/uploads/2016/06/Brookings
Pearlsteinv5_Revised-Feb-2014.pdf; for increase in global labor market, see
"The global labour market: United workers of the world," *The Economist,* June
16, 2012, http://www.economist.com/node/21556974.

4. Greg Sargent, "Who is to blame for Hillary Clinton's loss? A lot of people
are—James Comey included," *The Washington Post,* April 23, 2017, https://
www.washingtonpost.com/blogs/plum-line/wp/2017/04/23/who-is-to-blame
-for-hillary-clintons-loss-a-lot-of-people-are-james-comey-included/?utm
_term=.77e5d3959c71; Robert Griffin, John Halpin, and Ruy Teixeira, "Demo-
crats need to be the party of and for working people—of all races," *The American
Prospect,* June 1, 2017, http://prospect.org/article/democrats-need-be-party-and
-working-people%E2%80%94-all-races; Sean McElwee, "Millennials are significantly more progressive than their parents," *The Washington Post,* March
24, 2016, https://www.washingtonpost.com/news/in-theory/wp/2016/03/24
/millennials-are-significantly-more-progressive-than-their-parents/?utm_term
=.e77b639a6c0e; Zach Goldhammer and Sarah Leonard, "The young Left and
the Democrats," *Democracy,* Spring 2017, pp. 30–31; Lynn Vavreck, "Why this
election was not about the issues," *The New York Times,* November 23, 2016,
https://www.nytimes.com/2016/11/23/upshot/this-election-was-not-about
-the-issues-blame-the-candidates.html.

5. *Report of the Commission on Inclusive Prosperity,* cochaired by Lawrence H. Summers and Ed Balls, Center for American Progress, January 2015, https://cdn
.americanprogress.org/wp-content/uploads/2015/01/IPC-PDF-full.pdf; Joseph

Stiglitz, *Rewriting the Rules of the American Economy: An Agenda for Growth and Shared Prosperity,* Roosevelt Institute, May 2015, http://rooseveltinstitute.org /rewriting-rules-report/; Stanley Greenberg, "The Democrats' 'working-class problem'," *American Prospect,* June 1, 2017, http://prospect.org/article/demo crats%E2%80%99-%E2%80%98working-class-problem%E2%80%99.

6. Arthur M. Schlesinger, Jr., *The Cycles of American History* (Boston: Mariner Books, 1999), p. 274; E.J. Dionne, Jr., "Political memo: Dukakis remains on course, dismissing polls and advice," *The New York Times,* July 11, 1988, http://www.nytimes.com/1988/07/11/us/political-memo-dukakis-remains-on -course-dismissing-polls-and-advice.html.

7. Ben Casselman, "Manufacturing jobs are never coming back," *FiveThirtyEight,* March 18, 2016, https://fivethirtyeight.com/features/manufacturing-jobs-are -never-coming-back/; Steve Dennis, "What if retail traffic declines last for-ever?" *Forbes,* February 16, 2017, https://www.forbes.com/sites/stevendennis /2017/02/16/what-if-retail-traffic-declines-last-forever/#698189d362c0; Derek Thompson, "The missing men," *The Atlantic,* June 27, 2016, https://www.the atlantic.com/business/archive/2016/06/the-missing-men/488858/; Richard V. Reeves, "The dangerous separation of the American upper middle class," Brookings Institution, September 3, 2015, https://www.brookings.edu/resea rch/the-dangerous-separation-of-the-american-upper-middle-class/; Dennis J. Snower, "The US' failure to provide vocational training is a massive policy fail-ure which supports Donald Trump," London School of Economics US Cen-tre, November 8, 2016, http://blogs.lse.ac.uk/usappblog/2016/11/08/the-us -failure-to-provide-vocational-training-is-a-massive-policy-failure-which-sup ports-donald-trump/.

8. Andy Stern, *Raising the Floor: How a Universal Basic Income Can Renew Our Economy and Rebuild the American Dream* (New York: PublicAffairs, 2016); Charles Murray, *In Our Hands: A Plan to Replace the Welfare State* (Washing-ton, DC: American Enterprise Institute Press, 2016); Henry Clay, "In defense of the American system," 1832, https://www.senate.gov/artandhistory/history /common/generic/Speeches_ClayAmericanSystem.htm; Jeff Spross, "You're hired!" *Democracy: A Journal of Ideas,* No. 44, Spring 2017, http://democracy journal.org/magazine/44/youre-hired/; Matthew Yglesias, "Silicon Valley's ba-sic income fans should spare a minute to defend the actual safety net," *Vox,* June 1, 2017, https://www.vox.com/policy-and-politics/2017/6/1/15694194 /silicon-valley-ubi; Jared Bernstein, "Is there an emerging democratic agenda?" *The New York Times,* June 5, 2017, https://www.nytimes.com/2017/06/05 /opinion/democratic-party-inequality-child-allowance.html?_r=0.

9. Remarks by Senator Sherrod Brown, "Working too hard for too little: A plan for restoring the value of work in America," March 3, 2017, https://www.brown .senate.gov/newsroom/press/release/brown-unveils-plan-to-restore-value-of -work-in-america; Office of Senator Kristen Gillibrand, *American Opportunity Agenda,* https://www.gillibrand.senate.gov/imo/media/doc/Gillibrand_Wom ens%20booklet.pdf; Remarks by Senator Elizabeth Warren, "Strengthening the basic bargain for workers in the modern economy," New America Annual Conference, May 19, 2016, https://www.warren.senate.gov/files/documents /2016-5-19_Warren_New_America_Remarks.pdf.

10. Michael R. Strain, "A new jobs agenda," *National Review,* June 3, 2013, https://www.nationalreview.com/nrd/articles/348502/new-jobs-agenda; AEI/Brookings Working Group on Poverty and Opportunity, *Opportu-nity, Responsibility, and Security: A Consensus Plan for Reducing Poverty and Restoring the American Dream* (Washington, DC: American Enterprise In-stitute for Public Policy Research and the Brookings Institution, 2015), https://www.brookings.edu/wp-content/uploads/2016/07/Full-Report.pdf;

for current uninsured rate, see Robert Pear, "G.O.P. Health Bill would leave 23 million more uninsured in a decade, C.B.O. says," *The New York Times,* May 24, 2017, https://www.nytimes.com/2017/05/24/us/politics/cbo-congres sional-budget-office-health-care.html?mcubz=1; Ezra Klein, "Republicans are about to make Medicare-for-all much more likely," *Vox,* June 15, 2017, https:// www.vox.com/policy-and-politics/2017/6/15/15787626/mitch-mcconnell -single-payer-medicare-all.

11. For "supporting the police," see remarks by President Trump at the National Rifle Association Leadership Forum, April 28, 2017, https://www.whitehouse .gov/the-press-office/2017/04/28/remarks-president-trump-national-rifle -association-leadership-forum; for Sessions's actions on criminal justice reform, see Sari Horwitz, Mark Berman, and Wesley Lowery, "Sessions orders Justice Department to review all police reform agreements," *The Washington Post,* April 3, 2017, https://www.washingtonpost.com/world/national-security/ses sions-orders-justice-department-to-review-all-police-reform-agreements/2017 /04/03/ba934058-18bd-11e7-9887-1a5314b56a08_story.html?tid=a_inl&utm _term=.dafb5a1c8837.

12. Suzanne Mettler, *Soldiers to Citizens: The G.I. Bill and the Making of the Greatest Generation* (New York: Oxford University Press, 2005), pp. 6–7, 11.

13. Steven Pearlstein, "Businesses' focus on maximizing shareholder value has numerous costs," *The Washington Post,* September 6, 2013, https://www .washingtonpost.com/business/economy/businesses-focus-on-maximizing -shareholder-value-has-numerous-costs/2013/09/05/bcdc664e-045f-11e3-a07f -49ddc7417125_story.html?utm_term=.175fb3d0ae0c; William A. Galston and Elaine C. Kamarck, "More builders and fewer traders: A growth strategy for the American economy," Brookings Institution, June 2015, https://www .brookings.edu/wp-content/uploads/2016/06/CEPMGlastonKarmarck4.pdf.

14. For criticism of Clinton's platform, see Todd S. Purdum, "How Hillary could win the election—and lose the country," *Politico,* May 1, 2016, http://www .politico.com/magazine/story/2016/04/how-hillary-could-win-the-electio nand-lose-the-country-213852; Bureau of Labor Statistics, "Unemployment rate," https://data.bls.gov/timeseries/LNS14000000.

CHAPTER EIGHT

1. "Boston marathon terror attack fast facts," *CNN,* March 29, 2017, http://www .cnn.com/2013/06/03/us/boston-marathon-terror-attack-fast-facts/; Michael Lind, "The case for American nationalism," *The National Interest,* May 17, 2015, http://nationalinterest.org/feature/the-case-american-nationalism-103 28; George Orwell, "Notes on nationalism," in *The Collected Essays, Journalism and Letters of George Orwell, Volume III: As I Please 1943–1945,* ed. Sonia Orwell and Ian Angus (London: Penguin Books, 1970), p. 411.

2. For Yascha Mounk's quotes, see Chicago Council on Global Affairs, "Democracy in retreat," YouTube, April 11, 2017, https://www.youtube.com/watch ?v=uz-xL2xM3Mc&t=4308s [Video].

3. Remarks by Franklin Roosevelt to the Daughters of the American Revolution, April 21, 1938, retrieved from the American Presidency Project, http://www .presidency.ucsb.edu/ws/?pid=15631.

4. Mona Charen, "Patriotism not nationalism," *National Review,* February 17, 2017, http://www.nationalreview.com/article/445004/national-reviews-nation alism-debate; Jonah Goldberg, "The trouble with nationalism," *National Review,* February 7, 2017, http://www.nationalreview.com/article/444694/nati onalism-patriotism-donald-trump-response-national-review-cover-story.

5. Krishnadev Calamur, "A short history of 'America First,'" *The Atlantic,* January 21, 2017, https://www.theatlantic.com/politics/archive/2017/01/trump-amer ica-first/514037/; for Hillel's quote, see Melissa Kansky, "'If I am not for myself, who will be for me?' A discussion for developing a practice of self-care," *Hillel International,* February 28, 2017, http://www.hillel.org/about/news-views /news-views—blog/news-and-views/2017/02/28/-if-i-am-not-for-myself-who -will-be-for-me-a-discussion-for-developing-a-practice-of-self-care; The White House, "Statement by President Trump on the Paris Climate Accord," June 1, 2017, https://www.whitehouse.gov/the-press-office/2017/06/01/statement -president-trump-paris-climate-accord; Richard Hofstadter, "The paranoid style in American politics," *Harper's Magazine,* November 1964, https://harpers .org/archive/1964/11/the-paranoid-style-in-american-politics/.

6. Mara Liasson, "5 Takeaways from Trump's first foreign trip as president," *NPR,* May 27, 2017, http://www.npr.org/2017/05/27/530297900/5-takeaways-from -trumps-first-foreign-trip-as-president; David Sanger and Maggie Haberman, "Trump praises Duterte for Philippine drug crackdown in call transcript," *The New York Times,* May 23, 2017, https://www.nytimes.com/2017/05/23 /us/politics/trump-duterte-phone-transcript-philippine-drug-crackdown .html?mcubz=1; for Max Boot's quote, see *The Last Word with Lawrence O'Donnell,* "Why Trump gave up 'leader of free world,'" *MSNBC,* June 2, 2017, http://www.msnbc.com/the-last-word; Michael Birnbaum and Damian Paletta, "At G-20, world aligns against Trump policies ranging from free trade to climate change," *Washington Post* (July 7, 2017). https://www.washingtonpost .com/amphtml/world/at-g-20-eu-warns-of-trade-war-if-trump-imposes -restrictions-on-steel/2017/07/07/0ffae390–62f4–11e7-a6c7-f769fa1d5691 _story.html.

7. Remarks by Stephen Bannon at the 2017 Conservative Political Action Conference; "How to address the EU's democratic deficit," *The Economist,* March 23, 2017, http://www.economist.com/news/special-report/21719196-institutions -need-reform-how-address-eus-democratic-deficit; *Reuters,* "Britain's Johnson says Brexit means taking back control of immigration," published in *Business Insider,* December 1, 2016, http://www.businessinsider.com/r-britains-johnson -says-brexit-means-taking-back-control-of-immigration-2016-12.

8. Kwame Anthony Appiah, *Cosmopolitanism: Ethics in a World of Strangers* (New York: W. W. Norton, 2006), p. xv; for "neighborhood people," see Andrew M. Greeley, *Love Affair: A Prayer Journal,* excerpted for *Spirituality & Practice: Resources for Spiritual Journeys,* http://www.spiritualityandpractice.com/book -reviews/excerpts/view/14219; Andy Beckett, "From Trump to Brexit, power has leaked from cities to the countryside," *The Guardian,* December 12, 2016, https://www.theguardian.com/commentisfree/2016/dec/12/trump-brexit -cities-countryside-rural-voters.

9. For "tradition" and racism, see Bruce Levine, "The Confederate flag was always racist," *Politico,* June 27, 2015, http://www.politico.com/magazine/story /2015/06/confederate-flag-always-racist-119481; for "tradition" and gay marriage, see Garrett Epps, "Is there any rational case for banning gay marriage?" *The Atlantic,* September 4, 2014, https://www.theatlantic.com/politics/archive /2014/09/posner-gay-marriage/379667/; Karl Marx and Friedrich Engels, *The Communist Manifesto,* 1848, https://www.marxists.org/archive/marx/works /download/pdf/Manifesto.pdf.

10. Michael Walzer, *The Company of Critics: Social Criticism and Political Commitment in the Twentieth Century* (New York: Basic Books, 2002), p. 16; James T. Kloppenberg, *Toward Democracy: The Struggle for Self-Rule in European and American Thought* (New York: Oxford University Press, 2016), p. 709.

11. Sari Horwitz, Mark Berman, and Wesley Lowery, "Sessions orders Justice Department to review all police reform agreements," *The Washington Post,* April 3, 2017, https://www.washingtonpost.com/world/national-security/sessions-orders-justice-department-to-review-all-police-reform-agreements/2017/04/03/ba934058-18bd-11e7-9887-1a5314b56a08_story.html?tid=a_inl&utm_term=.dafb5a1c8837; Jeremy W. Peters, Jo Becker, and Julie Hirschfeld Davis, "Trump rescinds rules on bathrooms for transgender students," *The New York Times,* February 22, 2017, https://www.nytimes.com/2017/02/22/us/politics/devos-sessions-transgender-students-rights.html; Dietrich Bonhoeffer, *Witness to Jesus Christ,* ed. John W. De Gruchy (Minneapolis, MN: Fortress Press, 1991), p. 262; Martin Luther King, Jr., "I have a dream" speech, August 28, 1963, retrieved from the Martin Luther King, Jr., Research and Education Institute at Stanford University, https://kinginstitute.stanford.edu/king-papers/documents/i-have-dream-address-delivered-march-washington-jobs-and-freedom.

CHAPTER NINE

1. Kai T. Erikson, *Everything in Its Path: Destruction of Community in the Buffalo Creek Flood* (New York: Simon & Schuster, 1976), pp. 193–194; Entry: "Communis," *Cassell's Latin Dictionary* (London: Cassell, 1897), p. 112; Daron Acemoglu, "We are the last defense against Trump," *Foreign Policy,* January 18, 2017, http://foreignpolicy.com/2017/01/18/we-are-the-last-defense-against-trump-institutions/.

2. Gallup, "Confidence in institutions," June 26, 2017, http://www.gallup.com/poll/1597/confidence-institutions.aspx; Rob Goodman, "What the king of Hawaii can teach us about Trump," *Politico,* January 4, 2017, http://www.politico.com/magazine/story/2017/01/what-trump-taught-us-about-american-democracy-214596; Ganesh Sitaraman, *The Crisis of the Middle-Class Constitution: Why Economic Inequality Threatens Our Republic* (New York: Alfred A. Knopf, 2017), p. 9; for figure on trust in each other, see Josh Morgan, "The decline of trust in the United States: A look at the trend and what can be done about it," *Medium,* May 20, 2014, https://medium.com/@monarchjogs/the-decline-of-trust-in-the-united-states-fb8ab719b82a.

3. Robert D. Putnam, *Bowling Alone: The Collapse and Revival of American Community* (New York: Simon & Schuster, 2000); Robert A. Nisbet, *Tradition and Revolt* (New Brunswick: Transaction, 1999), p. 132; William Kornhauser, *The Politics of Mass Society* (New York: Routledge, reprint 2010), p. 73.

4. Yoni Appelbaum, "Why Donald Trump supporters are voting alone," *The Atlantic,* April 7, 2016, https://www.theatlantic.com/politics/archive/2016/04/voting-alone/477270/.

5. Bill Bishop, *The Big Sort: Why the Clustering of Like-Minded America Is Tearing Us Apart* (New York: Mariner Books, 2009); David Wasserman, "Purple America has all but disappeared," *FiveThirtyEight,* March 8, 2017, https://fivethirtyeight.com/features/purple-america-has-all-but-disappeared/; J. D. Vance, *Hillbilly Elegy: A Memoir of a Family and Culture in Crisis* (New York: HarperCollins, 2016).

6. Edmund Burke, *Reflections on the Revolution in France* (London: Everyman's Library, 1971), p. 44; U.S. Immigrations and Customs Enforcement, Memorandum on Enforcement Actions at or Focused on Sensitive Locations, 2011, https://www.ice.gov/doclib/ero-outreach/pdf/10029.2-policy.pdf; Elizabeth Evans and Yonat Shimron, "'Sanctuary churches' vow to shield immigrants

from Trump crackdown," *Religion News Service,* November 18, 2016, http://religionnews.com/2016/11/18/sanctuary-churches-vow-to-shield-immigrants-from-trump-crackdown/.

7. Jonathan Roos, "I'm a rabbi. Here's why my congregation offers sanctuary to undocumented immigrants," *The Washington Post,* April 14, 2017, https://www.washingtonpost.com/opinions/im-a-rabbi-heres-why-my-congregation-offers-sanctuary-to-undocumented-immigrants/2017/04/14/6109eb28-1ad8-11e7-9887-1a5314b56a08_story.html?utm_term=.a8c7617528d3; Madeline Farber, "Chicago's archbishop calls President Trump's immigration order 'a dark moment in U.S. history,'" *Time,* January 29, 2017, http://time.com/4652942/chicago-archbishop-donald-trump-immigration-ban/; Craig McCarthy, "Trump's anti-immigration orders are 'inhuman,' says Newark archbishop," *NJ.com,* January 28, 2017, http://www.nj.com/essex/index.ssf/2017/01/archbishop_of_newark_anti-immigration_orders_are_i.html; Brian Roewe, "In powerful speech, San Diego bishop challenges organizers to disrupt, rebuild," *National Catholic Reporter,* February 19, 2017, https://www.ncronline.org/news/justice/powerful-speech-san-diego-bishop-challenges-organizers-disrupt-rebuild.

8. For the letter from Catholic law school deans, see http://www.stthomas.edu/media/schooloflaw/pdf/catholiclawschooldeanslettertoLSC.pdf; for Matthew 25 Pledge, see Jim Wallis, "We've got a month until Inauguration Day. Here's what we can do right now," *Sojourners,* December 15, 2016, https://sojo.net/articles/weve-got-month-until-inauguration-day-heres-what-we-can-do-right-now; for Circle of Protection, see http://circleofprotection.us/; for Rev. Barber, see Bruce Henderson, "He made Moral Mondays a weekly jab at GOP. Now he's headed to a national stage," *The Charlotte Observer,* May 11, 2017, http://www.charlotteobserver.com/news/local/article149945162.html.

9. Barbara Demick, "How Trump's policies and rhetoric are forging alliances between U.S. Jews and Muslims," *Los Angeles Times,* February 5, 2017, http://www.latimes.com/nation/la-na-jew-muslim-2017-story.html; Ruth Graham, "Why Hillary Clinton bombed with white evangelical voters," *Slate,* December 15, 2016, http://www.slate.com/articles/news_and_politics/politics/2016/12/why_hillary_clinton_bombed_with_evangelical_voters.html; Marcia Tavares Maack, "A pro bono groundswell after Trump's immigration order (perspective)," *Bloomberg Law,* February 28, 2017, https://bol.bna.com/a-pro-bono-groundswell-after-trumps-immigration-order-perspective/; for Painter and Eisen's work, see David A. Fahrenthold and Jonathan O'Connell, "Two plaintiffs join suit against Trump, alleging breach of emoluments clause," *The Washington Post,* April 17, 2017, https://www.washingtonpost.com/politics/two-plaintiffs-join-suit-against-trump-alleging-breach-of-emoluments-clause/2017/04/17/1d4aaa70-238a-11e7-a1b3-faff0034e2de_story.html?utm_term=.e6d68109ec30.

10. For a summary of arguments in favor of and against place-based policymaking, see Edward L. Glaeser and Joshua D. Gottlieb, "The economics of place-making policies," *Brookings Papers on Economic Activity,* Vol. 2008 (Spring 2008), pp. 155–239; for the North Carolina Research Triangle, see National Research Council, "Annex B: North Carolina's Research Triangle Park," *Best Practices in State and Regional Innovation Initiatives: Competing in the 21st Century,* ed. Charles W. Wessner (Washington, DC: The National Academies Press, 2013), pp. 229–240.

11. For details on Obama administration place-based policymaking, see the White House Office of Urban Affairs, "Neighborhood Revitalization Initiative," https://obamawhitehouse.archives.gov/administration/eop/oua/initiatives/neighborhood-revitalization; for Promise Zones, see the White House Office

of the Press Secretary, "Fact sheet: President Obama's Promise Zones Initiative," January 8, 2014, https://obamawhitehouse.archives.gov/the-press -office/2014/01/08/fact-sheet-president-obama-s-promise-zones-initiative; for Mission Promise Neighborhood, see Raquel Donoso, "President Obama's legacy of success: Neighborhoods of opportunity," Mission Promise Neighborhood Blog, January 18, 2017, https://missionpromise.org/president-obamas -legacy-success-neighborhoods-opportunity/; for Indianapolis Promise Zone, see the White House Office of the Press Secretary, "Obama administration announces final round of Promise Zone designations to expand access to opportunity in urban, rural and tribal communities," June 6, 2016, https:// obamawhitehouse.archives.gov/the-press-office/2016/06/06/obama-admin istration-announces-final-round-promise-zone-designations.

12. John M. Bridgeland, *Heart of the Nation: Volunteering and America's Civic Spirit* (Lanham, MD: Rowman & Littlefield, 2013); Leslie Lenkowsky and James L. Perry, "Reinventing government: The case of national service," *Public Administration Review*, Vol. 60, No. 4, July/August 2000, pp. 298–307; for Service Year Alliance goals, see https://serviceyear.org/serviceyearalliance/; for McChrystal's quote, see E. J. Dionne, Jr., "A call for national service," *The Washington Post*, July 3, 2013, https://www.washingtonpost.com/opinions/ej -dionne-jr-a-call-for-national-service/2013/07/03/a65bce5a-e402-11e2-a11e -c2ea876a8f30_story.html?utm_term=.4f90bc7707d1.

13. Gregory Wallace, "Proposed budget cuts for 2017 include AIDS, AmeriCorps programs," *CNN*, March 30, 2017, http://www.cnn.com/2017/03/29/politics /donald-trump-budget-cuts/; Jake Rosenfeld, Patrick Denice, and Jennifer Laird, "Union decline lowers wages of nonunion workers," Economic Policy Institute, August 30, 2016, http://www.epi.org/publication/union-decline-low ers-wages-of-nonunion-workers-the-overlooked-reason-why-wages-are-stuck -and-inequality-is-growing/.

14. Reuben Jacobson, "Community schools: A place-based approach to education and neighborhood change," Brookings Institution, November 2016, https:// www.brookings.edu/wp-content/uploads/2016/11/jacobson-final-layout-pub lished-11-16-16.pdf; James Fallows, "Eleven signs a city will succeed," *The Atlantic*, February 8, 2016, https://www.theatlantic.com/amp/article/426885/; for community colleges and civic engagement, see Carol Jeandron and Gail Robinson, *Creating a Climate for Service Learning Success*, American Association of Community Colleges, 2010, http://www.aacc.nche.edu/Resources/aacc programs/horizons/Documents/creatingaclimate_082010.pdf; American Association of Community Colleges, *Where Value Meets Values: The Economic Impact of Community Colleges*, February 2014, http://www.aacc.nche.edu /About/Documents/USA_AGG_MainReport_Final_021114.pdf; Harry Holzer, "Higher Education and Workforce Policy: Creating more skilled workers (and jobs for them to fill)," Brookings Institution, April 2015, https://www .brookings.edu/wp-content/uploads/2016/06/higher_ed_jobs_policy_holzer .pdf.

15. Theda Skocpol, "United States: From membership to advocacy," in *Democracies in Flux: The Evolution of Social Capital in Contemporary Society*, ed. Robert D. Putnam (New York: Oxford University Press, 2002), pp. 103–136; Anna O. Law, "This is how Trump's deportations differ from Obama's," *The Washington Post*, May 3, 2017, https://www.washingtonpost.com/news/monkey-cage /wp/2017/05/03/this-is-how-trumps-deportations-differ-from-obamas/?utm _term=.b83dcc877812; Priscilla Alvarez, "Trump ditches his promise to 'terminate' DACA," *The Atlantic*, June 16, 2017, https://www.theatlantic.com /politics/archive/2017/06/trump-dreamers-campaign-pledge/530598/.

CHAPTER TEN

1. Rustin quoted in Michael G. Long, "Bayard Rustin in his own words: 'I must resist,'" *The Huffington Post Blog*, February 2, 2016, http://www.huffington post.com/michael-g-long/bayard-rustin-in-his-own_b_2881057.html; Molly Ivins, *You Got to Dance with Them What Brung You* (New York: First Vintage Books, 1999), p. 81; U.S. Bill of Rights, Amendment I.

2. Brennan Center for Justice at New York University School of Law, "New voting restrictions in America," https://www.brennancenter.org/new-voting-restri ctions-america; Sari Horwitz, "Getting a photo ID so you can vote is easy. Unless you're poor, black, Latino or elderly," *The Washington Post*, May 23, 2016, https://www.washingtonpost.com/politics/courts_law/getting-a-photo-id -so-you-can-vote-is-easy-unless-youre-poor-black-latino-or-elderly/2016 /05/23/8d5474ec-20f0-11e6-8690-f14ca9de2972_story.html?utm_term=.df 9315468cff; Rene Marsh, "DOT launches investigation in Alabama over DMV closures," *CNN*, December 9, 2015, http://www.cnn.com/2015/12/09/politics /alabama-dmv-closures-voting-rights/; Manny Fernandez, "Federal judge says Texas voter ID law intentionally discriminates," *The New York Times*, April 10, 2017, https://www.nytimes.com/2017/04/10/us/federal-judge-strikes-down -texas-voter-id-law.html?_r=0; Robert Barnes and Ann E. Marimow, "Appeals court strikes down North Carolina's voter-ID law," *The Washington Post*, July 29, 2016, https://www.washingtonpost.com/local/public-safety/appeals-court -strikes-down-north-carolinas-voter-id-law/2016/07/29/810b5844-4f72-11e6 -aa14-e0c1087f7583_story.html?utm_term=.2680a7f97427.

3. Ari Berman, "A big win for voting rights in Texas and a big loss for Trump," *The Nation*, April 11, 2017, https://www.thenation.com/article/a-big-win-for -voting-rights-in-texas-and-a-big-loss-for-trump/; "Debunking the voter fraud myth," Brennan Center for Justice, January 31, 2017, http://www.brennan center.org/analysis/debunking-voter-fraud-myth; Tomas Lopez and Jennifer L. Clark, "Uncovering Kris Kobach's anti-voting history," Brennan Center for Justice, May 11, 2017, https://www.brennancenter.org/blog/uncovering-kris -kobach%E2%80%99s-anti-voting-history; Julie Hirschfeld Davis, "Trump picks voter ID advocate for election fraud panel," *The New York Times*, May 11, 2017, https://www.nytimes.com/2017/05/11/us/politics/trump-voter-fraud .html?mcubz=1; Ari Berman, "The Trump administration's voter-suppression plans are backfiring," *The Nation*, July 5, 2017, https://www.thenation.com /article/the-trump-administrations-voter-suppression-plans-are-backfiring -badly/; Jaime Fuller, "How has voting changed since *Shelby County v. Holder?*" *The Washington Post*, July 7, 2014, https://www.washingtonpost.com/news /the-fix/2014/07/07/how-has-voting-changed-since-shelby-county-v -holder/?utm_term=.aacfa75b3b66.

4. Selena Simmons-Duffin, "Why are elections on Tuesdays?" *NPR Morning Edition*, October 23, 2012, http://www.npr.org/sections/itsallpolitics/2012/10 /23/162484410/why-are-elections-on-tuesdays; for Bauer and Ginsberg recommendations, see *The American Voting Experience: Report and Recommendations of the Presidential Commission on Election Administration*, January 2014, http:// electionlawblog.org/wp-content/uploads/pcea-final-report.pdf; Stuart Stevens, July 5, 2017 [Tweet]; Pew Charitable Trusts, "Use of vote centers on the rise nationwide," January 15, 2015, http://www.pewtrusts.org/en/research-and -analysis/analysis/2015/01/15/use-of-vote-centers-on-the-rise-nationwide; for discussion of how U.S. election procedures compare to those in other mature democracies, see Pippa Norris, "Why American elections are flawed (and how to fix them)," Harvard Kennedy School Faculty Research Working Paper

series, September 2016, https://research.hks.harvard.edu/publications/getFile
.aspx?Id=1431.

5. Nick Harmsen, "Why do we have compulsory voting?" *Australian Broadcasting Corporation,* June 6, 2016, http://www.abc.net.au/news/2016-06-07/why
-do-we-have-compulsory-voting/7484390.

6. John Templon, "How the Electoral College favors white voters," *BuzzFeed,*
November 7, 2016, https://www.buzzfeed.com/johntemplon/how-the-electoral
-college-screws-hispanic-and-asian-voters?utm_term=.otL5d7jELK#.vcMgPR
28rb; for criticism of "faithless electors," see Robert Alexander, "'Faithless
electors'—not Electoral College—cause voter suppression," *The Hill,* January 3, 2017, http://thehill.com/blogs/pundits-blog/presidential-campaign/31
2549-faithless-electors-not-the-electoral-college-are.

7. Michael Barone, "The Electoral College prevents California from imposing imperial rule on the country," *National Review,* December 6, 2016, http://www
.nationalreview.com/article/442783/electoral-college-california-rules-america
-without-constitutions-system; David Wasserman, "2016 National Popular Vote
Tracker," *Cook Political Report,* https://docs.google.com/spreadsheets/d/1PV
-jK0kov7-w-xuj6DhyL7gP9VGKIv0-c_hY0UN1Un0/edit; for discussion of nationwide recount, see Trent England, "Eliminating the Electoral College would
corrupt our elections," *U.S. News and World Report,* October 1, 2012, https://
www.usnews.com/opinion/articles/2012/10/01/eliminating-the-electoral-col
lege-would-corrupt-our-elections; for National Popular Vote Interstate Compact, see Mark Joseph Stern, "Yes, we could effectively abolish the Electoral
College soon. But we probably won't," *Slate,* November 10, 2016, http://www
.slate.com/blogs/the_slatest/2016/11/10/the_electoral_college_could_be
_abolished_without_an_amendment.html.

8. Aaron Blake, "Why you should stop blaming gerrymandering so much. Really," *The Washington Post,* April 8, 2017, https://www.washingtonpost.com
/news/the-fix/wp/2017/04/08/why-you-should-stop-blaming-gerrymander
ing-so-much-really/?utm_term=.775d646d4ae2; Ryan D. Williamson, Michael Crespin, Maxwell Palmer, and Barry C. Edwards, "This is how to get
rid of gerrymandered districts," *The Washington Post,* March 17, 2017, https://
www.washingtonpost.com/news/monkey-cage/wp/2017/03/17/this-will-get
-rid-of-gerrymandered-districts/?utm_term=.d436a5843be3; Alexander Burns
and Jonathan Martin, "Eric Holder to lead Democrats' attack on Republican
gerrymandering," *The New York Times,* January 11, 2017, https://www.ny
times.com/2017/01/11/us/eric-holder-to-lead-democrats-attack-on-republican
-gerrymandering.html; for *Gill v. Whitford,* see Adam Liptak, "When does political gerrymandering cross a constitutional line," *The New York Times,* May
15, 2017, https://www.nytimes.com/2017/05/15/us/politics/when-does-politi
cal-gerrymandering-cross-a-constitutional-line.html.

9. Adam Liptak, "Justices to hear major challenge to partisan gerrymandering,"
The New York Times, June 19, 2017, https://www.nytimes.com/2017/06/19
/us/politics/justices-to-hear-major-challenge-to-partisan-gerrymandering
.html?smprod=nytcore-iphone&smid=nytcore-iphone-share; for Kennedy
on partisan gerrymandering, see Ed Kilgore, "Federal Court opens the door
to restrictions on partisan gerrymandering," *New York Magazine,* November
23, 2016, http://nymag.com/daily/intelligencer/2016/11/court-opens-door-to
-restrictions-on-partisan-gerrymandering.html; for a description of Illinois's
multimember districts, see Pietro Nivola and William G. Galston, "Toward
depolarization," in *Red and Blue Nation?* Vol. 2, ed. Pietro Nivola and David
W. Brady (Washington, DC: Brookings Institution Press, 2008), pp. 266–
267; Thomas F. Schaller, "Multi-member districts: Just a thing of the past?"

Sabato's CrystalBall, March 21, 2013, http://www.centerforpolitics.org/crystalball/articles/multi-member-legislative-districts-just-a-thing-of-the-past/.

10. For Gang of Fourteen, see Sheryl Gay Stolberg, "Swing senators face new test in Supreme Court fight," *The New York Times,* July 14, 2005, http://www.nytimes.com/2005/07/14/us/swing-senators-face-new-test-in-supreme-court-fight.html; Josh Chafetz, "The filibuster was already doomed before the nuclear option vote," *The Washington Post,* April 6, 2017, https://www.washingtonpost.com/posteverything/wp/2017/04/06/the-filibuster-was-already-doomed-before-the-nuclear-option-vote/?utm_term=.2d5e532c6a7d; Aaron Blake, "Frustrated by failures, Trump now demands more power," *The Washington Post,* May 2, 2017, https://www.washingtonpost.com/news/the-fix/wp/2017/04/29/trump-is-now-talking-about-consolidating-his-own-power/?utm_term=.ddd0dd532961.

11. For Trump's proposals for civil servants, see Joe Davidson, "Trump plans to fire feds faster," *The Washington Post,* November 21, 2016, https://www.washingtonpost.com/news/powerpost/wp/2016/11/21/trump-plans-to-fire-feds-faster/?utm_term=.e9d00b6da758; for "kakistocracy," see Paul Krugman, "With all due respect," *The New York Times,* January 16, 2017, https://www.nytimes.com/2017/01/16/opinion/with-all-due-disrespect.html.

12. Daniel Hensel, "New poll shows money in politics is a top voting concern," Issue One, June 29, 2016, https://www.issueone.org/new-poll-shows-money-in-politics-is-a-top-voting-concern/; Center for Responsive Politics, "Cost of election," https://www.opensecrets.org/overview/cost.php; Center for Responsive Politics, "Political nonprofits (dark money)," https://www.opensecrets.org/outsidespending/nonprof_summ.php; Ann M. Ravel, "Dysfunction and deadlock at the Federal Election Commission," *The New York Times,* February 20, 2017, https://www.nytimes.com/2017/02/20/opinion/dysfunction-and-deadlock-at-the-federal-election-commission.html; Eric Lichtblau, "I.R.S. expected to stand aside as nonprofits increase role in 2016 race," *The New York Times,* July 5, 2015, https://www.nytimes.com/2015/07/06/us/politics/irs-expected-to-stand-aside-as-nonprofits-increase-role-in-2016-race.html.

13. Senator Tom Udall, "Udall introduces constitutional amendment to overturn Citizens United and get big money out of politics," January 24, 2017, https://www.tomudall.senate.gov/news/press-releases/udall-introduces-constitutional-amendment-to-overturn-citizens-united-and-get-big-money-out-of-politics; Democracy 21, "Summary of Empowering Citizens Act," January 21, 2015, http://www.democracy21.org/legislative-action/press-releases-legislative-action/summary-of-empowering-citizens-act/; Jon Schwarz, "Rep. John Sarbanes and a campaign finance reform plan that might actually work," *The Intercept,* July 8, 2015, https://theintercept.com/2015/07/08/part-rep-john-sarbanes-government-people-act/; Pamela L. Finmark and William D. Chalmers, "'Patriot dollars' to reform politics," *Los Angeles Times,* January 5, 2009, http://www.latimes.com/la-oe-chalmers5-2009jan05-story.html; Russell Berman, "Seattle's experiment with campaign funding," *The Atlantic,* November 10, 2015, https://www.theatlantic.com/politics/archive/2015/11/seattle-experiments-with-campaign-funding/415026/; "*Buckley v. Valeo,*" Oyez, https://www.oyez.org/cases/1975/75-436.

14. Cass R. Sunstein, *#republic: Divided Democracy in the Age of Social Media* (Princeton, NJ: Princeton University Press, 2017), pp. ix, 216–229; for Zuckerberg's quote, see Hannah Boland, "Facebook shareholders reject fake news proposal," *The Telegraph,* June 1, 2017, http://www.telegraph.co.uk/technology/2017/06/01/facebook-shareholders-reject-fake-news-proposal/; Christopher Lasch, "Journalism, publicity and the lost art of argument," *Gannett*

Center Journal, Spring 1990, pp. 1–11; Daniel Ziblatt, *Conservative Parties and the Birth of Democracy* (New York: Cambridge University Press, 2017).

CHAPTER ELEVEN

1. "President Obama farewell address: full text," *CNN,* January 11, 2017, http://www.cnn.com/2017/01/10/politics/president-obama-farewell-speech/.

2. Kaveh Waddell, "The exhausting work of tallying America's largest protest," *The Atlantic,* January 23, 2017, https://www.theatlantic.com/technology/ar chive/2017/01/womens-march-protest-count/514166/; Donald J. Trump, "Professional anarchists, thugs and paid protesters are proving the point of the millions of people who voted to MAKE AMERICA GREAT AGAIN!" February 3, 2017 [Tweet]; E. J. Dionne, Jr., "The Women's March was a stand against complacency," *The Washington Post,* January 21, 2017, https://www.washingtonpost .com/blogs/post-partisan/wp/2017/01/21/the-womens-march-was-a-stand-ag ainst-complacency/?utm_term=.4caee0d647bd.

3. Mike Isaac, "Uber C.E.O. to leave Trump Advisory Council after criticism," *The New York Times,* February 2, 2017, https://www.nytimes.com/2017/02 /02/technology/uber-ceo-travis-kalanick-trump-advisory-council.html; for "wrong and unjust," see Aimee Rawlins, "Uber pushes back on Trump's order after #DeleteUber starts trending," *CNN,* January 29, 2017, http://money .cnn.com/2017/01/29/technology/uber-lyft-trump-muslim-ban/; Leslie Hook, "Uber loses ground in US as rival Lyft accelerates," *Financial Times,* June 19, 2017, https://www.ft.com/content/b4fb76a6-52dd-11e7-bfb8-997009366969; Amber Jamieson, "Tax March: How a law professor sparked a global event to demand Trump's returns," *The Guardian,* April 12, 2017, https://www.the guardian.com/us-news/2017/apr/12/tax-march-trump-tax-returns-activism -jennifer-taub; Joel Achenbach, Ben Guarino, and Sarah Kaplan, "Why people are marching for science: 'There is no planet B,'" *The Washington Post,* April 22, 2017, https://www.washingtonpost.com/national/health-science/big-turn out-expected-for-march-for-science-in-dc/2017/04/21/67cf7f90-237f-11e7 -bb9d-8cd6118e1409_story.html?utm_term=.d1f2746d777f; Nicholas Fandos, "Climate March draws thousands of protesters alarmed by Trump's environmental agenda," *The New York Times,* April 29, 2017, https://www.nytimes .com/2017/04/29/us/politics/peoples-climate-march-trump.html.

4. Trip Gabriel, Thomas Kaplan, Lizette Alvarez, and Emmarie Huetteman, "At town halls, doses of fury and a bottle of Tums," *The New York Times,* February 21, 2017, https://www.nytimes.com/2017/02/21/us/politics/town-hall-protests -obamacare.html; Charles M. Blow, "Resilience of the resistance," *The New York Times,* April 24, 2017, https://www.nytimes.com/2017/04/24/opinion/resil ience-of-the-resistance-donald-trump.html; Wilson Andrews, Matthew Bloch, and Haeyoun Park, "Who stopped the Republican Health Bill?" *The New York Times,* March 24, 2017, https://www.nytimes.com/interactive/2017/03/24/us /politics/republicans-opposed-health-care-bill.html; Scott Detrow, "Hostile town hall for congressman who helped save GOP Health Care Bill," *NPR Morning Edition,* May 11, 2017, http://www.npr.org/2017/05/11/527895032 /gop-representative-faces-constituents-angry-over-russia-and-health-care; Grace Hauck, Liz Stark, Gabby Deutch, and Emily Karl, "Activists protest GOP health care bill on Capitol Hill," *CNN,* June 28, 2017, http://www.cnn .com/2017/06/28/politics/capitol-hill-protest-planned-parenthood-health -care-bill/index.html.

5. Herb Scribner, "Kathryn Allen is the underdog running against Chaffetz. See why she's suddenly on the rise," *Deseret News,* March 8, 2017, http://

www.deseretnews.com/article/865675117/Kathryn-Allen-is-the-underdog -running-against-Chaffetz-See-why-shes-suddenly-on-the-rise.html; Elise Viebeck, "Chaffetz will leave behind Oversight panel he used to investigate Obama White House," *The Washington Post*, April 19, 2017, https://www .washingtonpost.com/politics/jason-chaffetz-announces-he-wont-run-for-of fice-in-2018/2017/04/19/aad10c75-1200-483c-8d7f-16f2a996866d_story .html?utm_term=.4826134fa823; John Cassidy, "The Trump resistance: A progress report," *The New Yorker*, April 17, 2017, http://www.newyorker.com /news/john-cassidy/the-trump-resistance-a-progress-report.

6. *Indivisible Guide,* https://www.indivisibleguide.com/; Michael Alison Chandler, "Capitol Hill mom directs thousands of anti-Trump activists with texts sent from her living room," *The Washington Post,* January 28, 2017, https:// www.washingtonpost.com/local/social-issues/a-capitol-hill-mom-directs -thousands-of-anti-trump-activists-by-sending-texts-from-her-living-room /2017/01/27/cf0538f2-e447-11e6-a547-5fb9411d332c_story.html?utm _term=.857321e7f026; Eric Liu, "A cure for post-election malaise," *The Atlantic,* December 10, 2016, https://www.theatlantic.com/politics/archive/2016 /12/the-cure-for-post-election-malaise/509807/.

7. For the relevance of the 2018 election, see Jennifer Rubin, "What stops Republicans from behaving rationally," *The Washington Post,* June 13, 2017, https:// www.washingtonpost.com/blogs/right-turn/wp/2017/06/13/what-stops-re publicans-from-behaving-rationally/?utm_term=.3a11ff011f1b; for La Guardia, see William H. Honan, "Mayor goes the 'fusion' tradition one better," *The New York Times,* November 8, 1981, http://www.nytimes.com/1981/11 /08/weekinreview/mayor-goes-the-fusion-tradition-one-better.html?page wanted=all; Eric Bradner, "Democrats' chances of flipping GOP House seats in 5 special elections, ranked," *CNN,* March 30, 2017, http://www.cnn .com/2017/03/30/politics/5-house-special-elections/; Claire Sasko, "Democratic write-in candidate Emilio Vazquez wins special election," *Philadelphia Magazine,* March 24, 2017, http://www.phillymag.com/news/2017/03/24 /democrat-emilio-vazquez-special-election/; David Weigel, "Here's what Democrats have won (and lost) in special elections this year," *The Washington Post,* March 1, 2017, https://www.washingtonpost.com/news/powerpost /wp/2017/03/01/heres-what-democrats-have-won-and-lost-in-special-elections -this-year/?utm_term=.4352559f20ea.

8. For Mark Shields, see "Trump's GOP opponents get nowhere fast at convention," *PBS Newshour,* July 18, 2016, http://www.pbs.org/newshour/bb/politics -mondtrumps-gop-opponentaas-get-nowhere-fast-at-conventionay-2/; Daniel Schlozman, *When Movements Anchor Parties: Electoral Alignments in American History* (Princeton, NJ: Princeton University Press, 2015), p. 256.

9. Peter Steinfels, *The Neoconservatives: The Origins of a Movement* (New York: Simon & Schuster, new edition 2013); Justin Vaïsse, *Neoconservatism: The Biography of a Movement* (Cambridge, MA: Belknap Press of Harvard University Press, 2010); Gary Dorrien, *The Neoconservative Mind: Politics, Culture, and the War of Ideology* (Philadelphia: Temple University Press, 1993); Evan McMullin, May 28, 2017 [Tweet]; Dennis Prager, "Why conservatives still attack Trump," *National Review,* May 30, 2017, http://www.national review.com/article/448086/never-trump-conservatives-donald-trump-still -opposed.

10. CNN 2016 Exit Polls; Chuck McCutcheon and David Mark, "Politics ain't beanbag," *Christian Science Monitor,* November 14, 2014, http://www.csmon itor.com/USA/Politics/Politics-Voices/2014/1114/Politics-ain-t-beanbag; Franklin D. Roosevelt, "Address at Marietta, Ohio," July 9, 1938, http:// www.presidency.ucsb.edu/ws/?pid=15672; Meghan Keneally, "Trump says

Putin better leader than Obama in Military Town Hall," *ABC News,* September 7, 2016, http://abcnews.go.com/Politics/trump-putin-leader-obama-military -town-hall/story?id=41936057.

11. Daniel L. Davis, "America should not act as the world's policeman," *The National Interest,* January 16, 2017, http://nationalinterest.org/feature/americans -lose-when-america-runs-world-order-19064; Krishnadev Calamur, "A short history of 'America first,'" *The Atlantic,* January 21, 2017, https://www.the atlantic.com/politics/archive/2017/01/trump-america-first/514037/; Henry Farrell, "Trump's election has undermined 'political correctness.' That might actually be a problem," *The Washington Post,* November 19, 2016, https://www .washingtonpost.com/news/monkey-cage/wp/2016/11/19/trumps-election-has -undermined-political-correctness-thats-a-huge-problem/?utm_term=.dfc7 04dc4503; Martin Luther King, Jr., "I have a dream" speech, August 28, 1963, retrieved from the Martin Luther King, Jr., Research and Education Institute at Stanford University, https://kinginstitute.stanford.edu/king-papers/docu ments/i-have-dream-address-delivered-march-washington-jobs-and-freedom.

INDEX